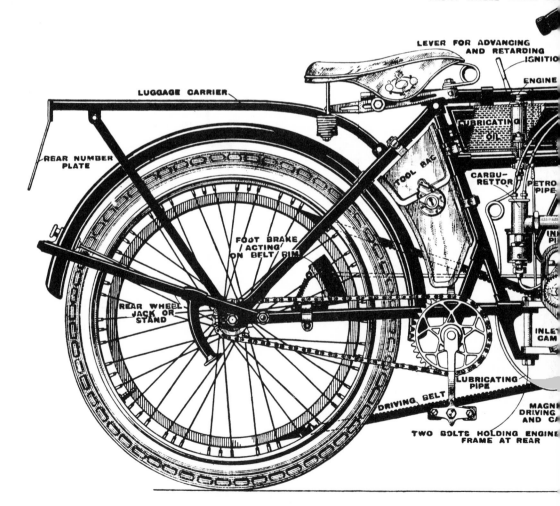

A copy of the fold-out sheet taken from *The Motor-Cyclist's Handbook* by "Phoenix" published by Percival Marshall & Co in the early 1900s

AIR

GAS LEVER OR THRO

FRONT WHEEL BRAKE LE

LEVER FOR ADVANCING
AND RETARDING
IGNITIO

ENGINE

LUGGAGE CARRIER

LUBRICATING
OIL

REAR NUMBER
PLATE

TOOL BAG

CARBU-
RETTOR

PETRO
PIPE

IN
PI

FOOT BRAKE
ACTING
ON BELT RIM

REAR WHEEL
JACK OR
STAND

INLET
CAM

LUBRICATING
PIPE

DRIVING BELT

MAGN
DRIVING
AND CA

TWO BOLTS HOLDING ENGINE
FRAME AT REAR

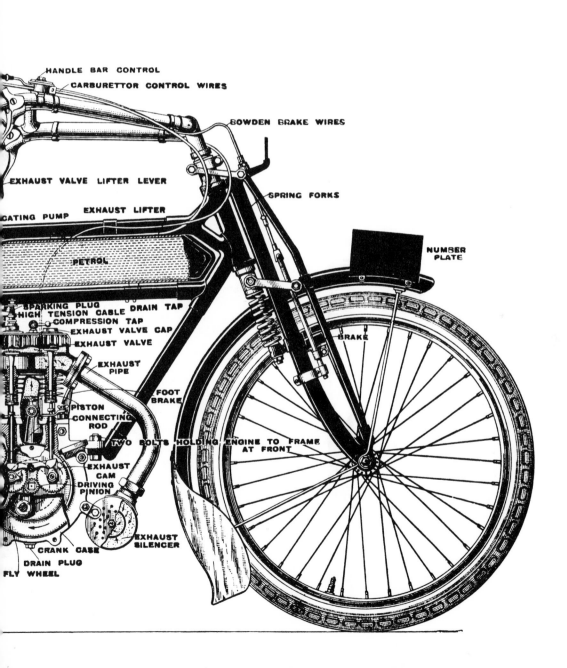

HANDLE BAR CONTROL

CARBURETTOR CONTROL WIRES

BOWDEN BRAKE WIRES

EXHAUST VALVE LIFTER LEVER

SPRING FORKS

CATING PUMP   EXHAUST LIFTER

NUMBER
PLATE

PETROL

SPARKING PLUG   DRAIN TAP
HIGH TENSION CABLE
COMPRESSION TAP
EXHAUST VALVE CAP
EXHAUST VALVE

BRAKE

EXHAUST
PIPE

FOOT
BRAKE

PISTON
CONNECTING
ROD

TWO BOLTS HOLDING ENGINE TO FRAME
AT FRONT

EXHAUST
CAM
DRIVING
PINION

EXHAUST
SILENCER

CRANK CASE

DRAIN PLUG

FLY WHEEL

The Restoration of Vintage & Thoroughbred MOTORCYCLES

Jeff Clew

ISBN 0 85429 185 7

First published November 1976
Reprinted 1977, 1978, 1982

© The Haynes Publishing Group 1976, 1977, 1978, 1982

The Haynes Publishing Group
Sparkford, Yeovil, Somerset BA22 7JJ, England

A FOULIS Motorcycling book

Printed by J H Haynes and Company Limited, Sparkford, Yeovil, Somerset BA22 7JJ

Editor Tim Parker

Distributed in North America by
Haynes Publications Incorporated
861 Lawrence Drive, Newbury Park, California 91320, USA

Dedication

To 'Twitch', who set a lasting, high standard, for the preservation and restoration of old motorcycles

The late H.O. Twitchen, with the machine he enjoyed restoring the most, a 1919 550cc model H Triumph

Foreword

Of the limited number of enthusiasts, with expert knowledge of early machines and their restoration, few can equal the lucid manner in which the author imparts it. So I hope that you will enjoy this volume as I have — that you will profit from its contents — and that your restoration project will be a source of pride and pleasure to you.

Philip S. Smith

Recognised authority on motorcycle restoration, much sought after concours judge and longstanding Vintage Motor Cycle Club member

PHILIP S. SMITH
Carmarthen
S. Wales
June 1976

Contents

Introduction

My first involvement with old motorcycles occurred during 1947, when I was in the RAF and stationed at Martlesham Heath, near Ipswich. My companion at that time was Roger Maughfling and we were sitting together in the NAAFI, trying to scrape-up enough to buy something to eat. Roger, who was penniless, suddenly had a flash of inspiration. Sensing that I was soon to go on leave, and would therefore have a penny or two, he offered to sell me the remains of a 1914 three-speed hub gear Triumph he had acquired some while ago. A bargain was struck and the machine changed hands for something like £5. Being incomplete, it was necessary to find another machine that would provide the much needed parts and eventually this, too, came to hand. I now had two 1914 Triumphs, one with a three-speed hub gear and the other a single-speeder. Only one problem remained; which one to rebuild, and with which parts.

The VMCC was still in its infancy and not too well equipped to answer problems of this magnitude, so I wrote to the late Graham Walker, then editor of *Motor Cycling*. He, in turn, put me in touch with the man he considered to be THE Triumph expert, the late H.O. Twitchen — known more affectionately as 'Twitch'. As a result of this meeting, a great friendship developed, which lasted until Twitch passed away in 1975. I spent countless hours with him, helping rebuild not only my own Triumph but many of his own machines — mostly vintage Triumphs, but with the occasional Norton or Sunbeam. When it came to renovation, there were few who could match his painstaking work and his desire for absolute authenticity. His machines were a showpiece wherever he went and he was in constant demand as a concours judge. Small wonder, therefore, that Graham Walker coined the word 'Twitchenise' when it came to reclaiming an old machine and presenting it in 'as new' condition. If anyone had written a book such as this, it should have been Twitch. Somehow, he never had the time, even though he would have relished the thought of encouraging others to set similarly high standards. And so I have stepped into his shoes, perhaps somewhat inadequately, translating everything I have witnessed in that shed in a back garden at Kingston-on-Thames, where we often worked late into the night, putting the finishing touches to his latest masterpiece. I owe him a tremendous debt for teaching me most of what I know about old motorcycles and I hope that perpetuation of the way he went about things, within the pages of this book, will help repay that debt just a little.

When I commenced work on the manuscript, I was a little surprised that no one else had written a book about the restoration of old machines, especially in view of the precedent set by 'Wheatley and Morgan' in their excellent reference work *The Restoration of Vintage and Thoroughbred Cars*. But as I progressed, I began to realise why. To go into the subject in any real depth, or to refer, in detail, to specific makes of machine, would result in a work of many volumes that could not be marketed at an economic price. If only by necessity, I realised that I would have to confine myself to generalities and mention only those instances where substantial deviations from normal practice have to be made. This in itself immediately creates problems on where to draw the line, a very faint line that is sure to be the subject of arguments. I was also aware that everyone has their own way of going about things and may not necessarily agree with the techniques I suggest. All I can say in mitigation is that they have all been tried and proven, and that I have used them myself, with some success. I did encounter one person who believed most sincerely that most paint defects were caused by the dust that adhered to one's clothes and that in order to achieve the perfect finish, he stripped naked before he applied the first coat of paint! Whilst I would hesitate to recommend this technique, it seemed to work for him and if you have used a certain method and know it works, that is the one to use again. It is the end result that counts. Whilst this book is aimed primarily at the newcomer to renovation, I hope, none the less, that many of the old hands at the game will find the odd wrinkle or two that will help make their future work even easier. If this proves so, then I shall have more than succeeded in my task.

JEFF CLEW
Queen Camel
Somerset
June 1976

The 1914 550cc Triumph, after restoration. It successfully completed five Sunbeam MCC Pioneer Runs ridden by the author, and is still going strong in the hands of the present owner

Acknowledgements

My grateful thanks are due to Dick Chalaye, of Velofello Motorcycles, who supplied the 1921 P & M and the 1952 Triumph Tiger 100, which are featured in some of the photographs. Both were restored to near original specification, to provide the practical, background data for this book. Les Brazier took the photographs and Brian Horsfall and Martin Penny assisted with the dismantling and renovation work. Stan Greenway kindly supplied information about electroplating and the electroplating kits that can be used in the home. Phil Smith and 'Tiny' Ayers, both of the VMCC, devoted much of their spare time reading through the completed manuscript and suggested ways in which the content could be improved, for which I am particularly indebted. Last, but certainly not least, may I thank my friends within the VMCC, the London Douglas MCC and the Scott Owners Club, whose helpful hints and suggestions have been incorporated in various parts of the text.

Chapter One

Finding a machine

It has been said that the greatest problem confronting anyone who has an interest in old motorcycles is not how to start, but when to stop. In a great many cases, the urge to obtain a machine that is no longer in production, yet has a certain appeal, starts quite innocently. There is, after all, a certain joy in owning something that has an air of distinction and character. Excellent though they are, today's motorcycles have become very sophisticated and tend to follow a broad design pattern that somehow manages to exclude individual characteristics, except amongst those in the highest price range. However, this does not mean that everything manufactured in the past is of good quality and worthy of preservation. Mass production techniques are not new, and there are many machines that were available twenty, thirty or even forty years ago that are best forgotten. Viewed in retrospect, the mind tends to remember only the better things that occurred during that time, and a machine that may have proved quite indifferent then, assumes the rosiest of hues when it is recalled. Nostalgia has to be reckoned with at all times; a second acquaintanceship often proves quite revealing. Many an expensive and time consuming reconditioning project has brought forth nothing but acute disappointment at its conclusion, simply because past memories were allowed to cloud the issue. And so the first requirement is a certain amount of self-discipline which, if sensibly applied, will tend to curb the temptation to buy every single thing that comes along.

Having decided to acquire an old machine, the next question is the extent to which it needs to be renovated. There is the world of difference between tidying up a machine, so that it looks reasonably presentable, and stripping it completely so that it is eventually restored to an 'as new' finish. To an extent, the decision to be made is governed by two factors — the amount of capital available and the extent of the renovator's enthusiasm. The achievement of a concours-winning presentation will have proved an expensive operation at its conclusion, since no corners can be cut, or anything skimped. Furthermore, the determination to see the job through must remain resolute, even when it reaches its lowest ebb. This is likely to occur at the stage when the machine has been stripped down into a multitude of rusty and worn parts, all awaiting attention. It is then that the real challenge becomes evident, and there are many that waver and fall by the wayside. Preparation of the various parts for plating and enamelling has its depressive effect too, for it is only by sheer devotion to the monotonous job in hand that perfection can be achieved. A poorly finished surface will always show through and many a work of restoration has been spoilt by impatience or lack of attention to detail. So, if there is any restriction on the amount of money available for the project or any doubt about the extent of one's enthusiasm, it is wise to set the sights much lower and present a machine that is rideable and has a clean and tidy appearance, without any pretence at challenging others in the concours finals. At least the basic objective will have been fulfilled — the preservation of yet another old machine that can give many hours of pleasure.

Two other major problems must also not be overlooked at this stage. The first is one's ability to cope with the restoration project, knowing how to use the various tools in a competent manner to produce a workman-like result. Not everyone has the necessary degree of mechanical ability, and whilst the work can be farmed out to others, the cost will be correspondingly larger. The second is the worry of knowing what is original and what is not, a matter discussed in more detail later in this Chapter. This can prove surprisingly difficult to anyone having their first encounter with an old machine, especially if it has been updated progressively by a previous owner, to keep abreast of current design changes.

The person looking for a machine can range from a first-time purchaser, to the hardened collector who has already amassed a considerable number of machines. Whilst the motives and experience will vary quite considerably, the available sources are fixed and the ways in which to procure a machine are much the same.

Unfortunately, the chances of finding a rare or interesting machine are getting steadily more and more remote. A great number of old machines went for scrap during the last war, when there was a drive for metal of all kinds to help the war effort. Those that survived were often in good hands and it was the emergence of the Vintage Motor Cycle Club during 1946 which did much to ensure their preservation. Not unexpectedly, some remain the cherished possessions of their owners, long after the latter's riding days are over, and a good many interesting machines remain hidden away under dust sheets. Sadly, they often deteriorate quite rapidly through lack of attention, and when the owner eventually passes on, the scrap man has an uncanny knack of getting there first so that the machine is cut up and weighed in for scrap, long before anyone else has a chance to make a bid. Others adopt a curious dog-in-the-manger attitude and would willingly see their cherished possession rot away, without giving anyone else the chance to rescue and restore it before it goes too far. And, of course, there is always the man who considers his machine is worth a quite fabulous sum of money, even if it is only a cheap, mass produced bike of the thirties. These, and many other instances, mitigate heavily against the chances of acquiring a machine for a modest sum, that can be made presentable without need for an overdraft from the bank. It is here that the specialist dealer fulfills a much needed role. By offering suitable machines at the going price, usually quite presentable and in reasonable running order, he can alleviate much of the heartache and frustrations experienced when trying to find a machine the hard way. At a price, of course, although no one runs a successful business without making a profit!

Even then, the option does not rest between the possibility of a chance-find or negotiating with a dealer. The Vintage Motor Cycle Club and many of the one-make clubs list machines for sale in their magazines, which are available to all bona fide members. Prices vary enormously and are invariably related to what is offered for sale, so it is soon apparent which machines are in the greatest demand. Often exchange or part-exchanges are offered, which can help reduce the outlay to a reasonable level, provided the old adage *caveat emptor* is applied. It is not always necessary to be a club member, for some magazines such as the ever-popular *Exchange and Mart* carry their own lists of advertisements. But it is always advisable to act very promptly if what appears to be a genuine bargain is to be followed up with success. There is always someone who purchased an early copy of the magazine, and by the time you have made your telephone call or visit, there may have been twenty before you who had similar objectives! Needless to say a degree of caution is necessary with all such transactions. You should make sure what you purchase is authentic and not misrepresented.

It is doubtful whether auctions will provide a good opportunity for purchase in view of the inflated prices that are often paid under these circumstances. In the heat of the moment it is quite easy to throw caution to the winds when trying to outbid others, so that you end up with a purchase at anything but a realistic price. Some of the machines offered need close inspection right at the very start, for if rust has taken a real hold, they may no longer be a restorable proposition. Remember that it is both a costly and a time-consuming process to restore any machine to a satisfactory standard. If the project is to be

A few, specialist, dealers can supply old machines in a fully or part-restored condition. Even the 'bubble' car outside will have its devotees

economically viable, a machine in need of complete restoration must be purchased for as low a sum as possible.

From the foregoing, it will be apparent that the best prospect for obtaining an old machine is to purchase it in circumstances where it has been 'found' by someone else at an earlier date. In other words, a planned search is likely to prove more positive and certainly much quicker than a chance find, even if the financial outlay is greater. But there is just one further point of which you should take heed. Unless you are really experienced in restoration, or know the model you are about to purchase particularly well, avoid buying a machine that has been completely dismantled, even if it is priced favourably and it is alleged that no parts are missing. The main disadvantage is the most obvious one — you will not have seen the machine whilst it was being dismantled and in consequence you will be purchasing what is little more than a huge do-it-yourself kit — without any instructions! It is also probable that despite what has been said, some parts will have been mislaid or perhaps substituted by others. It is too late to find out at the assembly stage that you are several vital parts short, or that some of the parts will not register correctly, for this is where the project will stop, often for quite a long period. Unfortunately, a large number of machines are ultimately sold in this form, simply because the previous owner let his enthusiasm run away with him and took every mortal piece apart, without regarding the project as a planned operation. When the initial burst of enthusiasm begins to wear a little thin, the folly of taking such rash action begins to emerge and there is nothing more off-putting than a huge pile of rusty or worn parts that will at some later stage have to be reassembled into a motorcycle. It is not long before the owner begins to have qualms, and soon the machine is again up for sale, this time at a greatly reduced figure. It can be said without fear of contradiction that more interesting machines have been lost this way than by any other.

15

Mecca of the bargain hunters! Yards such as this often contain some surprising finds and are worth while investigating

Buyers for this type of 'bargain' are thin on the ground and often by the time one does come along, the assortment of parts has degenerated to little more than a rusty mass, for the vendor has long since lost all interest in them. Make sure *you* do not follow a similar path after that initial flush of enthusiasm — it can happen only too easily.

Provided the financial outlay is kept within reasonable bounds, it is questionable whether too much accent should be placed on this aspect. Today's inflationary tendency suggests that tangibie assets such as *objets d'art* or even old vehicles, of one kind or another, are likely to appreciate in value at a greater rate than savings in the bank, and can therefore be regarded as an investment for the future. Whilst the true enthusiast is less likely to see the situation in this light, mainly because he collects his machines for the pleasure they give to him and is therefore unlikely to re-sell them, it is a comforting thought that the money is well spent, and can be realised to good advantage in times of dire need. It is not a position that is likely to change in the near future, either. As fewer and fewer old machines are discovered, those already preserved can be expected to continue to appreciate in value. Naturally those machines that are exceptionally rare, or have an interesting history that can be fully authenticated, will be the ones that appreciate most, a factor that should be kept in mind. Even a rare or unusual number plate will add considerably to the value of a machine these days. We have not yet reached the stage where a collection of well preserved old motorcycles will rival a private art collection, although it is not as remote a possibility as may have been considered a number of years ago.

The vital question of what to pay is one that is virtually impossible to answer, simply because there are so many factors that have to be taken into account. These include the age of the machine, the overall condition, whether the finish is original or restored, and whether the example concerned is one of many, or the only one. A rough guide can be obtained by looking through the vintage and veteran advertisements in the motorcycle weekly papers, as well as those in the *Official Journal of the Vintage Motor Cycle Club* and perhaps *Exchange and Mart*. Even so, this is only a very rough guide, for the prices asked are not necessarily those eventually received. There is always someone who sold his XYZ for £1,000, if only because he held out long enough and someone who was not *au fait* with current prices let his enthusiasm get the better of his cheque book! But it is not often that a multi-millionaire is attracted to pay an outrageous price for a chance purchase. Most asking prices are negotiable, especially those where the advertiser really chances his arm. For obvious reasons, there is even less in the way of a reliable guide in the case of a rare or one-off machine, or one that has a particularly interesting history. In cases such as these, some form of authentication is highly desirable, especially since nearly every racing Norton offered for sale is 'ex-Stanley Woods' or Velocette, 'ex-Freddie Frith'. Examples such as these are very difficult to substantiate, since there is rarely any written evidence and even the present owner may believe implicitly what was a complete fabrication when he originally purchased the machine himself. In some cases, a marque specialist can help, for his depth of experience with that particular make can usually be relied upon. But there is no such person in the case of a one-off or particularly obscure make, and in consequence, no really satisfactory answer. If a high price has to be paid, make sure a signed statement is obtained from the person selling the machine to you. Although a rather dubious safeguard, it is better than nothing, and may have some value if you ultimately decide to sell the machine yourself.

Never take the stated date of manufacture for granted, especially on a machine alleged to be a true veteran (pre-1915). A veteran machine acquires a special value because the owner is entitled to enter it in the annual Tattenham Corner to Brighton Run organised by the Sunbeam Motor Cycle Club, every March. Fortunately, a check is relatively easy to make because any machine considered eligible to compete in this historic event must have been awarded a Pioneer Machine Certificate by the Sunbeam MCC, to certify that it conforms to a specification that will exclude all post-1914 models, as well as modifications that take away the originality of the machine. No Certificate, no Run! It is as simple as that. And if there is no Certificate, there is a fair chance the machine has been rejected previously, provided it is not a 'new' discovery.

How the 1921 P&M featured in this book was found. Note how the back wheel has rotted away almost completely and the front wheel is about to follow suit. This machine was almost on the point of no return

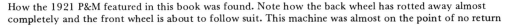

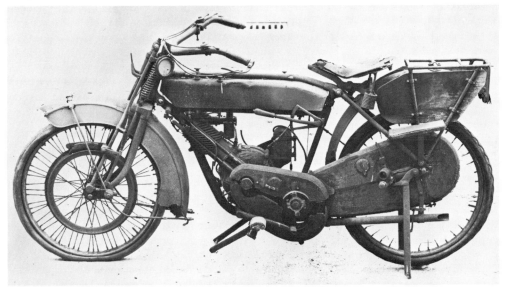

It is a little more difficult to 'date' a later model because there is no other demarkation line that can be so rigorously applied. The arbitrary border between vintage (1930) and post-vintage (1931) is very fine indeed and in the case of certain machines, it will require the aid of the marque specialist to give his verdict. Unfortunately the time has passed when many of the motorcycle manufacturers can verify the year of manufacture by checking the frame and engine numbers. Very few British manufacturers are in business and of those that have faded away, in a great many cases, their valuable service records have been lost for all time. Quite often, however, the marque specialist has evolved his own dating guide, based on these old records. But if you have occasion to write to him, do make sure you quote the engine and frame numbers in full, without omitting any of the prefixes or suffixes that may take the form of letters. They are often just as valuable as the number itself. Some manufacturers stamp the year of manufacture after the engine number. The early Velocette two-strokes, for example, carry an engine number something like 595/15, of which the '15' indicates the engine was manufactured during 1915. It also helps greatly if you can send two good, clear photographs, taken against a light background. A badly taken photograph that is out of focus, or has an ink-like background, is of no use at all, especially since it is often some of the smaller details that help identify the precise date of manufacture. Don't forget to enclose a stamped addressed envelope, either. The marque specialist may give up many hours of his spare time answering other people's enquiries. It is clearly unfair that he should be expected to subsidise the postage at the same time.

Generally speaking, it can be expected that where there is an area of doubt, the vendor will tend to date the machine on the early side, especially if the machine is considered likely to be a veteran. So it may be pertinent to list a few guidelines. For example, around 1913-14 it was customary to put a bend in the top frame tube above the petrol tank, at the rearward end, so that a lower riding position could be achieved. 'Open' type magnetos disappeared around 1911 and very few machines used a Bosch magneto after 1914, because the war put an end to their importation. Wired-on tyres appeared around 1927, when the beaded edge tyre faded out. Around the same period the saddle tank replaced the earlier wedge tank that is the hallmark of the true veteran or vintage machine. Chromium plating made its debut around 1929, at the time when the two-port cylinder head was becoming fashionable. There are, of course, always exceptions to the rule, but the foregoing are just a few examples that can be generally applied, to give a rough indication of the year of manufacture, when the machine is seen for the first time.

No mention has been made of the registration number, which again will give an approximate indication of the year of manufacture in the case of the later models. Unfortunately it was not a legal requirement to register a machine in the very early days and even if the machine was registered, owners often had occasion to transfer the number they were first allocated, to successive machines. I once owned a 1914 Triumph with the registration number BK 15, a number that was originally issued by the Portsmouth and Southsea authority to the previous owner's first machine, a Minerva, around the turn of the century. On this basis, the dating of the Triumph would have been at least fourteen years out! Also, of course, a machine may linger in a showroom for quite a long time until it is eventually so reduced in price that it becomes a bargain and is snapped up. According to the registration number it would appear to be a 1932 model, whereas in fact it is a genuine 1930 model. Examples such as this are, however, very much in the minority and will need careful checking.

If the machine has no registration number, further problems occur. Whilst it would seem unlikely that an old and rusty motorcycle awaiting complete restoration has been stolen, a receipt which quotes the frame and engine numbers should always be obtained, at the time of purchase. Proof of ownership will be required by the registration authority when application is made for the issue of a new registration number and, at the least, may save an unwelcome visit from the police who may need to check the machine details. Some local registration authorities are often sympathetic to the owners of old machines faced with this particular predicament and are willing to re-allocate an old number more in keeping with the

One of the author's early restorations, a 1922 499 cc Light Solo Sunbeam. Although purchased in an extremely rusty condition, it was 100% complete and original apart from the front hub brake.

This 1932 KSS Velocette was built from a 'do it yourself' kit of Velocette parts. When completed, it provided excellent reliable transport, and created no small amount of interest

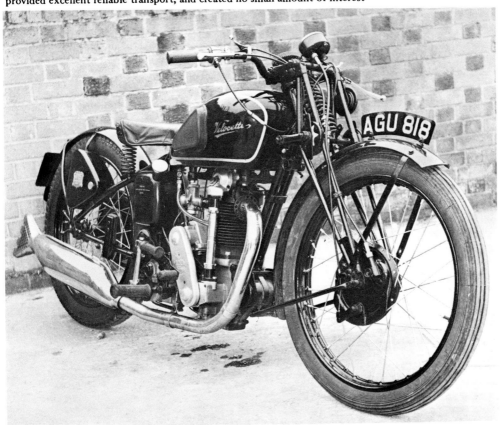

age of the machine, or reissue the original, if so requested. This cannot be taken for granted however, since the chances depend on the general attitude of the authority concerned and the manner in which the request is phrased; a nicely worded letter may work wonders! It would seem probable, however, that this facility will no longer be available in the near future, when the centralised computer takes over the vehicle licensing aspect of the local authorities. At the time of writing it is still possible to transfer a registration number, provided the registration authority concerned will agree, the number concerned has been in the hands of the owner for at least six months and the appropriate transfer fee is paid. It is, of course, also possible to purchase a 'personalised' number plate or one that is appropriate to the age of the machine in question, from one of the many number plate specialists who advertise regularly in the press. But this is a somewhat expensive means of acquiring a 'period' number in lieu of the 'modern' number that would normally be issued by the authority, when they are satisfied there is good cause for re-registering the machine.

Having dated the machine with reasonable accuracy, the next problem is to decide on the degree of originality, since if extensive modifications will have to be made to restore the machine to its original specification, further problems will occur. Quite apart from the fact that the original parts will be difficult and perhaps near impossible to obtain, a considerable outlay can be expected if the machine is far off standard — which in turn will necessitate a suitable reduction in the purchase price. The situation is even more critical in the case of what is basically a veteran machine, since the modifications will often exclude it from the Pioneer Machine Register; this, however, may not be important to you. Cases such as this are all too common, for many riders of the past preferred to update their machines from year to year by substituting parts from the later versions. Often these parts could be fitted with little difficulty and to the inexperienced purchaser, a machine so modified is difficult to detect. Some manufacturers, such as the Scott Motor Cycle Company, actually marketed updating kits so that owners of their machines who were not able to afford a new model could take advantage of some of the more recent design improvements. Here again, the marque specialist is the person to consult; he will know what to look for and will have a good knowledge of the chances of getting the machine back to specification.

It is a sad but inevitable fact that the attitude towards complete originality will have to be relaxed a little as time progresses, when the few remaining spares for the older machines are used up. Admittedly it is possible to reproduce certain parts from an original pattern, but only at a price which to some may prove quite unacceptable. One-off or small batch production is always costly because the setting up time cannot be spread over a long run.

When given to the author, this KTT had been raced continuously from 1930 to 1951, when it was registered for road use. By then it bore precious little resemblance to the original specification. It was fully restored when Veloce Limited confirmed it was the actual ex-Lamacraft Brooklands machine

20

Fortunately, there are still a great number of enthusiasts with their own home workshops, who are able to make parts to pattern as a favour for those who do not have similar facilities or experience. They are the backbone of the 'vintage and veteran movement' and long may they survive! Some quite incredible feats have been accomplished under these circumstances and there would be a great many machines permanently off the road if these mutual-aid facilities did not exist. Other parts are smuggled into factories and works, where 'homers' form part of the daily routine, albeit ignored by management. Without these facilities too, a good many machines and riders would be worse off, for it is possible to have quite intricate jobs undertaken on sophisticated machinery that is not normally available to the do-it-yourselfer. I can recall a works manager taking a keen interest in a frame straightening exercise that was completely 'outside' as far as the production schedule was concerned!

In yet another factory there was no need to ask who was the person experienced in truing-up flywheels — you just looked under the rows of lathes until you saw one with stacks of flywheels awaiting attention! It is to folk like these that we are all indebted, some time or other.

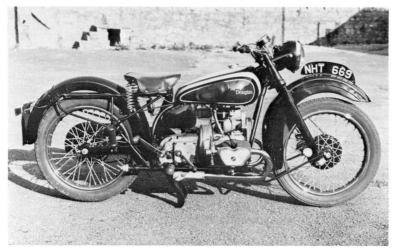

Not many left. This surprisingly original 1948 350cc Mark 3 Douglas was found by the author in Midsomer Norton, two years ago. Almost completely dismantled and in very derelict condition, it had been used by school children and even set fire to at one time. Now it is back on the road again, and used regularly

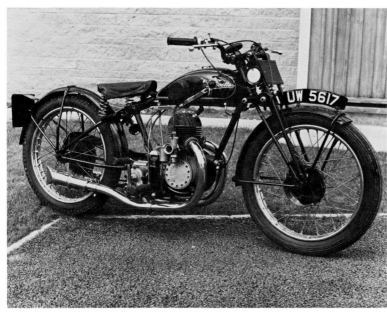

Parts of this 1929 249cc model USS Velocette two stroke were found in a chicken house at Oxted, Surrey. It is probably the only USS in Britain that is still in full running order, and used regularly

21

Two of the most difficult items to replace are magnetos and carburettors, both of which are subject to wear and become expendable. The Vintage Motor Cycle Club has already acted in a sensible way to this problem, and their specification for racing machines (which is very strict in most respects) permits an Amal pre-Monobloc carburettor to be used, if no other is available. A similar ruling applies in the case of the magneto. A later (post-war) type can be used, provided it is not one of the racing pattern. Obviously the problem is more acute with an early veteran, when it is hoped, that in an extreme case, a modern ignition coil and battery, suitably disguised, could be substituted for one of the old trembler coils. But there is no substitute for the surface carburettor which, hopefully, could be reconstructed with some skilled aid.

The other big problem is tyres, since it is no longer possible to obtain beaded edge tyres in certain sizes. Here there is no option other than to have the wheel rebuilt on a different type of rim so that matching, wired-on tyres can form a substitute. The change in specification is not too obvious and will at least keep a machine of historic value roadworthy for many years to come. Other problems loom as the result of the increased density of traffic on our roads. It is becoming more and more hazardous to venture out on a really old machine, with no clutch, only the sketchiest of brakes, and primitive lighting. Whilst it is fortunate that the DOE test contains certain provisions for the certification of old machines, the problem is only being deferred. Unfortunately any modifications to brakes in order to improve their efficiency, or the fitting of stop lamps and other safety devices, would drastically change the whole appearance and character of these historic vehicles. Fortunately, those who ride these machines are usually well aware of their limitations and have not, to the best of my knowledge, contributed in any way to an accident that will focus attention on their regular use. Even so, it is wise to realise that some machines may have been modified in certain respects so that they are more safe to use, if ridden regularly. Whether or not you are willing to accept and retain these modifications will depend on you alone.

Perhaps the most difficult problem of all is to know at what stage to completely restore a machine. A machine in its original finish is much to be desired, but sooner or later the finish deteriorates to such an extent that it becomes decidedly shabby and eventually a decision has to be made. In a sense, restoration destroys the originality, but on the other hand it can enhance the value of the machine, provided that it is in complete accord with the original scheme and is not over-done. It will be no revelation that many of the machines seen at concours events have been restored to a much higher specification than when they originally left the factory. Extra gold lines and sometimes even chromium plate in place of the original nickel, all gild the lily, detracting a little from the overall presentation and put a Concours judge on his guard. Even if this caution is heeded, a full-scale restoration will prove a time consuming and expensive proposition, for there is no room for a quick touch-up with paint, here and there, if the machine is to be made really presentable. So if complete restoration is considered, it should be taken into account when negotiating over the purchase price of the machine. A seemingly cheap, all-original machine can prove alarmingly expensive after the full treatment, even though the expenditure can be regarded as an investment, long term.

From the foregoing it will be apparent that there are many problems to consider when contemplating the purchase of an old motorcycle and that it is unwise to plunge blindly into restoration without at least being aware of a few of them. The main requirement seems to be the need for experienced advice and it would be a very wise initial move to join one of the clubs that have a particular interest in older machines, especially the Vintage Motor Cycle Club* which is a national club with over 4,000 members. The modest outlay on the annual subscription (which will be a mere fraction of what you may spend on the machine itself)

* The word 'Vintage' is perhaps off-putting to those who are contemplating post-second-war machines. The club is worth joining even if you might be restoring a Honda! The club's experience is in restoration, amongst other things.

will place you in contact with others who have similar interests and will entitle you to the facilities offered by the club, including a monthly magazine containing member's advertisements, the club library and regular meetings of whatever Section happens to be closest to your home address. More important still, you will have access to the services of the various marque specialists, who can be relied upon when help is most needed.

Finally, if a chance find comes your way, follow it up immediately. Tomorrow morning is not good enough; you have to get up and move there and then, or the opportunity may have passed. There is nothing more frustrating than to learn that the scrap man called yesterday and took it away; I once spent the best part of a day searching a stinking rubbish tip for a dirt track Douglas frame that had been given to the dustman and dumped. In vain too. Countless opportunities have been lost by the failure to get up and go, but on the other hand, do not appear over-enthusiastic when you arrive or the price may take an upward trend! Above all else, be very tactful in your negotiations, especially with elderly folk or those who are parting with the belongings of someone who has died recently. Only the other day I heard of someone who left the premises of an elderly farmer quite rapidly whilst the latter loaded his shotgun and took aim! Not everyone welcomes what they consider to be an intrusion into their private affairs!

Manufacturers often preserve some of their older models. Veloce Limited restored their classic 'Roarer', the 500cc supercharged vertical twin that was used during practice only for the 1939 Senior TT. The post-war ban on superchargers rendered the machine obsolete and it is indeed fortunate the one-off example was preserved

This rare 1946 596cc Scott was purchased by the author in a dismantled state. Even the hubs had been cut out of the wheel rims. To add to the problems there were no connecting rods and all the bearing rollers had rusted. It took two years to complete

23

Despite its condition, the old P&M was surprisingly original and lacked only few components. Evidence of earlier sidecar attachment can be seen from the fittings still bolted to the frame

The 'old P&M' again, after restoration. This machine illustrates well what can be done with a little money and lots of enthusiasm. This machine was restored with this book in mind

25

Although of more recent origin, the other machine featured—a 1952 Triumph Tiger 100—had suffered its fair amount of neglect too. Compare to the photograph found at the end of this book on page 204

Chapter Two

The workshop and renovation technique

Having acquired a machine, some thought should be given to the way in which the work-shop itself should be prepared so that the dismantling and examination routine can proceed without interruption. Much has been written about the composition of the ideal workshop, and indeed the way in which the workshop itself should be constructed. But in my experience it is rarely possible to achieve the ideal, because one has to accept what is available and make the best of it. I have seen some fantastic restoration work carried out in what is little more than a garden shed, and some quite poor work in a well-equipped workshop having every possible mechanical aid. It is one's own ability that counts, and right from the very beginning you should be honest with yourself and not attempt to tackle any job you consider may be beyond your capabilities. There is too much at stake when restoring something that is old and possibly unique, where risks cannot be entertained. There are always specialists able to undertake all aspects of repair and reclamation work although, of course, at a price that should reflect their know-how and general expertise. But this can be regarded as an insurance policy, if you like, to ensure a job is tackled the correct way and the part concerned given a new lease of life.

The basic requirements of any workshop are that it should be clean, well lit and both warm and dry. Preferably there should be a good working area, a substantial, well-built workbench fitted with a large vice, and a low machine bench, to avoid working at ground level. At least one power point should be available, close to the workbench, and even a radio, if you enjoy working with music in the background. It all adds up to working in a relaxed atmosphere, which is one of the keynotes of success. Earlier it has been stressed that one should work at a steady, though unhurried pace, without need to keep to a tight deadline. This cannot be over-emphasised, for it will be repeated again and again throughout this book. Never rush any job; there may be a reason why the part is difficult to remove, often because the dismantling operation is being tackled in the wrong sequence. Never be afraid to ask for advice, but do so only with an expert. More important, having sought advice, make good use of it. Experience counts for a great deal in restoration and if properly applied, can save you a great deal of unnecessary work and trouble in the long run.

The selection of a good set of tools is another important factor. Most probably you will already have a reasonable selection that have been gathered together over the years, so it will be a question of sorting out the good from the bad. As should be mentioned here, put out of reach the tools that are most likely to cause damage to the parts to which they are applied, namely the stillsons, vice-grips and adjustable spanners. Reject also any set spanners with splayed jaws, screwdrivers with broken or mis-shapen blades and the cheaper type of spanner that is often found in a lawnmower or motorcycle tool kit. Ideally, you should have a good quality set of socket, ring and set spanners in Whitworth sizes or, if

The need for good workshop facilities cannot be over-emphasised

the machine is of continental or Japanese origin, in metric sizes. You will also need several screwdrivers of various sizes (including a short, stumpy one, and some machines require an impact driver), a set of box spanners, a selection of drills and punches, a chain rivet extractor and a sprocket puller, with either interchangeable legs or a fairly wide range of adjustment, a hacksaw, a blow lamp and a selection of taps and dies. To this list can be added the other tools usually found in a workshop, such as a selection of files, several hammers of different weights, a rawhide or copper mallet, a drill of either the bench mounting or electric type, a soldering iron, internal and external calipers, a set of feeler gauges and a micrometer.

The workbench should be well lit and should stand quite firmly, preferably against a wall. The vice, already mentioned, should be bolted rigidly to the bench and should be fitted with soft clamps, so that the jaws do not bite into and mark the various components that are held tightly. It helps if the top of the bench is covered with a layer of sheet metal; I use gallon oil cans for this purpose, after they have been opened up, flattened and tacked to the workbench top. However, with a metal top to the bench, make sure any electrical tools or appliances you use are properly earthed. If you don't you may find out the hard way and then it may be too late! One of the worst culprits in this respect is an electric drill, although liberties should never be taken with any piece of electrical equipment.

Before commencing the actual dismantling work, it is as well to take stock of what follow-up operations are likely to be required. First, a certain amount of derusting and degreasing will be required and it is important to ensure you have the necessary facilities available or, if the amount of work involved is likely to prove too great, the necessary outside contacts. Provided the rust has not bitten too deeply into the metal, elbow work with strips of emery cloth will probably suffice. If the machine is little more than a rusty wreck, more drastic work will prove necessary and in this case it is best to enlist the help of someone with either sand or bead blasting equipment. The latter is to be preferred, since it is less harsh in action and will erode away less of the metal. It is imperative that all rust is removed, or it will rapidly reform and spread. It will also be necessary to apply some form of primer immediately after the metal has been cleaned of rust, otherwise even a damp atmosphere will encourage it to form again. There are a number of excellent brush-on primers available, some of which take the form of a clear liquid that will form a barrier to prevent the reformation of rust. The alternative, is to treat the metal with one of the several rust inhibitors available, some of which are phosphoric acid based and actually enter the surface slightly. There is some risk, however, from this, as, later on, they may cause the enamel to lift. Another alternative is to have the parts concerned zinc sprayed - a highly effective remedy.

As far as degreasing is concerned, one or other of the proprietary degreasing agents such as Gunk or Jizer should suffice. The technique is to apply the compound to the dry metalwork with a brush and if the grease is really thick, to work it in and allow it to penetrate the film of grease and oil before the wash-off with water. If more drastic action is required, a strong solution of caustic soda can be made up by dissolving 3 lb/1.4 kilo caustic soda pellets in 1 Imp gall/4.5 litre of COLD water. Great care is necessary when making up this highly corrosive solution and the pellets must be added to the water whilst stirring. Even then the solution will become very hot. Always wear rubber gloves when making up the solution and do not permit the solution to come into contact with bare skin or it will cause serious burns that are difficult to heal. Above all, take care of the eyes and seek immediate medical attention if they are splashed. It follows that a highly corrosive degreaser such as this should be used only as a last resort, when burnt on oil and grease is virtually immovable. NEVER use the solution on aluminium, which it will dissolve with great rapidity. An overnight soak is usually sufficient, followed by a wash with a copious quantity of water. Blocked two-stroke silencers can be cleaned very effectively using this technique, if one end is sealed off and the solution poured inside.

By far the most difficult oil to remove is one with a vegetable base such as Castrol R. It forms a hard, rubber-like skin on the outside of castings, which resists all attempts at removal. If methylated spirits will not remove it, the only really effective means of shifting it is to scrape it off with a knife, or if it is on a polished or plated surface, to use an abrasive cleaner such as wire wool or Brillo Pad. Many of the older machines were lubricated with oils of this type because, at that time, they were the only oils that would withstand great heat without breaking down and losing their lubricating properties.

Don't overlook the need for the good old paraffin bath, an essential requirement in the workshop of any renovator. Conveniently made up from an old, five gallon oil drum, a perforated drain tray can be added to permit the smaller components to be cleaned off without risk of being lost in the sludge at the bottom of the drum. Often, this form of treatment is more effective (and less expensive!) than the use of a degreasing agent, obviating the need for a final water wash.

After treatment of one kind or another, to remove oil and/or grease, alloy castings can often be restored to near new condition by immersing them in boiling detergent. Make sure the outer races of any bearings or any blind bushes have been removed prior to this treatment, otherwise they will suffer accordingly. Always wash off with plenty of water, after the castings have been allowed to cool. If the outer surface is corroded or covered with 'mould', clean this off first and burnish the surface, using three progressively fine grades of emery cloth.

Having got the cleaning and derusting out of the way, attention can be given to any parts that need to be straightened, repaired or built-up in some way, so that they are fit for continued use. Mild steel components such as footrests, handlebars, mudguard stays and other parts likely to suffer minor damage, can be straightened usually, in the workshop, by clamping them in a vice and applying local heat in the vicinity of the bend whilst correcting pressure is applied. This is not possible, however, with castings or any parts made of aluminium or zinc-based alloy, which will need expert attention if they are to be reclaimed successfully. This also applies to a major component, such as a frame or a set of forks. If true alignment is to be achieved, the whole assembly must be jigged up by an expert in this type of repair so that the minimum force is applied and yet everything is put back into correct

Penetrating oil will prove invaluable, when trying to remove rusted or seized parts. Always allow the oil ample time to soak in, making as many applications as necessary

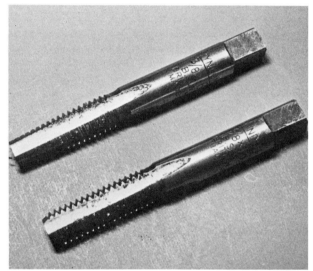

A set of good taps (and dies) will come in very useful, when the need arises to clean up damaged or badly rusted threads. Writing on stock denotes the thread size, type and number of threads per inch

Modern chemicals can be used with great success. A fibreglass kit such as this can be used to fill rust pits, or in some cases to build up damaged components to fill holes. Use according to the manufacturer's recommendations

alignment. The greatest risk is that of fatigue-failure, since the metal will already have deteriorated to a certain extent as a result of the continued road shocks to which it has been subjected over a long period. Greater care has to be taken in the case of components that have been accident damaged, the repair of which will almost certainly be handled by the same specialist. Pay particular attention to the frame of a machine that has been used for sidecar work. Even if the machine has not suffered accident damage, it is quite probable that the frame has been pulled out of line, if heavy loads have been carried in the sidecar.

Parts that have broken can quite often be repaired by welding, even aluminium alloy castings, although expert attention is required, preferably using the argon arc process. Before adopting this approach, however, it is advisable to make sure a replacement part cannot be obtained, since an effective repair by a highly skilled welder is of necessity a somewhat expensive operation. Nonetheless, many a rare and interesting machine has been reclaimed by the skillful use of a welding torch, and originality preserved. Welding (or in some cases brazing) can also be used to build-up worn parts, so that they can be re-machined and used for further service. There is also hard chroming and 'Metalisation' metal spraying. Often this is the only way in which a very old machine can be kept mobile. Again, special attention is required if the risk of heat changing the characteristics of the metal is to be avoided. The expert will often guarantee the repair, because he has confidence in the quality of his own workmanship. Hard chromium plating is better than metal spraying for building up spindles and other parts that suffer from rotational wear. Hard chromium plating is preferable, providing the wear is not too advanced or has taken place over a wide area. In the case of metal spraying, the technique is to build up a slight excess of metal and then grind or machine it down until the desired tolerances are obtained. With electro-plating, it is possible to maintain more accurate control. The rate of deposition can be calculated and then it is only a question of arranging the amount of time to suit. Electroplating comes into its own when heat will damage the part to be built up.

Often, further surface preparation is necessary after parts have been descaled or burnished with emery cloth, because pit marks will still remain from rust that has bitten deeply into the metal. This is always a matter of some concern especially if the frame and forks are affected, because if these pit marks are very deep, they may have seriously weakened the strength of the metal. There was a case not many years ago which emphasises the danger of over-estimating the strength of parts that have been unduly weakened by rust or general corrosion. A very early Ariel was pushed off its stand at the start of a Banbury Run, prior to the rider mounting and pedalling off. As both wheels contacted the ground, the whole front end of the machine broke off, to the amazement of the rider and onlookers alike. It was fortunate that the incident occurred when it did, for had the machine been on the road at the time, the consequences could have been far more serious.

A filler is normally employed to fill up the rust pits and other indentations which, when dry, can be rubbed down until a smooth, blemish-free surface is obtained. Needless to say this is a somewhat time-consuming and boring process, which is inclined to test one's enthusiam to the limit. Yet it has to be done properly, if a really good finish is ultimately to be obtained - there are no short cuts. Much the same basic technique has to be applied in the case of parts that have to be plated, but on this occasion a filler cannot be used since the electro-plate will not adhere to any surface that is not electrically conductive. Here it will be necessary to flow brazing metal into the pits and smooth it off, after it has cooled. The preparation of parts for plating is even more laborious, because the metal has to be smoothed down with files and then emery cloth until a really fine, smooth finish is obtained. This is of importance, because the deposited metal will follow every ripple and imperfection, giving anything but the desired effect, after polishing. This is the approach adopted by the specialist, who has the necessary equipment, although it can be applied only to parts that have deteriorated slightly. If deep pits were to be removed by this technique, the chances are that an inordinately large amount of metal would have to be abraded away before the desired finish is obtained. As mentioned earlier, a good surface finish is the only way in which plated parts can assume a professional appearance. If costs are to be kept within

When using fibreglass, a plane of the Surform type can be used to remove the excess, hardened material, before the final shaping and finishing off

An electric drill fitted with a linishing mop will provide a very effective means of restoring polished aluminium alloy surfaces

On smaller, less accessible surfaces, a good quality proprietary polish and plenty of elbow grease will achieve much the same effect

reasonable bounds, you are advised to undertake all the preparatory work yourself. Because it is a time consuming task, you will have greatly reduced the ultimate bill, of which labour charges would otherwise represent a sizeable part.

The question of what to plate and what not to plate is a vexed one. It can often best be resolved by carefully examining the parts concerned before they are derusted, to see whether any traces of original plating can be found. Some machines, such as the Velocette, used a very minimum of plated parts and any attempt at over-plating will be obvious immediately. Reference to catalogues of the period will often give some indication of the parts that were plated, especially in the machine specifications. Do not rely overmuch on the catalogue illustrations, which are often little more than an artist's impression of the new model. Quite often, some of the proposed styling changes were dropped before the new model went into production, and in consequence the impression is quite false, in certain respects. Good, clear period photographs are often much more difficult to obtain and even then cannot be completely relied upon. A highly polished enamelled surface can have a high level of reflectance, which can sometimes give the illusion of a plated surface. If necessary, fall back on the advice of the marque specialist. Quite a few machines have been eliminated in the final round of a concours judging because too much plating has been used. In other words, the machine was too good because it had been restored to a level better than that when it originally left the works.

In the case of a machine that has deteriorated badly with age, it is sometimes necessary to resort to an enamelled finish rather than have the part concerned plated. This course of action is usually necessary when so much metal has to be removed in order to provide the smooth surface essential for a good plated finish that the mechanical strength would be seriously impaired. A smooth, enamelled finish can be obtained as a satisfactory compromise by using a filler to mask all the imperfections, without need to reduce the thickness of the part concerned by any measurable amount. A good concours judge, however, would undoubtedly notice this deviation from standard.

Much has been written about electroplating and as mentioned earlier, a great deal depends on the thoroughness of the surface preparation prior to this form of treatment, since the slightest imperfections will tend to show up in the resulting finish. It is doubtful whether the cleaning-up process can be left to the plater, for two reasons. Firstly, the time expended in cleaning up to the standard required will add a very large premium to the overall cost. Secondly, and perhaps more important, the cleaning-up work is often undertaken by unskilled labour, who will not attach anything like the degree of importance to the job in hand. The indiscriminate use of emery bobs loaded with abrasive will tend to remove the fine edges and any design or wording that may be embossed in the surface of the metal to be plated. So, although the cleaning-up process is an irksome chore, it is far better to have it under your own control, so that you can set your own standards. An electric drill fitted with a hard rubber linishing pad and a selection of medium and fine emery discs will take much of the drudgery out of the work, provided the drill is man enough for the job without overheating, and there is good ventilation for all the metal dust. Remember the items being cleaned-up will get very hot during the process and frequent stops will have to be made to permit them to cool down. Work towards the finer grades of emery, so that at the conclusion of the operation, the parts have the appearance of polished chrome. Store them in a clean, dry place before they are sent off to the plater, for they will rust easily.

Areas will be found where the discs cannot penetrate, and it is here that some careful work will be needed with files, especially swiss files, for finishing off. It must be remembered that the quality of the finished plating can only be as good as the surface preparation, which underlines the need for a high degree of patience. The joy of seeing the newly plated parts in their eventual pristine state is more than adequate compensation for the monotony of the surface preparation work, so have courage!

It is possible to set up your own nickel plating plant, for a quite modest outlay, provided the area to be plated is not too large. If you have a number of small items to be plated, this is worth investigating, because quite professional results can be obtained with only a little experience. If the comprehensive instructions are followed carefully, it is possible to achieve a professional finish at comparatively low cost, as has been demonstrated on a number of occasions. A car battery is used to supply the current, and a domestic enamel bucket will act as the plating tank.

It is also advisable at this stage to arrive at a decision about the way in which the cycle parts are to be finished. Highly satisfactory results can be achieved by hand enamelling, provided you have the time and patience to follow the routine as described in the following Chapter. The alternative is to apply cellulose by brush, or to resort to stove enamelling, the technique that is normally used by most motorcycle manufacturers. It used to be said that only stove enamelling will give a really hard surface that will withstand the usual knocks to which a machine is subjected, without fear of damaging the paint film, whereas a hand applied paint or cellulose will mark very readily because the coating is comparatively soft. This was certainly true a number of years ago - until the advent of paints containing polyurethane. This additional ingredient gives the dried paint film a shock resistance tough-ness that is virtually on a par with a stove enamelled finish, so that the amateur can achieve near professional results in his own workshop. There are, of course, certain requirements that have to be met if an unblemished finish is to be achieved, as discussed later in this book, but it is true to say that with a little time, patience and devotion to the job in hand, quite professional results can be attained by hand painting, which are virtually indistinguishable from stove enamelling. It will be noticed that I have not mentioned the use of aerosol cans of paint because it is very difficult indeed to achieve a depth of finish that will in any way compare with the more traditional methods of surface coating. If runs are to be avoided, only a very thin layer of paint can be applied during each application of the aerosol can, and it will take many applications (and many cans of paint!) before a significant build-up can be achieved. I must stress, however, that these are only my own observations. I have no doubt that there are many who have achieved quite remarkable results with aerosol finishes through their determined efforts to pioneer this new approach.

The reason for considering all these problems at such an early stage is so that schedules can be planned for placing work with outside contractors. By planning the entire restoration project in advance, it is possible to arrange the inside and outside work to run simultaneously, so that hold-ups are reduced to a minimum. If one or other of the outside contractors over-runs, this is then unlikely to cause any undue problems, since other tasks can be undertaken as a fill-in. Do not, however, plan a very tight schedule so that the problem of meeting deadlines is created. Working to a strict time scale will encourage the taking of short cuts here and there, which inevitably will have their repercussions on the quality of the finished job. The chances to recondition completely a machine are only too rare and you should take every opportunity to ensure a first class job results, especially if you intend to compete seriously for major concours awards.

One final but nonetheless very important point. If the machine has been partly dismantled or stored for some lengthy period, it is quite probable that the engine or some other major component has seized and will have to be freed before further dismantling can take place. It is remarkable how many engines are left with the spark plug removed, so that dampness can get into the engine and cause the piston rings to rust to the cylinder bore. This bond is particularly difficult to break without risk of damage to the piston and/or rings, the latter of which will probably have to be scrapped in any case. Now is the time to add some penetrating oil, so that it has a chance to seep down the bore and break the bond. After each application of oil, try rocking the engine sprocket (or pulley) backwards and forwards, in the hope that a small amount of movement can be achieved. Once movement is detected, no matter how small, the problem is on the point of being overcome. Gradually, more and more movement can be made after repeated applications of oil, until the engine will once again turn over. Beware of applying too much force, however, especially in the early stages. Some very early models have somewhat spindly internal parts and it is easy to place a shear stress on a shaft if too much leverage is applied. A similar technique can be used for freeing most mechanical components and it is obviously best if a start is made as soon as possible.

Chapter Three

The restoration plan

Having brought your machine back to your garage or workshop, resist the temptation to tear it apart immediately it is off-loaded from the trailer, or whatever vehicle has been used to move it from its last resting place. The very first course of action should be to take several photographs of it from both sides, exactly as purchased, and preferably with a white sheet or some other light coloured background. Apart from the joy of having a set of before-and-after photographs at the conclusion of the restoration, they will prove useful in other respects. If the machine is a veteran and is not on the Pioneer Register, they can be sent to the registrar for confirmation that the machine is likely to be accepted when restoration is complete, and for his comments about modifications that may require attention before the machine can be accepted. They will also prove useful to the marque specialist, whom it is also advisable to contact at an early stage. Finally, they will also prove helpful as an *aide memoire* when reassembling the machine, since it is easy to forget how certain parts were arranged or accessories fitted. Use of a camera is almost a must throughout the entire restoration project, as discussed in greater detail at the end of this Chapter.

If the machine has no registration plates and no registration book, it is advisable to make application for registration at this early stage, with your local registration authority. Note, however, that if you wish to transfer an existing number, you will need to have retained and taxed the vehicle from which the number is to be transferred, for a minimum qualifying period of six months - assuming the authority concerned is willing to endorse the transfer. The re-registration of an old machine, or the transfer of a number to an old machine, will take time, since certain investigations have to be made before the authority is satisfied that all is above board. Sometimes it will help if you send photographs of the machine 'as found', with your application. At the very least you will need to record change of ownership; people have been fined on rare occasions for failing to give prompt notification, even when a registration book is available. Don't take it for granted, either, that your local registration authority will agree to a transfer of a number or will re-allocate an old number that is no longer in use. Neither of these actions is your right and if you upset them, you may end up with a 'modern' number and no option of a change.

Now is the time to give the machine a very thorough examination, in order to determine exactly what new cycle parts need fabricating, such as mudguards, mudguard stays, footrests and footrest bars to quote just a few examples. There is no point in commencing the restoration until you have a machine that is complete, otherwise you will find that the paintwork on some of the newly enamelled components is damaged by the need to make up brackets and other fittings that were overlooked at the time of dismantling.

Even more important is the need to check the overall specification of the machine for originality, and to make a list of all parts that need to be replaced by the original items, so that you will end up with a complete and original 'in period' machine. Never commence the stripdown if certain major components are missing altogether or if they have to be replaced by original items. It would clearly be a mistake to have the frame stove enamelled, for example, before finding the matching front forks. Sometimes, as mentioned later, more modern forks can be fitted as a temporary expedient to get the machine on the road. But even this has its disadvantages, quite distinct from the aesthetic viewpoint. Paintwork is invariably damaged during the dismantling and reassembly, no matter how careful you are. In consequence, you may need to have the frame re-stoved when the original forks come to hand because it is not possible to touch in the damaged areas.

If the machine was purchased in the completely or partially dismantled state, it is probably best to reassemble it at this stage, so that it is easier to determine what parts are missing and the originality of each of the major components. This approach has a hidden advantage, too. A knowledge of reassembly will pay dividends later since there is no worry about damaging the paintwork when working out at this stage the best method of assembly. Make a note of the routine, including any snags encountered.

The acquisition of missing parts or replacements for parts that are not of the correct period, will undoubtedly create one of the biggest problems of all. Advice is difficult to offer because there is no guarantee that any prescribed approach will have the desired results. If scanning the advertisements in the *Official Journal of the Vintage Motor Cycle Club*, the magazine of the appropriate one-make club and any other likely sources brings forth a blank, it often proves advantageous to advertise for the parts needed, describing them in some detail. If this fails too, it will be necessary to locate the former, main agents for the make of machine in question, and write to them individually, in the hope that they may still have some old parts in stock. If you are fortunate enough to locate a dealer who has a small stock of parts, it will pay dividends to pay him a visit by prior arrangement. You will possibly be in a better position to identify the parts you require, especially if the older members of the business have retired or if the business has changed hands. This is where patterns come in useful.

Sometimes, it is possible to locate parts outside the UK, on the shelves of dealers who at one time handled imported motorcycles. Although this approach is something of a long-shot, I once obtained a new petrol tank for a model EW Douglas that had stood on the shelf of a former Douglas dealer in Paris! It had been there so long that one side of the tank had faded visibly through constant exposure to sunlight. As far as foreign machines are concerned, the former UK concessionaire can often be traced without too much difficulty, or the person who bought up all the remaining stock of parts when the concessionaire ceased business. Never give up hope. A quite considerable amount of letter writing will be involved in most cases, and perhaps a number of quite fruitless visits. But if you persevere, sooner or later something will materialise that will make it worth while.

Before you set about the bike, clean it down as much as possible, using one of the proprietary cleaning aids such as Gunk or Jizer. Take special care that water does not get into any of the exposed parts when washing down, especially the carburettor and the electrics. If the old grease and oil is stubborn and reluctant to move, give the cleaner time to penetrate after working it in with a brush, before the water wash is applied. Allow the machine to dry thoroughly before proceeding further.

It is probable that many of the parts will have rusted in position, especially where iron and aluminium alloy come into contact with each other. Soak all the places considered likely to give trouble in penetrating oil, such as Plus Gas or similar proprietary products. I have heard of diesel oil and even vinegar being used to good effect for the same purpose - nearly everyone seems to have his own pet mixture. If the joint is badly corroded, try wire brushing it first, to remove all loose scale and rust. Be careful, however, of obliterating any transfers or lining that may need to be copied or preserved, if the original finish is to be reproduced. Leave all the treated parts to soak and if necessary, re-apply the lubricant if the joint commences to dry out.

The next requirement is an assortment of cardboard boxes, or better still tote bins, if they are available, in which to place the various parts as they are removed. Allocate each box to a specific major component of the machine, such as engine, gearbox etc, and mark the box clearly. Place the machine so that a good working area is available all around it, and stand it on sheets of clean newspaper, so that any parts dropped are easier to find. The main requirement is the ability to work at a leisurely pace, without trying to meet a tight deadline, so that plenty of time is available to cope with the more difficult jobs. If parts will not free easily, do not attempt to force them apart. Some parts may already have weakened as the result of metal fatigue, and in some cases relatively soft metals, such as brass, will have been used. It is only too easy to destroy some irreplaceable component by hasty action; often the application of local heat can be used to advantage. The bond between iron and aluminium alloy is often the worst to separate, due to the galvanic action between the two dissimilar metals which has caused corrosion to take place at their interface. Patience is the only answer. Repeated application of penetrating oil followed by local heating will often permit one of the components to move a fraction. Once movement is detected, the battle is over, because the part concerned can be worked steadily backwards and forwards, without force, so that the range of movement will steady increase until the joint separates. It takes time, but it is worth it in the end, because valuable parts are saved.

Do not succumb to the usual temptation and take every part of the machine to pieces, so that you are left with little more than a huge do-it-yourself kit. More motorcycles have been ruined this way than any other, because the owner eventually loses heart when faced with such an enormous problem of reassembly and invariably ends up selling the machine in this form - at a loss. Meanwhile, many of the smaller parts have been lost or misplaced, leaving the new owner with even greater problems. Start by breaking the machine down into a number of complete units, such as the engine, gearbox, frame, wheels etc. It is advisable to dismantle, recondition and reassemble each unit before passing to the next, but this is not always feasible when a full scale restoration is undertaken, because it is both easier and cheaper to send away all the parts for plating and enamelling at the same time.

When taking the machine apart in this fashion, do not trust to memory, or you will have some blanks when the time comes around for reassembly. Make sketches or drawings of the various assemblies when they come apart, so that the position of each washer, spacer and distance piece is known. This is particularly important in the case of a gearbox or a wheel bearing, where incorrect assembly can cause untold problems. Better still, use a camera to record the various stages of the dismantling sequence, provided you have the ability to use it correctly under indoor conditions. There are, of course, those who scorn any such procedure and gleefully tear a bike apart, knowing they can rely upon a retentive memory. I am one of them, although I must confess I have been caught out on the odd occasion when I have been temporarily stumped by some unrecognisable part. I have even encountered one person who can dismantle two or three machines simultaneously and throw all the parts into one huge heap, which will ultimately be sorted out correctly, without turning a hair! But this is not to be recommended. Memory does play tricks occasionally and it is best to play safe and have some reliable evidence handy, if need be.

Having broken the machine down into its major units, it is advisable to gather together as much information as possible, especially spare parts lists which show the component parts and will give an indication what is to be expected when dismantling commences. Again, work at a leisurely pace, make drawings and notes, or take photographs, at various stages. Watch out for nuts with a left-hand thread, often found on the timing pinion end of the crankshaft. They should be stamped LH to aid removal, but this does not always apply. If the nut is particularly stubborn to move, try turning it the other way. It could be threaded in the direction opposite to that expected. If the timing pinions are unmarked, make sure they are marked in some permanent way before they are withdrawn from the timing chest. This will ensure there is less difficulty in arriving at the correct setting when the engine has been reassembled. Mark all parts as they are removed, so that they are replaced in their original locations, when the engine is rebuilt. This is particularly important in the case of components such as the piston, push rods, cam followers and rocker gear. Where the screws

After bead blasting, any small imperfections should be filled in and smoothed off, as required. Unless primer is applied quickly, the newly exposed bright metal surface will rust very quickly

Now is the time to examine the frame and forks very carefully for cracks and general alignment. The photographer must be a Scott enthusiast, judging from the way in which he has arranged the P&M frame!

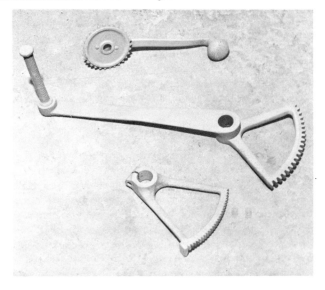

These components are badly pock-marked with rust pits, and will need special attention if a final, smooth finish, is to be obtained

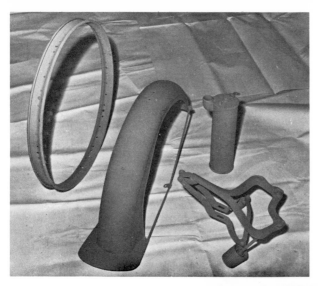

The undercoat will need to be built up and smoothed down again in a whole series of operations, if a really smooth, blemish-free surface is to result

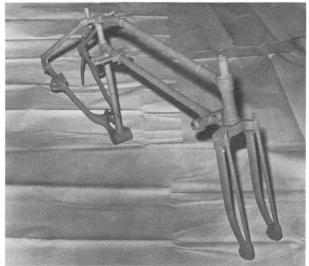

Although the surface looks good in the photograph, close examination would have shown otherwise. It was not until the top coat was applied that defects became evident — too late to take any remedial action

These parts would originally have been plated, but to remove all their pock marks would have weakened them considerably. Instead, they were stove enamelled

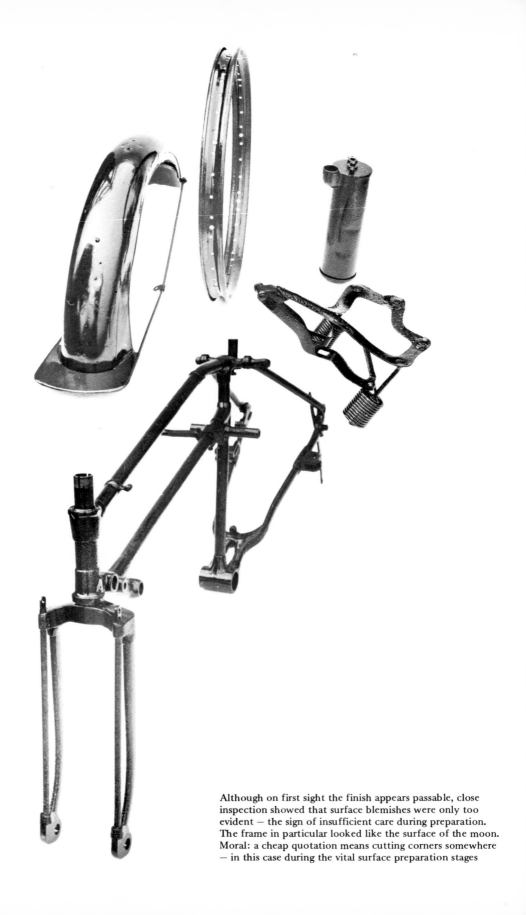

Although on first sight the finish appears passable, close inspection showed that surface blemishes were only too evident — the sign of insufficient care during preparation. The frame in particular looked like the surface of the moon. Moral: a cheap quotation means cutting corners somewhere — in this case during the vital surface preparation stages

40

The appearance of these parts had to be seen to be believed and it was obvious that the company concerned had little previous experience or understanding of renovation work. A cheap job suddenly became expensive; it had to be done all over again by somebody else

that retain a timing cover or an end cover of any kind are encountered, good use can be made of the lid from a cardboard box. If an outline of the cover is drawn on the lid, the bolts can be pushed through the cardboard in the same position, so that their correct location does not have to be worked out, by trial and error, during reassembly.

Unlike the instructions given when working on a modern motorcycle, throw nothing away, not even the piston circlips that should not be reused. Because spares will be anything but readily available, it may be necessary to use these parts as a pattern, to either identify them amongst other components in the same bin, or to be used as the basic for the fabrication of a new replacement. Even the gaskets should be retained, since it is advisable to have some record of their thickness and the type of material from which they are made. When the stripdown is complete, clean each part so that it is ready for close examination, before commencing work on the next unit. Store these parts under cover, so that they are in a clean and dry atmosphere and therefore unlikely to rust. I bought a Scott that had been completely dismantled and where the owner had taken care to place all the bearing rollers in polythene bags, carefully labelled right-hand and left-hand etc. Unfortunately, all his efforts had been in vain, because he left them lying on the garage floor. Rainwater trickled in during the winter, entered the bags and caused everything to rust quite severely. A moment's forethought would have prevented this from happening and not introduced the difficulty and cost of finding new replacements. If they had been stored on a shelf and greased or oiled first, they would probably still be in use today. Oil and/or grease are not always the best preservatives. It is often more effective to insert a small piece of paper impregnated with what is known as a vapour phase inhibitor to keep rust at bay. You may have encountered a small piece of brown coloured paper packed with precision instruments, such as micrometers and thread gauges. This is the same material, which can be purchased from paper specialists. I have often wondered why enthusiasts do not make better use of this particular product, for if a large piece of the treated paper is located near a motorcycle it will prevent the formation of rust, even in the dampest of conditions. Perhaps one of the reasons is that the treated paper can be purchased only in bulk, but even so, if a group of enthusiasts banded together and purchased the minimum quantity, it could prove quite economical and save a great deal of unnecessary winter cleaning and polishing.

During the cleaning up process that follows dismantling, care must be taken to ensure any of the original transfers are preserved along with any other decorative lines or panels. This often gives rise to many problems, since colours fade and there is no real indication that the finish may be the original. Although some transfers are available through the Vintage Motor Cycle Club transfer specialist, many are unobtainable and there is probably no record of what the original looked like. If sufficient of the transfer is left, it is a good idea to ask an artist to make a copy to scale, so that if necessary, the transfer can be reproduced by a skilled signwriter or even the artist himself. Make a note of the colour scheme too, at the same time, and a scale drawing of how the panels and lines are arranged. Sometimes it is possible to find just a fragment of the original paint that has not faded, such as that under a knee grip or some part shielded from the weather. If luck is with you in this respect, the colour can be matched by means of the British Standard Specification on paint colours. It is then easy to obtain a paint or a paint mix that will correspond with the BS number quoted. If, on the other hand, the machine is a mass of rust or has been painted with the usual bitumenous paint that nearly every unappreciative motorcyclist seems to apply at one time or another, you will have to rely upon our old friend, the marque specialist. He is sure to have been asked for advice about colour finishes on innumerable occasions. If you are particularly lucky, you will have found a Velocette or a Sunbeam, where the problem does not exist. An all-black finish with simple gold line relief is unlikely to give rise to any serious problems!

Having completely dismantled the various components on a sequential basis, closely examine each part so that you can draw up a list of what needs to be renewed and what can be reused. Here it is difficult to give any firm advice because it may be necessary to use parts that have worn to the extent where they would normally be rejected, simply because no replacements are available. More detailed information about how to get around this problem is given in the following Chapters, so I will not dwell on it unnecessarily at this stage. Let it suffice to say that a little more tolerance will have to be exercised when deciding whether a part is acceptable for further service. Again, throw nothing away; it may be needed as a pattern later.

Mention was made at the beginning of this Chapter concerning the use of a camera rather than drawing sketches, or making notes during the dismantling stage. I must confess that I have not previously been an advocate of this technique. However, since becoming involved with workshop manual production, I have begun to appreciate the value of the camera in this type of work. There have been occasions when it has been necessary to refer back to the photographs, which has proved my own memory is not infallible, if nothing else! It is better to take a precaution such as this rather than have to tear apart some component that has been reassembled with great care, solely because a misplaced washer or spring has caused it to malfunction.

Some experience with a camera is necessary, plus of course, a camera capable of producing good results. If you have only a box 'Brownie' and have taken nothing other than the occasional 'snap' at the seaside, the technique may prove none too successful. Worse still, the results of the exercise will not be apparent until after the film is developed, when it can be too late to adopt any alternative. So unless you feel competent enough to make use of the camera short-cut, don't take chances and keep to the pencil and paper. A guide of some kind is an essential requirement, especially if you have never undertaken a full scale renovation before.

Until now, I have assumed that the machine you are about to restore has been purchased as a complete unit, but sad to relate this is not often the case. At the very least, parts of it may have been removed at some earlier date, by persons unknown, so that all you have is a box of bits. Even worse, the whole machine may be completely dismantled. The Scott I mentioned earlier had even the wheels dismantled so that it was quite easy to transfer the complete machine in the boot of an Austin A40! In cases such as these, there is no chance of making notes that will help with the reassembly - it has to be carried out by a trial run before the project commences in earnest. Worse still, there will be no means of checking

Take care to preserve any transfers, since replacements may prove almost impossible to obtain. The Veloce steering head transfer shown is now stocked only by the Vintage MCC

whether any parts are missing or indeed, if the correct parts are contained in the boxes, without a well-illustrated copy of the original spare parts list or contact with someone who is familiar with the model concerned. I sometimes wonder why it is necessary to completely strip a machine in this fashion when in all probability only one or two of the main units required attention. Perhaps it is just curiosity, like the child who takes a clock or watch to pieces, to see what makes it tick. The outcome is the same, except that a motorcycle contains a great many more parts!

As mentioned in the previous Chapter, it is advisable to draw up a schedule for the entire renovation project, so that the various stages can be accomplished without undue delay. A certain amount of the work will have to be undertaken by outside contacts and some careful planning will ensure that whilst this work is under way, other work is being carried out in the home workshop. To a degree, economic considerations will govern the extent of the work that can be handled by others and it cannot be overstressed that an estimate should always be requested, along with a completion date. As in the insurance world, it pays to shop around, and not accept the first reasonable-looking quotation that comes along. Charges vary, even though the cheapest are not necessarily the ones to accept. Always work on a personal recommendation, whenever possible. Some of the photographs in this book show the folly of going to a 'specialist' who tries to cut corners and has little knowledge of what a good renovation job entails. They speak for themselves, because the whole job had to be done again by someone else, greatly increasing the original costing and adding quite considerably to the delay before reassembly could commence.

Each man must make his own plan, tailored to suit his individual requirements. And having made his plan, he should adhere to it. Each plan will, of necessity, be different and each sequence of events will be arranged in different order, in view of the need to rebuild in the minimum time and cost. Because of the almost infinite variety involved, successive Chapters can only deal with the major units in random order, leaving the reader to decide the sequence best suited to his own requirements.

A close-up of the reassembled P & M front forks. These forks have been shown elsewhere in various states of restoration

Chapter Four

The frame and forks

The order in which the various major assemblies of the machine are dismantled, examined and restored is of no real consequence. As far as I am concerned, it is usually the engine that holds the most interest and for this reason I tend to leave it until the cycle parts and gearbox have been dealt with, so that I have something to which I can look forward! There is the added advantage that if the cycle parts are restored first, reassembly of the machine can commence right from the start. By the time the wheels have been fitted to the frame and forks the assembly becomes mobile and can be moved about — a great advantage when working space is cramped.

Commencing with the frame, the first problem is the removal of all the old paint, so that eventually only the bare metal is exposed. If costs have to be kept to a minimum, the paint can be stripped off with an old knife, preferably warming (not heating) the area with a blow lamp, or by using a paint stripper, such as Nitromors, if it has particularly good adhesion. It is when the original paint is exposed that colours can be matched, so that the final finish is identical to that when the machine originally left the works. Now is the time to record such colours. Although the colour may have faded in the more exposed areas, traces can often be found in the vicinity of lugs or where accessories have previously been clamped, which give a much truer representation. Watch out also for any gold lining, which may have been applied to the frame of a particularly early model. Paint stripping by hand is a very tedious operation and a very messy one too, if paint stripper has to be used. If you find yourself getting bored, break the monotony by reverting to another job, coming back to the frame only when you have had time to relax a little.

The alternative is to have the frame sand blasted, or better still, bead blasted if it is heavily scaled and pitted with rust. There is less chance of abrading away metal when bead blasting is used, which is important if the strength of the frame structure is not to be impaired. Whatever technique is used, all traces of the old paint finish must be removed, so that the frame is cleaned down to the bare metal. Don't forget that many frames have a steering head transfer, which should be masked off or copied so that it can be reproduced by an artist or signwriter, assuming a replacement is not available.

If the frame is fitted with any form of rear suspension, this must be removed prior to any sand or bead blasting operation and any bushes masked off to protect them from damage. This is especially so in the case of a frame with a swinging arm, where traces of abrasive can cause very rapid wear of the pivoting fork bushes or spindle. Do not forget the bearing cups within the steering head of the frame, unless they are badly worn and have to be renewed.

Similar attention can be given to the front forks. If they are of the girder type, remove all the spindles and links first, so that the holes through which they pass can be masked off.

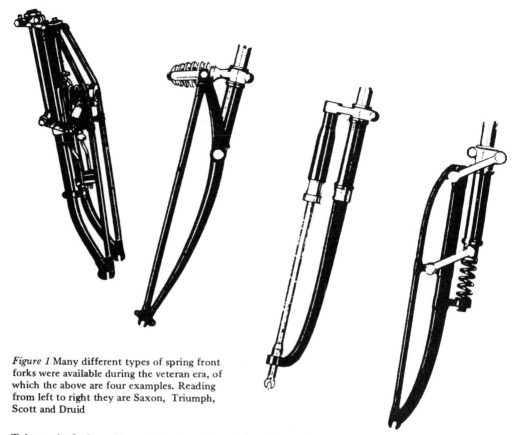

Figure 1 Many different types of spring front forks were available during the veteran era, of which the above are four examples. Reading from left to right they are Saxon, Triumph, Scott and Druid

Telescopic forks will need to be stripped completely first, unless they are found to be in good working order and only the upper shrouds require repainting. At the very least, the forks will have to be separated from the frame, irrespective of their type.

When all the paint has been removed, examine the frame and forks closely for cracks, damage or general misalignment. Cracks can usually be repaired in a very satisfactory manner by brazing or welding, although this type of repair should always be entrusted to a frame repair specialist. If they occur in an alloy component, however, such as the lower fork leg of a pair of telescopic forks, a repair of this type is much less practicable. Under these circumstances, a replacement part is the obvious answer, even if some difficulty is experienced in obtaining exactly what is required. Experience with a particular machine is often the best guide to where trouble is likely to be encountered. For example, the upper fork yoke casting of AMC Teledraulic forks is prone to cracking, if over-stressed, and the early camshaft Velocettes often fracture the rear chainstays immediately behind the channel section casting, to which the gearbox is bolted. Occasionally, a front down tube will part company with the steering head, a fracture that is not immediately obvious.

Always check the frame for alignment, especially the frame of an early model to which a sidecar has been attached. If the wheels are out of track, the machine can never be expected to handle correctly and worse still, there is risk of a 'speed wobble' developing if the machine is rebuilt without correcting the fault. Frame (and fork) alignment is a task for the specialist, who will have all the necessary jigs and mandrels, plus the experience. The basic objective is to use as little heat as possible and yet at the same time desist from applying too much force. The borderline is fine, and this is where expertise is necessary. Twisted girder forks are difficult to straighten, especially the strutted Webb type that have additional side bracing to give greater lateral rigidity.

Assuming the frame and forks are in correct alignment (or have been straightened), now is the time to effect any minor repairs which, if carried out at a later stage, may cause damage to the newly applied finish. If the machine has a centre stand that bolts to the frame, the bolt holes may have become elongated and need building up with brazing metal so that they can be redrilled to the correct size. If a swinging arm is fitted, now is a good opportunity to renew the pivot and bushes, if any wear is evident. In the case of girder forks, it is almost certain that wear will have developed in the fork spindles and in the holes in the fork blades through which they pass. Late-type forks have replaceable bushes, but if the forks are of an earlier pattern, two courses of action can be taken. The holes can be bored oversize and bushes turned up to fit, which will simplify the procedure when wear again dictates further action, at a later date. The alternative is to bore the holes oversize and fit oversize spindles. Whilst dealing with the forks, it is advisable to check the condition of the brake plate stop, which is often welded to the inside of one side of the fork blades. If wear has developed, the brake plate will move backwards and forwards when the front brake is applied, which will render the braking action much less effective. If wear is permitted to continue at this point, a shear stress will ultimately be imposed, which may cause the stop to break off, without warning, when the front brake is suddenly applied in an emergency. The consequences of this happening need not be elaborated.

Other points that may require attention at this stage are the steering head bearing cups, which usually have to be drifted out of position and their new replacements driven back in, and any tapped holes such as those in the rear forks into which the chain adjusters thread. It is easy to re-tap the thread or even to extract particles of broken bolts or studs, when the frame, or whatever component is being worked on, can be clamped in any position without having to worry about spoiling the finish. Don't forget to clean-up the frame again, especially if any welding or brazing has taken place. A set of small swiss files can often be used to advantage when removing a small amount of surplus metal or spatter in the vicinity of the repair.

Having attended to all the repair tasks, give the frame and forks a final smooth down with emery cloth. This should leave a good surface finish, apart from any rust pits, and provide a sufficiently good key to which any following surface coatings will adhere. Unfortunately it is not practicable to eliminate the rust pits, without removing too much of the surrounding metal and thereby weakening the whole structure. If the rust pits are numerous and inclined to be deep in places, it is imperative that professional advice is sought at this stage, for it is quite probable that the strength of the part in question is now seriously reduced. The Engineering Department of a large College of Further Education will often give advice on matters such as this for a quite nominal sum and may be able to carry out one or two special tests. If there is any cause for doubt in the results, always err on the safe side and renew the part concerned, if this is practicable. The alternative is to have the affected area(s) built up by metal spraying or, in the case of a frame, to remove the complete tube that is affected and fit another in its place. Although this is a job for the frame repair specialist, it is not quite as difficult as it sounds because most frames consist of lugs into which the various tubes are pinned and brazed. Special care must be taken if the machine is of the ladies type or one with an open frame. The absence of a cross-bracing top tube leaves a somewhat weaker frame structure under normal circumstances, unless the frame is constructed on triangulated lines.

Before applying filler or undercoat, it is advisable to rust proof the frame and forks by forming a chemical barrier through which rust cannot penetrate. Many a good finish has gradually deteriorated as time progresses through the appearance of small bubbles in the paint film that grow larger and eventually cause the finish to break down completely. They are caused by a build up of rust underneath the paint film as the result of moisture that has been trapped between the paint film and the untreated metal, permitting the metal to oxidise, and rust to re-form. Most rust proofing agents react with the metal surface, to produce a barrier which will inhibit the formation of rust. Quite often this is achieved by incorporating phosphoric acid in the agent, which attacks the metal surface to form a phosphate barrier. Wash primers work on a somewhat similar principle. The alternative is to apply a cold galvanizing primer, which uses a metal such as zinc to provide the barrier coat. There are many proprietary rust prevention compounds on the market and you will probably have your own pet choice. One of the best known is Jenolite. Allow the coating to dry thoroughly before passing to the next operation.

To fill any pit marks, clamp the assembly in a vice and apply by brush a coating of filler, using one with either a cellulose base if a cellulose finish is to be applied as the final top coat, or an oil base for paints of the enamel type. The finish and the condition of the brush used to apply the filler is unimportant at this stage because the basic requirement is to fill up the rust pits so that an even finish can be achieved on rubbing down. Several coats of filler will prove necessary, each one applied after the one preceding has had the chance to dry. As explained later, it will help if each alternate coat is coloured, by adding a small quantity of paint having the same base composition (eg cellulose or oil). It is not at all uncommon to apply as many as eight or even ten separate coats if the pitting is bad; the important fact is to fill the pits completely so that no trace remains after the rubbing down stage. Finish off with a coat of dark coloured undercoat, which again can be applied without too much care and attention. Now leave the part that has been treated in this manner to dry for at least a week, so that the various coats have an opportunity to harden. Storage in a warm, dry place will help the hardening process.

Commence rubbing down with what is known as 'wet and dry' paper, starting with 320 grade. Cut two pieces of this paper approximately 6 in/150mm by 8 in/200mm and rub them together for a few seconds to take off the initial sharp cut. Wet one piece and immerse the other in a bucket of water that is kept close by. Use plenty of water and keep interchanging the pieces of paper, so that the water cleans them off whilst immersed in the bucket. Avoid going through the primed surface at any point and continue rubbing down until the dark coloured undercoat has been removed, to give a smooth, even surface. It is advisable to work in the more inaccessible areas first and to cut in the edges of the lugs when the paper is well worn. Whilst the rubbing down continues, use a sponge to wash away the paste that is left behind from the operation, or it will pack into the various crevices and dry rock hard. If the job has been done correctly, a smooth surface will result over the entire surface of the assembly, with no trace of the rust pits or bare metal.

The reason for colouring the alternate coats of filler will now be evident because it is easy to tell when over zealous rubbing down is in danger of contacting the bare metal. Progress through the various coats will be visible like the rings of a tree and should give ample warning that the danger level is being approached, provided that you have counted the number of coats used. Give the assembly a final wash with water, to remove any remaining traces of the rubbing-down debris and allow it to dry thoroughly.

The first coat of the finishing enamel can now be applied by brush. Use a good quality 1 in/25mm brush that will not shed hairs, preferably one that has been used previously and is therefore broken in. Work in warm, dry surroundings, so that the paint will flow evenly as it is applied. If you are working on the frame, apply the paint along the tubes sideways to start with, so that it is 'laid on' in sufficient quantity. Beware of overloading the brush or the area to which the paint is applied, otherwise runs will develop which may later prove difficult to remove. Next, work the brush from end to end so that a more even distribution of the paint is achieved, reverting to the sideways movement when necessary to aid evenness of distribution. Finish off with an end to end 'smoothing' action using the weight of the brush alone to lay off the paint. If the operation has proved a success, a smooth mirror-like surface should be evident. Leave the assembly to dry thoroughly in warm, dry surroundings for at least three days.

When the top coat has dried and hardened, take another two pieces of 320 wet and dry paper and again rub them together for a few seconds to take off the initial cut. In this instance, water is not required. The paper is used on this occasion to dull the surface only without rubbing it down, so that it is easy to see whether the second coat has given complete coverage. Wash the assembly down to remove all traces of abrasive and allow it to dry, then apply the second coating of the finishing enamel in an identical manner to the first. Allow this second coat to dry and harden in a warm, dry atmosphere before passing on to the next stage.

The next stage is usually the final stage in the finishing sequence and it is important that certain precautions are taken if a blemish free surface is to be obtained. The main dangers are particles of dust or fluff which will settle in the paint film after it has been applied and mar an otherwise perfect surface. A little forethought will help alleviate the problem and perhaps eliminate the need for yet a further coat in order to make good the damage.

The main essential is the most obvious one — to keep the atmosphere as dust free as possible. Water the floor before you commence work in order to lay the dust and try and avoid applying the final coat on a windy day. Make sure the paint tin is clean before you open the lid, and when you commence work, transfer a quantity of the paint into a separate container such as a paint can or even an old cup, so that the brush is never inserted in the tin itself. In order to keep dust to a minimum, the parts should have been flatted and washed down the previous day, using 400 paper on this occasion.

Before applying the finishing coat, use a tack rag to remove all surface dust from the parts to be painted. Use the brush you have used previously, as it is now nicely broken in, but make sure it has been cleaned very thoroughly. One recommended technique is to wash it repeatedly with paraffin, throwing away the paraffin between each wash so that only fresh cleaner is used. If a white container, such as a pudding basin, is used to contain the paraffin wash, it is easy to spot any particles that would otherwise be carried over with the brush. This technique, using synthetic coach enamel, originates from Phil Smith of the Vintage MCC, a recognised authority on restoration and concours judging. Dry the brush by striking the metal part on the workbench several times, so that the excess paraffin is shaken off. Apply the finishing coat in similar fashion to the previous two coatings and leave the parts to dry and harden in a warm, dry atmosphere. Even now some particles of dust from the atmosphere will tend to settle on the still wet parts. I have found that if the parts can be enclosed in an empty cupboard as soon as they have been painted, the risk of contamination in this way is greatly reduced.

I have quite deliberately made no recommendations about the make of paint to use or even whether it is preferable to use an oil-base paint in preference to cellulose. Nearly everyone has their own preferences and I have seen excellent results obtained with all manner of proprietary finishes. If a cellulose finish is desired, it can be either brush applied or sprayed, but it is important to ensure the correct type of cellulose for the job is obtained. The brush-on finish is thicker in viscosity, to take into account the mode of application. I have found it is more difficult to eliminate brush marks with cellulose because it is quicker drying and one must resist the temptation to retouch the surface after it has flowed out. A more acute ventilation problem occurs when cellulose is being used, because the solvent vapours can prove overpowering within a confined space. There is also a greater fire risk because the material has a lower flash point than ordinary paint. It follows that a cellulose-base filler must be used, also a cellulose paint to tint the alternate coats of filler during the stopping up process.

Some practice is advisable before adopting the spray painting approach, to achieve a good finish, free from runs and without too much overspray that will waste the paint. The main requirement is to hold the spray gun the correct distance from the part to be painted and to use the 'little but often' technique so that a succession of thin coatings are built up on one another, allowing for drying in between. This is the only way in which any real depth of finish can be achieved.

As mentioned earlier, the main disadvantage with brush and spray coated finishes is that even when dry, the paint film is still relatively soft and is very easily chipped or scratched. Fortunately, advances in paint technology during recent years have resulted in the introduction of paints containing polyurethane, an ingredient that causes them to set rock hard with a gloss finish that is comparable to that of stove enamelling. In consequence, a paint with a polyurethane base can be used to advantage, or if the finish is cellulose, a final coat of clear polyurethane varnish can be applied after the cellulose has had the opportunity to dry thoroughly.

Although the foregoing techniques have the advantage of low cost, they are nonetheless time consuming and demand a high degree of self-discipline if the perfect finish is to be achieved. Not everyone has the time, patience or ability, in which case the alternative is to place the work with an outside contractor who will have stove enamelling facilities. Without doubt, this is the most durable of all the finishes, provided it is correctly applied, for it is the technique used by nearly every motorcycle manufacturer. The problem is to find someone who will take sufficient interest in the job to do a really first class job of work and who uses a dip tank — a somewhat rare item these days. Dipping is to be preferred to spraying, because a much more even coating will result, that penetrates all the crevices. This does not mean to say that satisfactory results cannot be achieved by spray coating before stoving; if the contractor knows his job the difference will not be very marked. But you may need to give him a more detailed brief because many jobs that would appear passable to the novice would be rejected out of hand during a concours judging. A personal recommendation is best, rather than a hunt through the yellow pages with a pin. Make sure you obtain an estimate beforehand, however, or you could be in for a nasty surprise. If you have done your preparation well, you will have the satisfaction of knowing labour charges have been kept to a bare minimum.

One or two minor points to keep in mind may not be amiss at this point, especially since they will all help achieve perfection. If you suspend parts during either the painting or drying stage, use wire and not rope. This will prevent particles from the rope contaminating the finish. Forks can often be held by clamping a long metal rod in the vice and inserting this through one of the fork spindle holes, as can handlebars and other components. When the final coat has dried thoroughly, give the surface several coats of wax polish to protect it from accidental damage. Make sure, however, that if transfers are to be affixed, they are applied first. When parts have been finished, move them well away from the working area and stand them up so that they cannot accidentally fall over and suffer damage. It is very difficult indeed to touch in a damaged area without drawing unwanted attention to it.

Mention has already been made of the need to rebush girder forks when they have been stripped of paint. The old bushes should be drifted out of position, often a somewhat delicate operation. The problem can be eased if a small hacksaw blade is inserted and the bush cut through in two places, so that it can be picked out in two separate pieces. Take care when inserting the new bushes, which are easily burred if excess force is used. They will probably require in-line reaming when they are in position, so that the fork spindle is a good sliding fit.

Fork spindles are also prone to wear badly, especially if they are not greased at regular intervals. Frequently they seize in their bushes and prove very difficult to remove without risk of causing damage. Heat and the repeated application of penetrating oil is one of the best ways in which to free a badly seized spindle, using a spanner to turn the squared end of the spindle after the locknuts have been removed. If it proves necessary to make up a new spindle, make sure the correct grade of nickel steel is used. A very serious accident is likely to occur if a fork spindle happens to shear whilst the machine is in use, since the forks will fold forwards and all steering action will be lost. Often, this will throw the rider over the front of the machine as the frame grounds, and it is no coincidence that grass track sidecar outfits used to have a stout chain fitted across the upper and lower fork shackles when girder forks were in fashion. Only a special high tensile steel will successfully withstand the stresses and it is imperative that a material of this type is always used. The spindle must be a good sliding fit within the fork bushes, without any perceptible play. There must be room for grease as a lubricant, if risk of seizure is to be avoided.

Damping of girder forks is effected by means of side-mounted adjustable friction dampers. Special friction discs, made of a material similar in composition to that used for brake linings perform this action. Unfortunately they are now very difficult to obtain. The

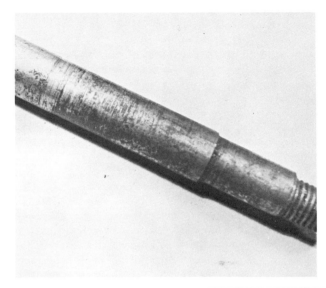

Lack of grease has caused this fork spindle to seize on some previous occasion, giving rise to these characteristic score marks. Forks should be lubricated regularly, until grease exudes from ends of spindle housings

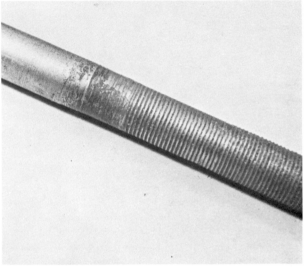

Loose spindle nuts and lack of attention has caused this spindle to chatter and wear away the thread. It is now of scrap value only

Some examples of replaceable girder fork bushes. Great care is needed when inserting them, as they are thin walled. They will need to be reamed to size, when pressed into position

Brake plate stops will need building up and reshaping if there is any play between the brake plate and the stop

Adjust fork spindles by slackening off nuts and turning the square end of the spindle. Adjuster behind operates on separate thread, to tension the side damper

There are many designs of friction damper. This one has the adjuster and damper assembly on the inside of the fork link

original discs should be retained if at all possible, provided they are not impregnated with grease or oil. If they have worn thin, the use of packing washers to apply additional pressure can sometimes be used to advantage. The parts most likely to strip are the hand adjusters, because the thread will wear after extensive use. It is very difficult to reclaim the thread without a major machining operation and often the use of packing washers can solve the problem, with the advantage that this modification is not at all easy to detect.

Telescopic forks will require a different form of attention before they are reassembled. All oil seals, dust seals and bushes should be renewed as a matter of principle, unless replacements are difficult to obtain. Under these circumstances, only parts that are 100% fit for further service should be refitted. If seals leak or have hardened, they must be renewed — they cannot be reconditioned for further use. Worn bushes must not be replaced, either. Check that the fork springs have not taken a permanent set and that both are of equal length, wound from the same gauge of material. The manufacturer's service manual or handbook will often give the various wear limits, which indicate the point at which renewal of the part concerned should be made. Always renew fork springs as a pair, never singly. The damper unit within each fork leg is another item that must be checked, otherwise the machine will give a very lively ride if there is no effective damping. It is easy to check by moving the damper rod smartly; if little or no resistance is offered, some form of repair or replacement is necessary. The course of action that has to be taken will depend on the make of machine. On some, only the complete damper unit can be renewed; on others, the piston assembly can be dismantled and the worn or damaged parts renewed.

Steering dampers, fitted to most machines that have any pretention to a sports specification, and to large capacity models capable of hauling a sidecar, can be likened in construction to the side dampers of girder forks, even though a multi-plate assembly may be used. The friction discs use the same type of material and are brought into closer contact with the metal plate on which they bear by means of the steering damper knob in this instance. It is unlikely that the steering damper assembly will have worn to anything like the extent of the fork dampers, but a check should be made nonetheless to ensure none of the parts is badly worn or distorted. A steering damper assembly that binds in places can give a machine peculiar handling characteristics and the cause of the trouble can prove difficult to detect. On some of the older machines a steering damper is a necessity, to ward off the chances of a 'speed wobble' which will gradually increase in amplitude and make the machine uncontrollable.

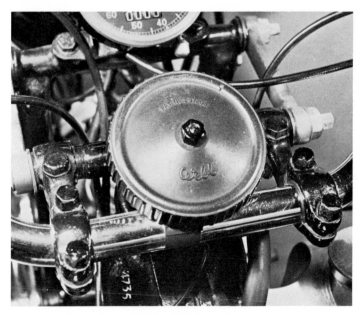

Characteristic steering damper knob, fitted to forks of Webb manufacture. Not usually required when a machine is ridden solo

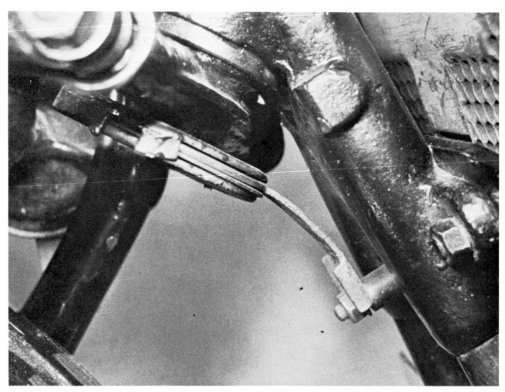

Friction plates of steering damper unit can be found at the base of the steering head. Note how the centre, fixed plates, locate with stud on the frame

Steering dampers of the Andre type are more common on racing machines. Friction plates are mounted on top of steering head; petrol tank has special stud for anchorage of central, fixed plate

Chapter Five

Wheels, tyres, brakes and mudguards

This Chapter deals with the parts of the motorcycle that are likely to suffer most from neglect, and especially corrosion, if the machine has been left in the open or in an atmosphere that is particularly damp. In nine cases out of ten, the tyres will be unfit for further use, even if they can be pumped up and appear to hold air. This is because the rubber compound will have hardened and perished with age, leading to cracking of the sidewalls and general deterioration. Furthermore, the wheels themselves will also have weakened because the spokes have rusted, effectively reducing their gauge. In short, whilst the wheels and tyres will aid the removal of the machine to the workshop where it is to be stripped down (provided the spokes have not rusted too far!), this is usually the limit of their usefulness.

Having separated the wheels from the remainder of the machine, the first requirement is to make careful note of the type, diameter and section of tyre fitted to each wheel, so that the correct replacements can be obtained. This is particularly important in the case of the older, beaded edge tyres, which, although still obtainable, are available in only a relatively small selection of sizes. It is, of course, assumed the correct tyres were fitted by the previous owner of the machine, but if any doubts exist, it is best to check with a catalogue specification or with the marque specialist. Beaded edge tyres are normally made in small batches these days, so it is important to place an order for new replacements as soon as possible. This also applies to the later, wired-on tyres, if they are of unusual size or section. In this instance you will have to rely on Ken Cobbing, who runs the Vintage MCC tyre scheme,* or on finding old stock. However, since there is not yet sufficient demand to justify limited manufacture in the more unusual sizes, often, a replacement of remould quality can sometimes provide the best answer.

Tyres that have hardened with age are difficult to remove by conventional means and for this reason, careful work with a hacksaw will usually achieve the desired results! If the tyre has perished, it is more than likely that the inner tube has suffered a similar fate, so there is little point in trying to preserve it. Don't forget to unscrew the collar that retains the valve in position where it protrudes through the wheel rim and any security bolts that may otherwise hold the tyre firmly in position.

The next operation is to dismantle the wheel bearings so that they can be examined, and if necessary, new parts obtained. Make careful note of the arrangement of any spacers or distance pieces. Do not rely on memory. Adjustable bearings of the cup and cone type were used extensively on older machines and can be likened to enlarged versions of those normally found on the average bicycle. Often, the locknuts for the adjustable cone have

* Ken Cobbing has invested little short of a personal fortune in keeping open the manufacture of beaded edge and obsolete size tyres. His efforts deserve the support of everyone in need of tyres for old vehicles.

left-hand threads; this is a point that should not be overlooked. Furthermore, the spindle and wheel nuts usually have a very fine thread, which is easily stripped if excessive force is used. If the nuts will not turn one way, try turning them the other.

Wear invariably takes the form of a track worn in both the cups and the cones, which may have broken through the hardened surface. Provided the wear is not too deep, it is often possible to reclaim the cups and cones by having them re-ground and hardened. If, however, they are beyond redemption, the only alternative is to have the hub machined so that it will accept more modern bearings of either the ball journal or taper roller type. Cup and cone bearings are now virtually unobtainable. Irrespective of their condition, it is a wise precaution to renew all the loose ball bearings, especially on account of their low cost. Take careful note of the number of ball bearings in each race and note that they are not packed tightly together. There should always be room for one extra ball, so that those within the race can revolve freely without skidding or rubbing against each other.

Ball journal or taper roller bearings are easier to replace. The former can be drifted out of position with very little difficulty; in the case of the latter, only the outer race will remain within the hub as the inner race usually comes away with the wheel spindle. Like a ball journal bearing, the outer race has to be drifted out of position. Renew any bearings that have play in them, after they have been washed free of grease and oil to enable a proper check for play. Always renew as a pair, never singly. If the bearings show signs of rotating in their housings, it will be necessary to apply a coating of Loctite Bearing Sealant to the clean surface, before the new replacement is located correctly. This should be obtained in advance, so that the instructions can be studied carefully.

A decision must now be made whether the wheel can be cleaned-up and re-used, or whether rust has taken its toll and it will be necessary to rebuild the wheel using new spokes and, perhaps, a new wheel rim. Wheel building is a specialised art, for not only must the wheel be true but it must also be laced and tensioned correctly. Comparatively few have the ability to rebuild a wheel with confidence and for this reason it is recommended that a wheel building expert is brought in at this stage. Apart from being able to advise whether the wheel will have sufficient strength when it has been cleaned-up, he will also require the wheel intact if it is to be rebuilt. Factors such as whether the wheel rim is offset in relation to the hub, how the spokes are laced and even their gauge when new, are lost if the wheel is dismantled in gay abandon by simply cutting through the spokes! Yet, quite a number meet this fate and thereafter present a considerable problem to all concerned. If the wheel rim is of the type necessary for a beaded edge tyre, the chances are that it cannot be replaced very easily and will have to be saved if at all possible. And if both the tyre size and the wheel rim are obsolete and irreplaceable, it may be necessary to rebuild on a modern rim, using a wired-on tyre of the size nearest to the original. Although not favoured by concours judges, this course of action will at least get an old machine mobile and will not detract from its appearance, other than to the very knowledgeable.

If the rims and hubs are painted, they should be reconditioned whilst the wheel builder has the wheel apart, since it is very difficult to achieve anything like a good finish after the wheel has been rebuilt. Apart from the application of a general finish to the rim or perhaps a different colour band to the raised portion of a well-base rim, any hand lining is best left until the wheel is rebuilt so that the thin line can be applied by brush as the wheel is revolved.

Another problem is that of the replacement spokes to be used. Today, it is customary to use much thicker spokes and these will look out of place in the wheel of an early machine, no matter how well the wheel has been restored. Try to match the original gauge as closely as possible and if possible, use spokes of the rustless type. They can always be painted afterwards if the originals had a dull or painted finish. Lightly remove cadmium plating with fine emery cloth before painting, as paint will not adhere for long to cadmium finish. Make sure both wheels are rebuilt in similar fashion; many a concours entry has been spoilt by having one wheel with plated spokes and the other in which the spokes have been painted. It is attention to fine detail such as this that often swings a concours decision.

This is one wheel that will never turn again. Even in this state it will still provide evidence of the lacing pattern — invaluable to the person who has to build up a replacement

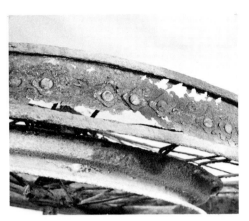

Even the rim has rusted through in places — a pity because rims suitable for beaded edge tyres are difficult to find. Note the little square plates that act as a seating for the spoke nipples and help seal the rim

Typical bearings of the cup and cone type. Only one cone is adjustable — that on the right, which has a flat for a thin spanner

Vintage oil seals were little more than a joke. These wheel bearing seals should have a circle of felt in the channel section, which will absorb the escaping grease and oil

This rear wheel sprocket has seen better days and will quickly ruin any chain. It should have been replaced long before it reached this state

Triumph sprung hub spring box carries its own warning. Heed it, or serious injury may well result

Older wheels will have a belt rim or a brake rim of the so-called 'dummy belt rim' type built into them, in which case the rim will have to be cleaned up separately and repainted before it is laced into the wheel. Problems occur if the rim has rusted through in places or has worn very thin, in which case considerable ingenuity will have to be used; there will not be a replacement available. Repairs with fibreglass and resin are practicable provided there is sufficient metal present in the first instance. Unfortunately it is not possible to change either the braking or transmission system without seriously detracting from the machine's originality. Brazing or perhaps even complete refabrication of the rim seem the only possible alternatives, in an extreme case.

Often, the brake drum forms part of one or perhaps both wheel hubs, and if the brake drum is badly scored, it is advisable to have it skimmed out in a lathe whilst the wheel is dismantled. Not everyone has a lathe large enough to swing a complete wheel and attention to this point could save a great deal of trouble later on. Sometimes the rear wheel sprocket is integral with the rear brake drum too, and this may require attention at the same time. There are one or two specialists who will re-tooth a worn sprocket, by skimming off all the old teeth and shrinking on a new toothed 'ring' in its place. Here again it would otherwise be necessary to dismantle a wheel for this operation to be completed with any success, unless the brake drum is of the 'bolt-on' variety.

Mention should also be made of the rear wheel hub fitted to a wide range of pre-1915 motorcycles which contain either a three speed gear of the epicyclic type, a multi-plate clutch, or a combination of both. There is also the sprung hub, fitted to many of the post world war 2 Triumph twins. It is wise to strip and examine these special types of hub whilst the wheel is dismantled, so that there is greater freedom of access when the hub itself becomes a handleable unit. But do not dismantle them unnecessarily; if they function correctly, **leave well alone**. A three-speed hub is a very tricky item to strip and rebuild correctly without some previous experience, whilst the Triumph sprung hub will need specialist attention. If the springs are not released under controlled conditions, a very nasty accident can result. I have seen holes in a garage roof caused by the unexpected release of the springs from a Triumph hub; fortunately the person dismantling the hub was not in the firing line at the time!

When the time comes for reassembly, make sure all the old grease is removed from the hub, and then pack it with fresh, high melting point grease. Cup and cone wheel bearings should be adjusted so that there is a just perceptible amount of play detectable at the wheel rim, otherwise there will be too much pressure on the bearing and rapid wear will set in. Wheel bearings of the taper roller type should be adjusted so that all play is removed — but only just. It is easy to apply unwittingly a loading of several tons even though the wheel will still revolve, unless the adjustment is made gradually to the point where the last small amount of play finally disappears. Ball journal bearings are non-adjustable. When driving the outer race of a taper roller bearing into place, or a ball journal bearing into its housing, hit the outer race only. If the inner race is hit at all hard, the bearing is likely to fail after a comparatively short life. Fit all ball journal bearings with the identification numbers facing outwards. This face is specially hardened to withstand the impact as the bearing is driven into position. Do not forget to replace any oil seals or felts that prevent oil or grease from reaching the brakes.

Before the tyre and tube is fitted, check whether the spoke ends have been ground-off where they protrude through the base of each spoke nipple. If not, they will eventually chafe through the inner tube and cause a puncture. Fit a new rim tape and use French chalk, in preference to liquid detergent, as an aid to tyre fitting. Although both are equally effective, the liquid detergent has the disadvantage that it will initiate rusting of the rim, underneath the tyre and inner tube.

Follow the tyre manufacturer's instructions when refitting a tyre. A few moments study of their recommended procedure, prior to fitting, will make the task very much easier. Try and avoid the use of tyre levers except as a last resort; they should not normally be necessary with a tyre of the beaded edge type. Do not omit any security bolts that were

A security bolt is often fitted to machines of the more sporting type, to ensure the rear tyre is clamped to the wheel rim and cannot rotate and therefore tear out the tyre valve. Necessary, even if it makes tyre removal and refitting a little more difficult

fitted previously, for they were fitted for a purpose. Most wired-on tyres prove difficult to fit if the bead is not worked down into the well of the wheel rim, to give the extra amount of clearance required. After fitting, pump to the required pressure and check that the tyre is seating evenly all round the rim. There is usually a moulded-on rib that can be used as a reference point. On most machines, it may be necessary to balance the front wheel, by adding weights opposite to the tyre value so that the wheel will stop in ANY random position after it has been spun. This will obviate any tendency for the wheel to 'hammer' at speed, as a result of the out-of-balance forces brought in to play.

Tyres are not always of good appearance, especially when the machine has been used on the road for a while. Their appearance can be enhanced by applying tyre paint, made by Dunlop, amongst others, — a special formulation that is flexible and suitable for application to a rubber surface. A black, shiny finish will result, like that seen on the tyres of motorcycles at the various exhibitions. Whether you pick out the tyre manufacturer's name and other details in a different colour, such as silver, white or gold, is up to you. It could be considered by some as gilding the lily, as discussed in one of the concluding Chapters.

It is not possible to generalise on braking systems because so many different types have been employed since the birth of the motorcycle. Early models usually have a stirrup-type front brake, similar to that found on most bicycles. It satisfies the law in name only, and can be disregarded in terms of effectiveness. Indeed, on occasions it can prove highly dangerous since if incorrectly aligned, it will remove the spokes from the front wheel with amazing efficiency! The back brake on these models inevitably takes the form of a pad of some friction material that is brought into contact with the inside of the belt rim, when the brake pedal is depressed. This too is not very effective because sooner or later oil from the engine or the exhaust system finds itself on the rim, thus providing an excellent lubricant where it is least needed. In the wet, the brake may not function at all, until it has dried out from frictional heat. The dummy belt rim type of brake, when fitted to the front wheel, represented an advance on the earlier types of brake, although only marginally so. Unfortunately, the brake was still rendered less effective by the presence of water. Internal expanding drum brakes also had commenced to come into fashion at the same time, although initially the brake drum was of microscopic size when compared to those in use today. There was also the Research Association brake (a form of disc brake in which the role of the pad and disc were reversed) and the servo-action drum brake — both closely associated with the Douglas marque. Other variants included the band brake used on the early model P Triumphs, interconnected brakes (usually associated with the Rudge) and, in rare instances, two independently operated brakes, both acting on the rear wheel. This latter arrangement was usually adopted when leading link forks were fitted.

It is fortunate that the DOE test contains special provision for early motor vehicles, otherwise very few would be able to achieve the minimum efficiency figure without need for drastic modifications to the existing brakes. This relaxation of the minimum efficiency figure to one that is correspondingly lower, permits even the veteran category of machine to stand a reasonable chance of being accepted. In terms of the brake itself, maximum braking efficiency can be attained only if the maximum amount of the frictional material of the brake shoe or pad is in firm contact with the braking surface. Thus if the brake drum is scored, or the brake pad worn or deformed, a loss of contact will prove inevitable, with a resulting reduction in braking efficiency. Mention of the DOE test brings forth the realisation that the stirrup front brake will have to be applied in the case of an elderly machine, so if the front wheel has been painted, it is as well to ensure it has a good, hard top coating. The brake blocks will rub through the paint film very easily if the front wheel commences to revolve as the spring balance pulls the machine along.

By far the greatest problem when restoring brakes of the pad type is the location of replacement brake blocks or some material suitable for the purpose that can be shaped to fit. Fibrax Limited used to make brake blocks and pads suitable for machines manufactured before the 1914-18 war but no stocks are held now. The choice of a lining material with the correct characteristics for the job in hand is one that is quite vital. Usually, a brake lining specialist can help in some way or other, without destroying originality to any noticeable extent. If not, you may be in for a lengthy search, with no central point of contact.

Much the same advice applies in the case of other unconventional brakes, such as the band brake or the servo-assisted brake that has an exceptionally long continuous strip of flexible brake lining material. Save what you can, even if the original is badly worn. It may be possible to reface it in some way, if all attempts to secure a replacement fail.

Internal expanding drum brakes are much easier to restore to peak efficiency, since this type of brake is still in widespread use. Although it is unlikely that replacement brake shoe linings will be available from stock, especially those of the rivet-on type, it is frequently possible to adapt other linings to fit and bond them on to the existing shoes with an expoy resin that heat hardens.

The condition of the brake drum itself is as important as the brake lining and it is imperative that the braking surface is free of score marks and other blemishes that will affect braking efficiency. If the surface is scored, or is rusty as the result of exposure, it can be reclaimed by lightly skimming it in a lathe. Only a very small amount of material should be removed, otherwise the point will quickly be reached where it is no longer possible to achieve maximum efficiency. The radius of the skimmed drum must closely approximate that of the brake shoe itself, or the linings will no longer be able to make full contact. Note that when the brake is reassembled it will be necessary to add extra end pads to the brake shoes, so that they are packed out to compensate for the small increase in diameter of the brake drum.

It is also worth mentioning that when full width hubs came into fashion during the mid-fifties, a spate of braking problems became apparent as the result of elliptical brake drums. The trouble was eventually tracked down to the wheel building stage, when the tensioning of the spokes tended to cause the distortion. The problem was eliminated by skimming the brake drum after the wheel had been built, a course of action that may again prove necessary when the wheel is subsequently rebuilt on another rim. Ultimately, the problem was cured by a different spoking arrangement, where the spokes no longer had a direct pull on the hub and brake drum.

The grade of linings used is also of importance and it is on this point that the advice of a brake lining specialist should be sought. Some linings are prone to fade if the build-up of frictional heat impairs their stability. Others are effective at high speeds only, or are adversely affected by water. There is usually a grade of lining to meet the problems in hand, without having to accept a compromise. Do not forget to relieve the leading edges by chamfering them, or there is risk of the brake locking-on when it is first applied.

Machines capable of high speeds or those where it has proved difficult to obtain good

Stirrup-type front brake fitted to early motorcycles was of ornamental value only, to satisfy the requirements of the law. If poorly aligned, it will rip spokes from the front wheel

The post-war Scott of 1946 onwards was one of several machines to have a twin front brake. Some form of compensating device, such as the Scott balance box shown, is necessary to ensure both brakes are applied simultaneously

Most rear brakes are rod operated. Note unusual brake plate anchorage and strengthened housing around brake operating cam, typical of Veloce attention to detail

Some machines, especially those with rear suspension, favour a cable-operated rear brake. In the example shown, Douglas use a similar method for brake plate anchorage to that adopted by Veloce

Cable adjusters are usually found on the brake plate and may, or may not, incorporate a return spring. Scotts have an unusual cam stop for the end of the brake operating arm

Not often found today is the volute spring, used by Douglas to help return the front brake operating arm

61

braking efficiency, often benefit from the treatment that is applied when racing preparation is undertaken. Under these circumstances it is customary to fit new linings to the brake shoes and then fit the complete assembly to the brake plate, which is set up in a lathe. By lightly skimming the linings whilst they are rotating, it can be ensured that the shoes will make maximum contact with the brake drum when they are applied. Anyone who has ridden a machine before and after this treatment will need no convincing. Irrespective of how the relined brake shoes are set up, always ensure the return springs are in good order and that aluminium alloy brake shoes have their hardened end pads replaced.

The way in which the brake plate is anchored is another point that should have particular attention. If the anchorage works loose, is inaccurately located, or breaks, there is every possibility of a serious accident. This is because the brake plate will then tend to revolve with the wheel and apply the brake in the full-on position, causing a skid that can be quite frightening. There must be no measurable play at the brake stop, if it is of the peg and slot type. When wear develops at this point, the rate will be greatly accelerated by the constant backwards and forwards motion, which in itself will impair braking efficiency. Eventually a shear stress will be applied to the peg, causing it to break off without prior warning. It follows that brake torque arms should be examined at regular intervals and never drilled in an attempt to lighten the machine. All bolts and nuts must have good threads and be tightened securely, preferably with a spring washer interposed. It is no coincidence that the Japanese, who pay fine attention to detail, drill anchor bolts and fit a split pin, so that the retaining nut cannot work loose and be lost. Only high tensile nuts and bolts should be used.

Some brake plates are surprisingly thin and can be seen to flex when the brake is applied heavily. Provided there is room, they should be ribbed internally, to stiffen them up. It has always been a Velocette characteristic to either web the projection on the rear brake plate through which the operating cam spindle protrudes, or to fit an external link piece between this projection and the wheel spindle. Both approaches help eliminate any flexing that may occur during heavy braking, in a very practical manner.

Do not forget that thin brake cables or operating rods with bends in them can give the illusion of spongy braking as the result of unwanted extension. A heavier gauge cable, or one of the Bowdenex type, will cure the former; if the brake rod needs to have bends in it, it should be gussetted for extra strength, particularly if the rod is of only thin gauge.

Mudguards are the components likely to have suffered most on an old motorcycle, because they are usually of comparatively thin gauge metal and will have corroded from both sides if the machine has been stored for any appreciable time. Unfortunately, they are also one of the most difficult items to replace, if the new mudguard is to follow the original specification. Often, with a heavily beaded edge and side valences of one kind or another, there is nothing remotely similar in current production. In consequence, it is necessary to either repair the original (which may involve the patching of substantial portions with modern, resin-based materials of the flexible type) or to fabricate an entirely new mudguard, using whatever can be utilised of the correct basic shape.

Provided the original will withstand such treatment, it should be bead blasted so that all rust and scale is removed, exposing the bright metal surface. If the surface has not gone through in places or is exceptionally thin, the surface can be built-up with filler and then enamelled and sprayed by following the technique outlined for the restoration of the frame and forks. This is another task that will demand great patience, for the polished surface that ultimately results will otherwise show any blemishes or imperfections. It will also be necessary to undertake a certain amount of other preparatory work, to ensure that the lugs which attach the mudguard to the forks and frame are not loose or in danger of working loose. This also applies to any brackets for the attachment of mudguard stays or a stand of some kind, and in the case of the rear mudguard only, to any portion that is made quickly detachable to aid wheel removal. Number plate attachments are another item; on early Triumph models, to quote but one example, they took the form of an aluminium alloy casting attached to the front mudguard, which is prone to corrode badly or even crack.

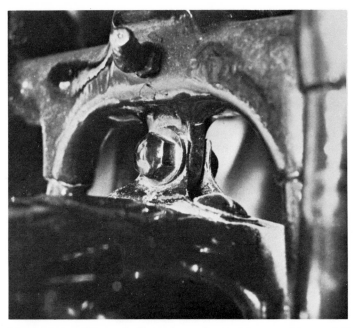

Mudguards must be positively anchored to the forks, so that they cannot rotate with the stays. This centre bracket fitting is typical of Webb girder fork practice

Almost invariably such fitments are rivetted into position and if allowed to work loose, they eventually elongate the rivet holes, making a repair quite difficult. In an extreme case, a large amount of mudguard may pull through altogether, leaving a sizeable hole. Cracks or splits can be welded and filed flat again.

Quite often it is the rear mudguard that is in the worst shape, because it will have been drilled in various places, perhaps following the efforts of a previous owner to fit a pillion seat, rear carrier or pannier bags. When removed from the machine, such a mudguard will resemble a Gruyere cheese; even club badges necessitate the drilling of one or two holes. Take heed, however, if any transfer was affixed to the mudguard and note, or better still, copy the form and size, before the clean-up commences. Quite a number of manufacturers added a smaller version of the petrol tank transfer, or perhaps a badge or sales slogan of some kind. This will need to be reproduced during the final stages of the restoration.

In the case of a badly holed or thin mudguard which is unavailable, a very effective repair that is difficult to detect, can be achieved by the use of the fibreglass technique, using either an epoxy or a polyester resin. A complete repair kit of this type can be purchased for a reasonable sum, sufficient in quantity to cover most repairs of this nature on the machine. The main essentials are the need to work in a clean, dry atmosphere, to pay careful attention to the instructions provided with every repair kit, especially with regard to the mixing procedure, and to have the surface to be patched, clean, rust and scale-free, prior to application of the resinous compound. Briefly, the usual technique is to mix the resin with the recommended amount of promoter and catalyst so that it will start to harden after a set period of time. Too much, and it will set too rapidly; too little and it may never harden at all but merely reach a gel-like stage and progress no further. This is just one reason why the kit instructions should be properly understood and followed to the letter. If a hole has to be patched, it is customary to lay a piece of glass fibre mat over the hole so that it covers a reasonable amount of the surround as well as the hole itself. Resin is then worked into the mat with a brush and allowed to harden. Successive layers can be built up in this manner, if required, and it is possible to obtain a good smooth top surface that will not require too much attention, if a fine grade of glass fibre mat is used for the top layer. Larger holes require different attention and it is often necessary to use perforated metal to bridge the gap, into which is worked resin, loaded with filler. The great advantage of this type of repair is that it can be carried out quite successfully by anyone unable to repair damaged metalwork by the more traditional techniques of panel beating or welding — provided the instructions are followed closely. The resultant 'patch' is easy to smooth down and blend in with the surround, after it has hardened. Excess material can be removed with a coarse file or a Surform plane tool and then finished off with emery cloth of increasing fineness. If sufficient care and patience is used, the repair will be indistinguishable from the original surround, after re-enamelling. Just one reminder. Never work in a damp atmosphere or on a very wet day. Water vapour will prevent the resin from curing correctly, and it may not even set at all.

The foregoing does not necessarily mean that the fibreglass approach has completely superseded the more traditional types of repair work, which can be carried out equally effectively by someone experienced in either panel beating or welding and brazing. It merely brings this type of repair work within the scope of the person who has little or no experience of metalworking processes, so that unskilled hands can take advantage of modern techniques to obtain a professional finish.

It is still possible to purchase steel mudguards in a limited variety of cross-sections from at least one supplier. It would be comparatively easy for anyone skilled with brazing equipment to attach valences, lugs and other attachments so that a replica of the original could be fabricated from scratch. Competition machines and others with quite brief mudguards present far less of a problem. It is still possible to purchase light alloy mudguards, front and rear, of the type that were fitted to competition machines after the second war. These are drilled easily and adapted to fit. For machines other than competition models, they can be black enamelled to disguise their origin. It will be necessary to 'kill' the highly polished surface to get the paint to adhere; a favourite dodge is to wipe the surface with a rag soaked in vinegar and allow it to dry off before the first coat is applied. It would seem unlikely that the more modern fibreglass or plastic mudguards can be adapted for use in similar fashion, because their styling is far removed from that which would be found on the older type of machine.

Mudguard stays are easy to make up from tube, with the ends flattened and drilled, from mild steel strip or threaded rod, to form a replica of the original pattern. Do not overlook the fact that the front mudguard must always be positively located with some part of the front forks, so that it is prevented from rotating. Numerous instances have occurred where a front mudguard unsupported in this fashion has moved unexpectedly, and has made contact with the tyre, which has caused it to rotate and form a skid immediately under the front wheel. The dire consequences of this happening need not be elaborated. In the case of girder forks, there must always be a shaped bracket which links the centre of the mudguard with the main part of the fork blades — often taking the form of a small lug immediately below the fork spring mounting. On telescopic forks, it is customary to have a special stay that joins both fork sliders and passes either over or under the centre of the mudguard, to which it is also bolted. There are, however, many variations on this basic theme, depending on how the mudguard itself is suspended.

Do not be tempted to use alloy mudguard stays, even with competition mudguards, unless lightness of weight is essential and the machine is to have limited, off-road use only. This type of mudguard stay will fracture very easily, usually as the result of vibration transmitted to the front or rear of the machine. This also applies to bridge pieces to which the mudguard stays or other fitments may be connected.

At the points of attachment of the mudguard, use very large diameter washers under the bolt heads that are located inside the mudguard. This will spread the load as the bolts are tightened and prevent them from pulling through the thin section metal. It is possible to obtain special mudguard washers supplied specifically for this purpose, that are coated with an anti-rust finish. Make sure the washer is curved to conform to the inner contour of the mudguard, otherwise it may deform the shape as the bolt is tightened. It is also advisable to use a spring or a shakeproof washer under each mudguard nut, so that the chances of the nuts and bolts working loose are greatly reduced.

Number plate holders and any other fitments that bolt direct to the mudguard should be fixed in position after the mudguard itself has been renovated, enamelled and attached to the machine. In many cases it will not be possible to fit them after the wheel has been replaced, or to tighten them sufficiently without having to remove the wheel temporarily. Some permanent fixtures, such as club badges, can have their retaining studs or bolts wired together under the mudguard, as a safeguard against them working loose or being stolen. Make sure, however, that the rear tyre will have sufficient clearance, especially when the machine has a spring frame. Tyre fling itself can account for a surprising increase in the diameter of a tyre when it is rotating. If it is necessary to shorten bolts, file them square again afterwards. Concours judges frequently look underneath mudguards too, especially when looking for a tie-breaker in a closely fought presentation.

In many respects it is advisable to treat the underside of both mudguards with underseal or some other form of bituminous compound to offset the effects of future corrosion. Unfortunately, it would seem that treatment of this nature may actually mitigate against the owner of an otherwise perfectly prepared concours machine, simply because this form of protection was not applied by the manufacturer when the machine was new. Most concours judges expect to see a shiny black surface on the underside of the mudguards if the owner of the machine has prepared it for display in the proper fashion. Whilst it can be argued quite convincingly that the basic objective of a real concours finish is to preserve a machine and to present it in an 'as new' condition, it can also be argued that the application of underseal will aid the preservation aspect and is not at all conspicuous. I would prefer not to comment on this one. The borderline between sheer originality and common sense is indeed very fine!

Rigid frame machines are usually fitted with two stands, a rear stand that is often of the spring-up type and a front stand that takes the place of the lower front mudguard stays. For some strange reason, it is the stands that are frequently missing from machines that have been left neglected, the more so on sporting or competition models where they may have formed an unnecessary attachment in terms of extra weight. The front stand is usually quite easy to make from scratch since it is virtually two lengths of tubing joined near the extremity by a cross-piece. There are, of course, variations on this theme, even though none would prove too difficult to fabricate from scratch. After a lengthy period of service, the closed ends of the two main tubes will begin to wear through and many a restoration job has been rendered imperfect by failure to have the ends filled with brazing metal and reshaped before re-enamelling. Note that there is usually a lug welded to the cross-piece, so that the stand can be held to the bottom of the front mudguard. The customary arrangement takes the form of a bolt or stud projecting from the lower end of the front mudguard, which will pass through a slot cut in the lug welded to the cross-piece of the stand. The stand is fastened in many cases by a peculiar but instantly recognisable nut, shaped rather like half a wing nut. The arm welded to the nut provides the necessary leverage for the nut to be tightened securely to hold the stand in the 'up' position, without need to use a spanner.

The rear stand is more difficult to fabricate in a great many cases, because the side arms take the form of two stout castings or forgings, held together by a cross-piece similar to that of the front stand. On many machines, the stand is spring-loaded and will revert to the 'up' position immediately the weight of the machine is taken off it. This is accomplished in most cases by an extension spring mounted between a lug on the frame and a lug on one of the stand legs. If the stand is not of the spring-up type, it will be retained by a special spring-loaded clip attached to the end of the rear mudguard, or in some cases, may be bolted direct to two small lugs extending from the end of the rear mudguard. Here again, the ends of the side members will tend to wear through as time progresses and should be filled with brazing metal prior to application of the finish. If the stand has to be removed, difficulty is sure to be experienced if it is one of the spring-loaded type and the spring has to be re-tensioned. Many dodges have been suggested ranging from the use of small wedges driven through the coils of the spring to expand it, to the use of a stout wire puller or even a screwdriver to ease the end of the spring over one or other of the lugs. Make sure both stand bolts have been replaced and tightened before the spring is coupled up, otherwise it is only

65

too easy to strip the bolt threads when trying to get correct alignment of the bolt and the hole into which it is to fit, whilst pulling against the spring tension. The stand bolts must be tight or a similar problem will occur if one or other happens to drop out.

It is often possible to adapt a rear stand from another machine, provided the main essentials are correct; ie, the length of the side arms and the angle at which the stand rests when it is in the lowered position. There may also be secondary problems with regard to silencer clearance, although most problems can be overcome with a little ingenuity. Apart from making the machine complete, a stand is an essential requirement when it is necessary to park the machine, and even more so, when it is necessary to remove the rear wheel on the road.

To preserve original appearance, it is sometimes necessary to reproduce the small lug into which the stand tubes are brazed, or even a specially shaped forging. It is possible to overcome this problem by making up wooden patterns and having it cast in bronze. When made-up into the stand, and painted, it will be indistinguishable from new.

A great many older machines were fitted with some form of rear carrier, which quite often formed an integral part of the rear mudguard stay assembly. There is also a unique form of rear carrier that when inverted, forms the rear wheel stand. Most carriers are constructed of tubing and should prove relatively easy to repair, or if necessary, to fabricate from an original pattern. The mudguard will probably be retained to the carrier by half-clips, which are very easy to make.

Another item associated with the rear carrier on early machines, or with the rear mudguard stays on most post-1930 models, is the tool bag or tool box, in which to carry the machine's tool kit and any spares likely to be needed for emergency roadside repairs. Where a rear carrier is fitted, it is often the practice to mount a pair of identical tool bags, one on each side of the frame, held in place with metal clips. The bag itself may be made entirely of leather or may have a leather front only, the remainder taking the form of a metal box. It is rarely possible to resurrect the leather if it has remained untreated for a number of years and furthermore, it is highly probable that the stitching will have rotted. Fortunately, there are still a handful of specialists engaged in leatherwork of one kind or another, who may be prepared to make a replica of the original, so do not discard the remains — they will probably be useful as a pattern. A saddler or upholsterer is the person to contact, preferably an older man who runs a small business and may be interested to take on the job for the novelty aspect. But do ask for a quotation first, or you could be in for a nasty shock! Needless to say, the type of tool bag with a leather front only causes much less trouble, for it is quite easy to fabricate a new metal box and then attach a replica of the front. Sometimes the disabled are well equipped and willing to undertake small jobs of this nature, so it is well worth while making a few local enquiries.

Metal tool boxes come in all shapes and sizes, and it is not too difficult to obtain a replacement close to the original design or, if needs be, to make up a replica. On sporting or competition models, the tool box is another item that is likely to have been taken-off in order to save weight. In consequence, it may be necessary to refer to the original catalogue, so that the shape and general dimensions of the tool box can be ascertained.

No mention has been made of centre stands which, in the main, are fitted to spring frame machines where a rear stand would no longer be practicable. A centre stand is usually attached to a lug on the underside of the frame or to an extension of the rear engine plates, and is arranged to spring into the fully retracted position when the weight of the machine is taken from it. Wear will occur in the pivot bolt and in either the lug or the holes in the engine plates, the latter tending to become elongated. It is important that any wear is eliminated at this stage by building up with brazing metal and redrilling, if necessary, or perhaps by bushing. The latter approach has the advantage that future repairs are easier to carry out. Make sure the extension spring is in good condition too. If the stand drops whilst the machine is in motion, especially when cornering, the rider will be unseated only too easily. Prop stands should receive similar attention, with regard to both their pivot and the extension spring that returns them to the folded position. The latter are not much in

Early stands performed the dual role of a rear carrier, when they were retracted. The Anglian shown here is just one of many examples

Front wheel stand was at one time considered essential, and proved a godsend in the event of a front wheel puncture. Fitted to a vintage racer, this stand has been wired into position

For some peculiar reason, most of the older machines found today have the rear stand missing. It provides by far the best means of parking the machine safely, on a hard surface

This special quick-release clip retains the stand in the retracted position, whilst the machine is on the move

The rear carrier was a built-on feature of most elderly machines. Apart from luggage carrying duties, it often offered provision for the carriage of a pillion passenger, when the only concession to comfort was a strapped-on cushion

Neat leather toolbags were suspended from the carrier and used to carry whatever tools and spare parts were necessary for roadside repairs. Some needed the equivalent of a Gladstone bag for this purpose!

evidence on pre-1930 models. Mention should also be made of proprietary fittings that were in common use after the second world war, such as the 'Esway', a telescopic form of prop stand that will cause a very nasty accident if the rider forgets to retract it before starting off. It clips to the frame in a vertical position, and does not retract of its own accord when the weight of the machine is taken from it.

Some machines, such as the post-war Douglas twins, have an aluminium alloy centre stand of substantial dimensions, which is subject to fatigue failure after long service. It is worth noting that the London Douglas MCC have had a batch of new centre stands cast, which are available to members at moderate cost — yet another benefit to be gained from joining a one-make club. Most other types of centre stand can be straightened under the influence of heat, and welding or brazing used to make a permanent repair. A centre stand is the first item to suffer from the effects of laying the bike over on fast corners.

Like the rear stand, the centre stand fitted to spring frame models needs a firm base on which to support the machine securely

Chapter Six

Reconditioning petrol and oil tanks

The petrol tank is the part of a motorcycle that receives the most attention when the machine is looked at for the first time. Usually of a pleasing and colourful design, or of a distinctive shape, it forms the focal point, so that special care and attention to detail with the presentation will be more than amply repaid. A good first impression counts for much, irrespective of whether the machine is for sale, is being judged in a concours competition, or simply represents the owner's efforts to make good, from the usual pile of rusty junk that seems to await most restorers.

The oil tank is less likely to be an eye-catcher because it presents a smaller surface area and is often mounted in a much less conspicuous position. There are, however, exceptions such as the type of oil tank fitted to the so-called 'garden gate' Manx Norton. Even a black enamelled oil tank, relieved only by a gold transfer showing the recommended oil level, can add something extra to a machine, if it has received the same amount of care and attention as the petrol tank.

Before stripping the old paint from a petrol or oil tank, make a detailed sketch of any panels or lining, the design of lettering and size of any transfers used. The thickness of the lining and the exact shape of the panels must be recorded for the preservation of originality, also the exact detail of the transfers. It is often wise to enlist the help of an artist at this stage because some of the older transfers are unobtainable and may have to be signwritten, when the tank has been refinished. The question of colour matching will also arise, a difficult problem as the original finish will have faded. Often, traces of the original colour can be found on the underside of petrol and oil tanks, where a film of oil has provided a protective coating over the ages or by gently rubbing the surface with wetted 400 grade wet and dry paper to remove the original top coat of varnish applied to the older 'flat' tanks. It will have yellowed with age and dulled down the colours. If knee grips are fitted or if the tank is retained in position by means of clips, traces of the original paint can sometimes be found in these locations too. To obtain a correct colour match, use the British Standard (BS) for paint colours. Once you have a reference number, a paint or cellulose having the same BS number will provide the correct match to the original finish. A good example of how it is possible to misinterpret a true match without such a means of reference can be gained by looking at vintage Triumph petrol tanks, at any substantial gathering of old motorcycles. The original green/grey finish is very difficult to match and the number of variations to be found is quite staggering.

Having stripped the tank of the original finish and removed any rust or scale, the tank should next be examined for any dents or scratches that will have to be filled or knocked out. The decision on which course of action to take may be influenced by any other problems that may be apparent, such as loose baffles within the tank (to prevent petrol

Manufacturers sometimes have their own distinctive shapes of petrol tank. That used on the Scott is instantly recognisable, even if the transfers have long since disappeared

The early post-war Douglas has its own style too, low mounted and finished in the traditional Douglas colours of blue and silver

surge), or as happens quite often in many of the older tanks, a leakage between the main petrol compartment of the tank and the smaller compartment that contains engine oil. In either case it may be necessary to cut the bottom out of the tank in order to effect the necessary repairs, making it easy for an experienced panel beater to remove any dents or other blemishes from the surface. This is the technique used by most professional tank repairers, irrespective of whether the internal parts of the tank need attention too. After knocking out the dents, the bottom of the tank is replaced and then leak tested, prior to refinishing.

Early tanks are made from tinplate and have soft-soldered joints, so that anyone skilled with a soldering iron can usually make an effective repair. Experience is, however, essential as too much heat may cause the whole seam to run and you will end up with a pile of nicely cut tinplate sheets that originally formed the tank! Later tanks, especially those of the saddle type, have welded seams, making the use of welding equipment necessary to repair anything more than a small pinhole. A few saddle tanks have soft-soldered seams and are usually characterised by a wavy or scalloped edge - the Manx Norton petrol tank is a good example.

Petrol vapour is extremely explosive and it cannot be over-emphasised that every possible precaution must be taken during tank repairs, particularly if a blowlamp or welding torch is used. Drain the tank completely, then fill it with water several times, to make sure all traces of petrol are removed. Alternatively, the exhaust gases from a car exhaust pipe can be led into the tank and left to flush out the petrol vapour by keeping the engine running for a while. This, however, is an 'open air technique' usually seen at competition events when emergency repairs are essential. An engine should never be run within a confined space for quite obvious reasons. Whatever method you use, do check that the tank is vapour-free before you start work with a naked flame. Even the most skilled tank repairer will always hold a welding torch at arms length over the open filler before he commences work. If an explosion is likely to occur, it is better that it should happen under controlled conditions.

Small dents or scratches can be filled by using the fibreglass technique mentioned in the previous Chapter for the repair of mudguards. It is also possible to use cellulose filler, and even soft solder. Make sure, however, that any material used to fill in the dent has a good 'key' with the metal surface, so that there is no danger of it falling out at a later date. Dents can sometimes be pulled out by the simple expedient of temporarily soldering a bolt to the centre of the depression and using it for the pull. Often petrol tanks are left empty with the filler cap removed and in due course the tank will commence to rust from the inside. This can create problems if there is no necessity to open up the bottom of the tank, because the rust and scale that have formed will otherwise prove quite difficult to remove. Much of the loose material can be removed by placing a number of nuts inside the tank and shaking it around quite vigorously so that the nuts remove all the loose rust and scale, permitting it to be shaken out of the filler cap orifice. What remains can be sealed into position by pouring a resinous material such as Petseal* into the tank which, when swilled around will distribute itself in the form of a thin layer over the whole of the inside of the tank and set hard to provide a protective coating. This is also an effective means of leak-proofing a petrol tank when it is desired to preserve the existing finish. The total cost of treatment in this fashion is very low.

Sometimes it proves necessary to remove old oil from a combined petrol and oil tank, where the oil has thickened considerably as a result of its long storage. Heat may help reduce the viscosity so that it can be poured out more easily, but if it has gone too thick, it may have to be scraped out and then the residue removed with strong caustic soda solution. Before resorting to any such action, withdraw the handpump and any other fitments that may suffer damage from heat or the action of the caustic soda solution. A vegetable base oil, such as Castrol R, is especially difficult to deal with successfully in this respect, although methylated spirits may prove helpful.

It is less likely that aluminium alloy petrol tanks will be encountered, which is just as well, because they require specialist attention if leaks develop or if dents have to be removed. NEVER use caustic soda to clean out a tank of aluminium alloy because it will react violently with the alloy and etch it away at a very rapid rate.

Before the tank is smoothed down prior to the application of the primer coat, check that the mounting lugs (if any) are in sound condition and their point of attachment has not cracked or split. Usually this takes the form of a welded joint. Cracking or splitting is liable to occur as the result of vibration and often manufacturers fit a bracing strip across the underside of the tank, close to the nose, to prevent any flexing that may occur. As this is a bolt-on item, fitted after the tank is in position, it is often omitted by owners, especially as it hinders removal of the tank on a future occasion. If the attachment studs are there and the strip is not, one should be made up and fitted, since it serves a useful purpose.

When a tank is attached to the frame by means of bolts that pass through frame lugs into threaded inserts within the bottom of the tank, two types of problem can occur. If the original shouldered bolts are lost and not replaced with bolts of identical type, it is possible to tighten the unshouldered replacements to such an extent that they burst through the

* Solent Plastics Ltd

bottom of the insert and cause an instant escape of petrol. Also, if bolts of incorrect thread are fitted, it is quite easy to strip the thread from the insert, so that the tank can no longer be secured easily at this point. In both cases a repair is difficult to execute, because it is virtually impossible to reseal the bottom of the insert without cutting the tank open or because there is insufficient metal to tap oversize. The most practical remedy for the former problem is to make what in effect is a very shallow grub screw that can be threaded into the insert until it reaches the former limit of travel. If the grub screw is then sealed into position with either an epoxy resin such as Araldite or soft solder, the leak will be resealed and the original length of bolt can be reused provided it is shortened the correct amount. The latter problem is best remedied by reclaiming the thread by means of a Helicoil insert, and by making sure that bolts of corresponding thread size are always fitted in the future. The threaded inserts for a hand gear change gate can be repaired in similar manner. Petrol and oil unions that need replacing usually can be soft or hard soldered into position - brazing is impracticable because invariably they are made of brass

Always leak-test a repaired tank by blocking up the various outlet points and then applying air from a foot pump so that there is a small build-up of pressure within. If an air line is used, take great care to avoid a build-up of pressure which may make the sides of the tank bulge and distort permanently. Only a slight build-up of pressure within should prove necessary; the leaks (if any) can be detected by applying a detergent/soap solution along the seams and joints and looking for bubbles.

This is also the time to repair any damage to the stud(s) attached to the sides of the petrol tank to which the plates holding knee grip rubbers are attached. A special form of stud that resembles a very large, flat-headed screw is often used for this purpose, which is soft-soldered into position. Make sure it is located in the correct position first and that the studs are exactly in line on both sides of the tank.

No specific mention has been made of oil tank repairs because identical techniques are used. Problems may occur, however, when soldering or brazing, due to the tendency for residual oil to seep through the joint or section that is being repaired, through the action of heat. For this reason it is always best to clean the oil tank thoroughly at the very commencement of operations, if only to remove any sludge and sediment that has accumulated whilst the machine was in use. Oil filters should be removed and cleaned separately, irrespective of whether they are of the gauze or fabric type. Note that if a final wash out is given with petrol or paraffin, a serious fire/explosion risk will again be evident, as in the case of the petrol tank; it should be dealt with in a similar manner. Soldering problems can often be eased by using one of the proprietary surface cleansers such as Bakers Fluid, which will help make the solder flow more readily. In the case of brazing a compound known as Easiflow will have similar beneficial results.

Oil tank attachment points should be examined with particular care because they are more likely to fracture than those of the petrol tank; the oil tank suffers more from the effects of vibration. Check that any vent pipes and breathers are free from obstructions, otherwise a pressure build-up may occur within the tank, giving rise to oil leaks and possibly even obstructing the free flow of oil from the main outlet. Some oil tanks are rubber mounted, in which case the mountings should be checked to ensure they have not perished or hardened.

The base colour of the tank can be applied after the customary surface preparation, which should closely follow that prescribed in Chapter 4, for the frame and forks. That is, unless the tank has areas of plating, in which case it must be plated all over first. Any subsequent panelling and lining requires a certain amount of expertise and a steady hand, using masking tape wherever possible. Even the smallest imperfection or lack of attention to detail will immediately be obvious, so unless you consider yourself competent enough to see the job through and present a professional finish, it is wiser to call in a signwriter at this stage. It is now that the detailed sketches made at an earlier date will prove invaluable as a guide, especially when there is some need for an indication of the correct profile and size of the panel(s), the shape and thickness of any lining and its distance from the edge of the tank.

Usual method of attachment is by means of bolts that locate with threaded inserts in base. Bolts pass through rubber washers, to cushion vibration and shocks

Kneegrips fit over plates which bolt to threaded insert(s) in side of tank. Sometimes, they bolt to tank direct, without plates

Tap fitted to the oil tank main outlet prevents oil from seeping through the pump to fill the crankcase, when the machine is standing. Usually fitted to the old racing machines. Forget to turn on and engine is ruined

Some taps use a cork as the sealing medium, and are of the push-pull type

Lever-type taps give a higher rate of flow and are invariably found on the more sporting models. A ground, taper joint provides the leakproof seal between tap body and rotor

As a tank is made in two halves, it is often necessary to connect the two halves by an underpipe, as shown. A single petrol tap can then be used. Disadvantage is the need to drain the tank, prior to removal from machine

Make quite sure that any paint used in this context will be completely petrol and oil-proof when dry - an important consideration that could easily be overlooked. If the tank has been plated first, it may be necessary to dull the plating in the area of the enamelled panels just a little, using 400 grade paper, so that the enamel has a good 'key'. Allow the tank to dry thoroughly in a dust-free atmosphere and then give it several good coats of polish, but not in the areas where any transfers are to be affixed.

If you undertake the panelling and lining work yourself, use good quality brushes and especially the long haired lining brush the professional uses, or a lining wheel, for the application of the lines. Mask off the areas to be painted wherever possible with masking tape, so that a clearly defined edge is obtained, free from any ripples or waves. Do not remove masking tape until the paint is hard and do not be afraid to erase any mistakes and start all over again; the visual effect has to be correct if a really good presentation is to result.

Whilst the paint is drying, attention can be given to the various tank fittings, which will have been removed at an earlier stage. Filler caps are invariably plated, but before going to the trouble of cleaning up the originals, check that replacements are not available over the counter. If they are, this invariably proves much cheaper and will save a lot of unnecessary, monotonous work. Check also that the cap seats effectively, to prevent spillage of petrol or oil whilst the machine is in motion. Most use some form of cork or compressible synthetic rubber seal for this purpose, which should be renewed if it has hardened with age. Make sure that the new seal does not block the tank vent in the filler cap, however, or an obscure fault will be evident when the machine is first used. If air cannot enter the closed compartment, the flow of fluid will eventually cease and the cause of the resultant air lock will prove very elusive to track down. If the filler cap is of the snap release type, make sure it turns easily and that the pivot pin is not badly worn. A badly fitting cap will produce an annoying rattle, as the result of vibration.

Machines of the earlier type often have a hand pump in either the petrol tank or the oil tank - the former, if the petrol tank contains a special oil compartment. The pump usually threads on to a circular extension that projects from the oil compartment or oil tank and can be unscrewed to release the plunger mechanism which draws oil from the reservoir and delivers it to the engine and/or gearbox either directly, or via a drip feed regulator, and a sight glass. If the pump does not work, the chances are that the leather washer on the end of the plunger has split or deteriorated so that it no longer forms an effective seal. The plunger is, in fact, virtually a miniature version of the bicycle pump and utilises the same form of washer. The pump plunger assembly will have to be dismantled so that the end caps, plunger knob and rod can be plated, together with the ancillary parts such as the sight glass holder, drip feed adjuster and union nut and the oil pipe(s) and tap(s) that form part of the complete lubrication system. Fortunately, these parts are invariably made of brass, which means they will plate very easily after they have been cleaned up and smoothed down.

Before the oil pipes or taps are plated, they should be checked to ensure leakage is unlikely to occur. Loose nipples should be re-soldered into position and if the taps are of the lever type, the rotating portion should be ground into the main body, using very fine grinding paste. If the pipes have any sharp bends or are tending to flatten in the vicinity of a bend, it is best to make up a replacement, since it is very difficult indeed to resurrect a pipe that is deformed in this manner. Copper tubing is easy to bend once it has been annealed; all that is necessary is to heat the tubing in the area where it is to be bent, until it colours, and then plunge the pipe into a bowl of cold water. It can now be worked very easily. To harden the tubing again, re-heat it and allow it to air cool. It is customary to have one complete circular bend (in the horizontal plane) in a petrol pipe or a long oil pipe, to give a certain amount of resilience. Without this, the pipe would eventually fracture, as copper tends to work harden as it ages.

It will probably be necessary to give the pipes a thorough clean out by blowing them through with air, and to clean any filter gauzes or other strainers in the system. Old petrol

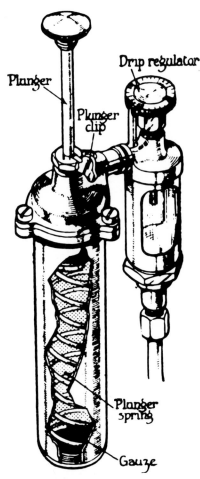

Plunger

Drip regulator

Plunger clip

Plunger spring

Gauze

Figure 2 Early lubrication systems relied upon a drip feed lubrication and hand pump, built in to the oil compartment of the petrol tank. Most popular was the Best and Lloyd semi-automatic design, shown in cutaway form above

will dry, leaving behind a gummy residue, which is quite capable of blocking any fine holes or restricted pipe bends. It is important that filters are retained in the system, or added if they are absent. If a machine is used again after a lapse of several years, small particles will inevitably break away from the inner surface of the petrol or oil tank, creating a series of blockages that are extremely annoying and difficult to clear. It is doubtful, however, whether it is still necessary to retain filters in the petrol and oil filler inlets, other than for appearances' sake. There is far less danger today of petrol or oil sold in bulk being contaminated, than it was many years ago.

Where oil is fed to the crankcase by external means other than by an oil pump that maintains a constant pressure, it is customary to include some form of one-way valve in the system, so that the gases within the crankcase cannot pass back up the pipe and create an air lock. Usually this takes the form of a simple disc valve, found in the base of the sight feed chamber. If the sight glass tends to fill with oil or becomes aerated, the chances are that the disc is not moving freely. It is easily dismantled for cleaning purposes by separating the two locknuts that comprise the body. Do not lose the disc, which is very small, and make sure it is clean and seating correctly before the unit is reassembled. Check by blowing through it. Air should pass one way, and be cut-off the other. If oil leaks tend to occur around the pump plunger or the drip feed adjuster, the gland should be repacked with a small quantity of packing - asbestos string can often be used quite successfully. It should not be necessary to tighten the union nut too tightly to obtain a good seal, since this will make operation of the plunger or adjuster difficult.

75

If the engine is water-cooled, the cylinder block will have a drain tap fitted. It is preferable to wire it into position; the temptation for bystanders to fiddle with it can lead to disaster. This tap originated from a Jaguar car engine

Never change from a vegetable base oil to one of the mineral base type that is in common use today, without cleaning out the entire system. Vegetable and mineral base oils do not mix and under the influence of heat will form a rubber-like sediment which rapidly cause blockages and prove very difficult to remove. In point of fact, there is no longer any advantage to be gained from using vegetable base oils such as Castrol R since today's mineral oils have been developed to such an extent that they are more than an adequate substitute. They have the advantage of being much cheaper, can be obtained at every roadside garage and are far easier to remove if they find their way to the exterior of the machine. More important, they are not so prone to absorb water and in consequence there is much less risk of internal engine corrosion, especially if the machine is laid up for any period of time.

A fuel gauge is sometimes included in the petrol tank of some early machines, which takes the form of either a sight level indicator or a dial gauge that operates on the rising float principle. Neither is likely to give trouble unless an actual breakage occurs. At least one early model, the Royal Enfield vee twin, utilises an all-glass oil tank. Needless to say, every possible care has to be taken with any glass component, especially since glass tends to become more brittle with age. Sunbeam, amongst others, used a glass insert in the top of the petrol and oil filler caps - yet another variation on means of keeping a visual check on the contents without having to remove the cap.

Here it should be mentioned that some lubrication systems are designed to work on the suction or pressure principle and if air leaks are evident, the system will fail, with dire consequences. Two such systems, of quite different design, were used on some of the Villiers engined lightweights of the late twenties and early thirties and on the early versions of the model EW Douglas, circa 1925. Although evidence of continuity of supply was provided by a sight glass in each case, the system had its shortcomings and was ultimately superseded by a different arrangement that proved more reliable. Anyone having a machine fitted with a suction system of this type is well advised to familiarise himself with the manufacturer's instructions and to keep a constant lookout for the first signs of failure.

Knee grips of one kind or another are fitted to most petrol tanks, so that the clothing around the knees of the rider does not abrade the sides of the tank and wear through the finish, to leave an unsightly-looking patch. Early knee grips are of the leather or rubber type that clamp around the sides of a flat tank by means of a lacing arrangement, or webbing straps. This arrangement was superseded by having a metal plate attached to each side of the tank, over which a separate knee grip rubber is located. The plate is held away from the side of the tank to give sufficient clearance for the knee grip overlap, by means of a stud or studs welded or soldered to the tank itself. Later still, when strong adhesives were more readily available, the grip was stuck to the side of the tank, or in some cases held in position by a screw or screws that located with threaded inserts in the side of the tank. Only competition models and the more sporting types of machine did not have their tanks protected in this manner, although proprietary stick-on rubbers of the ultra-slim type were available for this purpose from John Bull and others. Even stick-on boot soles have been used successfully by a few riders, which are equally effective from the protective point of view but hardly in keeping with an otherwise high quality finish! If it is desired not to deviate from the original finish in this latter case, a coating of clear polyurethane varnish would seem to offer the best solution, as it is very wear resistant.

It need not be stressed that plastic tubing and some of the modern, more decorative synthetic rubber tubing, should not be used for oil or petrol pipelines under any circumstances unless, of course, the machine is of recent origin. It is still possible to buy the dull black synthetic rubber tubing that was in common use many years ago, from many accessory stockists, and from refrigeration and compressed air engineers. Make sure, however, that the tubing is both petrol and oil proof before it is used. Natural rubber swells very rapidly when immersed in petrol and the flow would soon be restricted or even shut off completely. Worse still, the internal surface of the tube would eventually begin to break up, so that particles of rubber find their way into the fuel or lubrication system. Special clips are made to hold the tube in place when it is pushed over a metal pipe or similar outlet. They should be used in preference to worm drive clips that are much more unsightly; wire itself should never be used. Anyone who has a car fitted with wire clamps around the radiator hoses will know how soon they cut through the hose and give rise to problems when they are least expected. Wherever possible, use copper tubing for the petrol pipe and for any short runs of the oil lines, since the widespread use of plastic tubing on production models is a comparatively recent innovation. Synthetic rubber tubing should be used only where some degree of flexibility is necessary, and even then, for the transfer of oil. It was not widely used for other purposes and is found mainly on post-vintage machines.

No specific mention has been made of the small cross-pipe, often found on the underside of petrol tanks, to interconnect the two separate halves of the tank. This is the pipe that will tend to collect sediment from the tank and if the flow of petrol is impeded, only one half of the tank contents may prove usable. The cross-pipe is fitted to saddle tanks or pannier tanks only, and should always be cleaned out thoroughly and blown through with compressed air before it is refitted, after plating.

At some time or other, your petrol tank is likely to spring a leak, which can prove serious if there is danger of petrol dropping on to the exhaust pipe or cylinder head. As a leak is bound to occur whilst the machine is in use and there is little chance of an immediate permanent repair, it is worth noting that a very effective temporary seal can often be made with soap or plasticine. This is a dodge that has been used successfully over the years, to the extent that many a difficult competition schedule has been completed on time without loss of marks. If soap is used, it must be worked into a very thick paste so that it will penetrate the leak, before it has a chance to dry out and set. Fibreglass is the more modern answer to the same problem, although a small repair kit of this kind is less easy to find in an emergency.

The overall presentation of a petrol or oil tank is enhanced by the transfers that formed part of the original specification. It is surprising how many of the original transfers can still be obtained, even for many of seemingly long forgotten models. The Vintage Motor Cycle Club, for example, has had a tank transfer scheme going for several years, where exact copies of the original designs have been made on a limited basis, for sale to members. This is the most obvious source, before resorting to signwriting.

A special technique has to be used if the transfers are to be applied in a presentable manner, and it is first necessary to determine whether the transfers are of the varnish or waterslide type. The latter can be identified because they 'read' the same way in which they will appear when applied to the surface of the tank. Varnish transfers appear in reverse, because the varnish has to be applied to the back of the transfer, prior to application.

To fix a waterslide transfer, immerse the transfer in cold water for a few minutes, until the transfer is free from its backing paper. It should slide along the backing paper with ease, but should not become detached and float in the water. Do not soak too long and test that the transfer is free with the greatest of care, because the ultra-thin transfer is very easily damaged at this stage.

Assuming the surface to which the transfer is to be applied is clean and smooth, slide the moistened transfer from the backing paper on to the tank surface, into the correct location. Carefully smooth it out, so that any air trapped beneath is expelled from the edges. It is best to use a dampened cloth for this purpose, working from the centre of the transfer to the edges. Avoid creasing or moving the transfer. This too is a very delicate operation, as the transfer is only too easily broken. When the transfer is perfectly flat, leave it to dry thoroughly. When it is dry, give a final, very light rub over with a damp rag, to remove any traces of adhesive. Added protection must be given by applying a very thin coating of clear varnish, after the transfer surface has again dried thoroughly.

A varnish transfer needs an entirely different technique. First, peel away one corner of the backing paper so that the whole of the backing paper can be stripped off easily at a later stage. Then apply a thin coating of clear varnish to the transfer itself, making sure all portions of it are covered. Lay the transfer aside until the varnish is touch dry. Clean the surface to which the transfer is to be applied, then peel off the backing paper and apply the transfer to its location. Smooth it out with a dry rag, working from the centre outwards until all the air bubbles are dispersed from the edges. This is a very delicate operation, especially if creasing is to be avoided. Leave the transfer to dry thoroughly, preferably overnight. When it has dried, moisten the tissue backing with a damp rag and when it is soaked, peel it off from the transfer. Allow the surface to dry, then wipe over the surface of the transfer with the same damp rag to remove traces of adhesive. Again, great care should be taken, or the transfer will break up. When the surface is dry once again, give the transfer a light coating of clear varnish.

A third type of transfer is sometimes available - a spirit transfer which is similar in most respects to the varnish type. In this instance, the transfer is applied after giving it a light coating of a mixture comprising 75% methylated spirits and 25% water. A final light coating of clear varnish will aid its preservation, if applied after the transfer is dry. All transfers should be supplied with fixing instructions, or at the very least, an indication of their type. I have found a clear, polyurethane varnish gives the best protective coating, which is less inclined to yellow with age.

It is possible to obtain pin striping in long runs, which can also be applied by the varnish technique, and will aid the lining of a petrol or oil tank. A coachbuilder is probably the best contact for this type of transfer. Roll-on lines, backed by plastic strips, are usually available at good car accessory shops. I have heard of the thin gold line around cigarette carton wrappings being used quite successfully, too - there is no limit to ingenuity.

It follows that similar techniques are applied for transfers affixed to steering heads, mudguards and sidecars.

Chapter Seven

Seating

In the early days, solo machines were fitted with only one seat — for the rider! This usually took the form of a leather covered saddle rather like that fitted to an ordinary bicycle, which had similar springs and a single, adjustable pillar fitting. The saddle was of small dimensions so that the rider could dismount easily, as proved a necessity when frequent breakdowns occurred or it was necessary to dismount and run alongside on hills. Gradually the size of the saddle increased and improvements in the springing occurred at the same time. As machines became more powerful, it became possible to carry a pillion passenger, and in due course a second seat, bolted to the rear carrier or mudguard, came into fashion. This, too, had some form of springing and the addition of a pair of clip-on footrests completed the ensemble. The move towards a twin seat came from racing requirements, for it was necessary to arrange a separate pillion seat in close proximity to, and in line with the saddle, so that the rider could slide back to lessen his wind resistance. But it was not until after the second war that the dualseat as we know it today became the vogue. It was

Figure 3 All manner of seating arrangements have been used over the years, in an endeavour to improve rider comfort. On early machines, the saddle size had to be kept small, so that the rider could dismount with ease, when confronted by a hill. In such instances, various forms of springing were used; this telescopic saddle pillar used by the manufacturers of the Rex is particularly ingenious

intended as an added refinement to spring frame models, which began appearing around the late forties and early fifties, but many adapted them to fit rigid frame machines, only to find that anything but a comfortable ride was the end result. The majority of the dualseats available had no spring mounting, relying upon the spring frame itself to cushion road shocks. Even so, the conventional and much more comfortable saddle, disappeared almost overnight on rigid frame machines, such is the power of fashion. This explains why so many of the early post-war models are found equipped in this fashion and why there is such difficulty in obtaining a replacement saddle. They were deemed old fashioned and discarded, without so much as a second thought about the standard of comfort they provided.

The covering of a saddle is the item likely to suffer most, especially if the machine has been exposed in the open for any length of time. Leather will usually harden and split, but may also grow mildew and disintegrate if permitted to remain permanently damp. Some quite remarkable jobs of restoration have been accomplished by treating an old saddle top with Neatsfoot Oil or saddle soap, obtainable from a saddler or stockist of horse tackle, who is one person well qualified to give advice. But if the top has gone beyond the point of redemption, a new replacement will have to be made, using the original as a pattern. Surprisingly, this is not as difficult as it sounds, although the exercise may prove a trifle expensive. Many saddlers, upholsterers and even schools for the disabled may be sufficiently interested to tackle the job on a one-off basis. Unfortunately, it is not practicable to fit a later saddle of the mattress-top type, because most have a three-point and not a single stem fitting. Furthermore, they look out of context on an early machine.

Saddle springs of the coil type are fairly easy to obtain, even today, but there is no easy means of replacing the long centre spring that often extends forwards from the nose of some early saddles, giving the impression that horrible injuries await the rider if he slips off the saddle whilst giving light pedal assistance! There are some cases where a departure from originality may actually prove desirable!

Saddles of the mattress type came into general use during the late twenties and early thirties. Of larger size and providing a greater standard of comfort, a three-point fixing was now considered necessary, with attachment lugs welded to the frame. Apart from the two coil springs used for the rear mountings, additional comfort was provided by means of springs or aero elastic running from the front to the rear of the saddle, to form the actual seat. This was covered by a felt-lined, shaped leatherette saddle top of the detachable type, held in position by metal clips that looped around the saddle frame. The leatherette cover will deteriorate very rapidly if the machine lies neglected, without some form of protection, and at the very least will wear and become somewhat shabby in appearance, if the machine is in regular use. A few replacement covers are reportedly available, otherwise a dualseat recoverer can sometimes be prevailed upon to make up a cover as a one-off task. Get an estimate first!

Broken or missing mattress springs will prove difficult to replace, although it is sometimes possible to find substitutes amongst the boxes of assorted springs found in tool shops and motor accessory stockists. The alternative is to use aero elastics of the type used for retaining luggage on a carrier which, in some designs of saddle, were fitted as standard. They will be hidden by the saddle cover and if tensioned correctly, will perform their duty well. The main essential is to use clips that will not cut through the rubber strands, especially if the elastic has to be looped backwards and forwards several times on account of its length. Use as broad a clip as possible to spread the load, free of sharp edges.

The saddle frame is usually of rivetted construction and does not often give trouble. Fractures can be repaired by either welding or brazing; the lugs used for the attachment of the two main springs at the rear of the saddle are normally rivetted to the main frame and can be moved if the saddle has to be fitted where the fixing points do not correspond exactly. Do not overlook the pivot bolt through the nose of the saddle, which is seldom lubricated and in consequence will wear quite badly. If the lug on the frame has worn too, it can be drilled oversize and a slim bush pressed in, so that it is sleeved back to the original dimensions. It is a good policy to drill and tap a hole at the same time, so that a standard

Early saddles were a slightly enlarged version of the bicycle type. Note the unsightly (and dangerous!) spring at the nose

An all-original saddle fitted to an American vee-twin. The way in which the rear springs operate is somewhat unusual

This early pillar-mounted saddle appears to have been recovered by someone who really knows his job

During the late twenties, saddles relied upon a three-point fixing. This is the nose mounting, through a lug attached to the top of the frame. Greasing here is essential, or rapid wear will occur, making the saddle insecure

A pair of plated springs invariably provide the rear mountings, their lower end being attached to conveniently placed frame lugs

The Veloce ohc models have three alternative location points for the rear springs, to give an alternative in riding position

Leatherette-type saddle tops clip on and are replaceable. Note the spring mattress below

Hardly to be taken seriously as a pillion seat, this so-called 'bum pad' found most favour with the racing fraternity, to give a more acceptable racing crouch

The sponge rubber pillion seat that was so popular in the thirties and late forties. It bolted direct to the rear mudguard but was hardly the acme of comfort

grease nipple can be threaded into the lug, thus lessening the risk of neglect in the future. A loose or badly worn saddle pivot can give the impression that the roadholding qualities of the machine leave much to be desired.

Dualseats take the form of a moulded sponge rubber layer of the required shape, covered by a close fitting grained or embossed plastic cover that is normally not detachable. The dualseat bolts direct to the frame and has no springing of its own, apart from a few early examples of the mattress type that were designed specifically for rigid frame machines. After an extended period of use, the cover will split or the stitches rot, so that the seat soon becomes unsightly. Worse still, it will no longer be waterproof, since rainwater will enter and be absorbed by the sponge rubber within. It is rarely necessary to renew a dualseat that has worn badly in this manner unless the metal undertray has rusted badly or has begun to split or crack in places. Several companies offer a dualseat recovering service and it is often possible to purchase a replacement cover of the correct shape that will fit over the original.

The introduction of the dualseat completely obviated the need for a separate pillion seat which, at that time, formed part of the standard equipment of many motorcycles. Although pillion seats had been made in two distinctive forms — a shaped sponge rubber pad to conform to the curvature of the mudguard, and a mattress type of seat supported on springs — various sizes were available that provided different standards of comfort. Reputedly the most comfortable was the Tan Sad mattress type, which was in quite common use during the twenties. It was designed to permit the pillion passenger to ride side saddle if desired, a practice that was at that time permissible by law. From the thirties onwards, the pillion seat seemed to diminish in size, without too much thought for the passenger's comfort. The type most commonly in use at that time (and immediately after world war 2) was the sponge rubber type.

Greater difficulty will be experienced if the pillion seat has to be recovered or replaced, because such items are now quite rare. Replacement covers are not available, which in itself creates problems since the cover is invariably used to retain the sponge rubber pad to the metal base which bolts to the mudguard. The mattress top is equally difficult to replace, so that one has the option of removing the pillion seat altogether (and filling up the mounting holes drilled in the rear mudguard), or trying to find a new replacement. Presumably anyone experienced in upholstery work could be prevailed upon to recover a pillion seat that is badly worn or damaged in some way, even though there is no recovering service as such. This is an area where ingenuity will have to be exercised if originality is to be retained.

Mention should be made of what may be regarded as a third form of pillion seat, which is virtually an extension of the existing saddle. It was used almost exclusively on racing machines so that the rider could slide rearwards to adopt a racing crouch and was arranged to pivot from a mounting on the rear of the saddle so that the rider could make use of the saddle springs. This type of racing seat is very rare today, but is easily recognised on account of the front pivot mounting and the thin but constant section of the covered sponge rubber pad. It is also worth noting that many competition models had a special rubber topped saddle, in which the moulded rubber top was rivetted direct to the saddle frame. This type of saddle will withstand rough usage and exposure to the elements better than any other, but may give rise to problems if the somewhat small headed rivets pull through the top cover. It will then be necessary to patch the underside in the region of the damage and re-rivet the cover into place, using rivets with a larger diameter head.

It is a legal requirement to have pillion footrests if a pillion passenger is carried — a requirement that causes very few problems with most post-world war 2 machines where pillion footrests form part of the standard equipment. Machines manufactured during the late thirties often had lugs provided on the frame to which pillion footrests, available as optional extras, could be bolted. Before that, bolt-on footrests were the order of the day, using a system of clamp brackets and clips that could be adapted to fit almost every make of machine.

It follows, of course, that the appropriate design of pillion footrests should be used wherever practicable, especially the clip-on type for the very early machines. The only problem is likely to be the footrest rubbers, which will prove almost impossible to match with any success if the originals are beyond redemption.

The law requires permanently-fitted pillion footrests, if a pillion passenger is carried. For some unknown reason, a few manufacturers fitted the mounting point to the swinging arm, which makes the footrests move up and down with the suspension

Chapter Eight

Gearboxes

At the start of the development of the motorcycle, it soon became apparent that some form of variable speed drive would be necessary if maximum advantage was to be made of the somewhat limited amount of power available from the engine. Apart from a number of arrangements made to vary the size of the engine pulley, such as the Zenith Gradua and Rudge Multi described later in this Chapter, most attention was directed towards the hub gear, an arrangement of the sun and planet wheel type that was built into the hub of the rear wheel. This so-called epicyclic arrangement can be regarded as little more than a scaled-up version of the three-speed hub found on many modern bicycles, but with one important addition. It was also necessary to include some form of internal clutch or band brake so that the load could be taken off the somewhat diminutive internal mechanism during the gear changing process. Supplied with the machine, most hub gears were proprietary fittings, usually of Sturmey Archer or Armstrong manufacture. They were bought in by the manufacturer and built into the rear wheels of his variable speed models.

Not every manufacturer had adopted the hub gears that were so popular in the period immediately before the 1914-18 war. A few had opted for the countershaft gearbox in preference which, although of simple design and without either a clutch or kickstarter, was destined to be the forerunner of the motorcycle gearbox that is widely used today. The countershaft gearbox came into prominence immediately after the war, when the limitations of the hub gear became apparent. Even then there were still other approaches to the same problem, such as the two-speed gear of the internal expanding type, made popular by Scott and P & M, and the friction disc drive, used in the Ner-a-Car. Eventually, it was the countershaft gearbox that was universally adopted, a design that lends itself particularly well to unit-construction layout.

The repair of hub gears of the epicyclic type will undoubtedly create problems, and a check should first be made to ensure adjustment of the operating rod is correct, since this will have a direct influence on the selection of the gears. Adjustment is correct when the bell crank lever on the left-hand side of the wheel spindle has about 1/32 in (0.80mm) clearance from the indicating pin, when the latter is in the low gear position. The gears should be quiet when they are selected, and the rear wheel is turned by hand. A grating sound indicates the sun pinions are slipping past the clutches and adjustment should be made at the control rod until this noise disappears. Plenty of oil is necessary for the correct operation of the gears — a light machine oil. It should be injected every 200 miles and the hub flushed out with clean paraffin before the third or fourth application. There is little danger of over-lubricating the hub if only a light machine oil is used. Whilst oiling the hub, check that the clutch has not been too tightly adjusted so that there is no free play in the push rod, and that the wheel

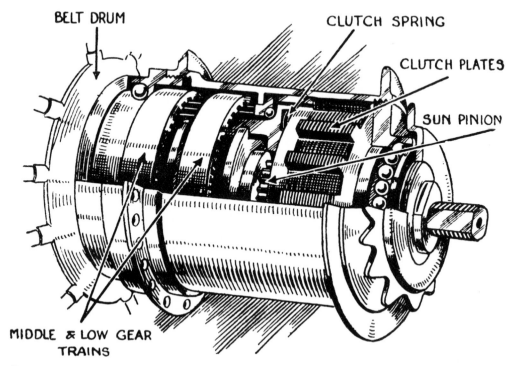

BELT DRUM

CLUTCH SPRING

CLUTCH PLATES

SUN PINION

MIDDLE & LOW GEAR
TRAINS

Figure 4 Before the countershaft gearbox became widely established, most manufacturers pinned their faith in the three-speed hub gear, which also contained a foot-operated clutch. The Sturmey Archer design , featured above, was probably the most popular and was fitted as standard by numerous manufacturers, including Triumph

bearings have not slackened off. Both these adjustments are normally made from the right-hand side of the machine.

Do not dismantle the hub gear unless absolutely necessary. It is difficult to reassemble without some previous experience, due to the use of uncaged ball races. The troubles most likely to be encountered, such as damaged pinions or sheared clutch plates will, however, necessitate a stripdown, in which case it should be carried out methodically and without undue use of force. Make detailed notes to aid reassembly, after the appropriate repairs have been carried out. It is extremely unlikely that replacement parts will be available, hence there is need to preserve anything that can be reclaimed. Often, a thorough wash-out with paraffin, followed by lubrication with thin oil and readjustment of the control rod, will work wonders. This type of gear was surprisingly robust if the size of the internal working parts is taken into account, so give the gear this treatment and recheck its action first, before taking it apart.

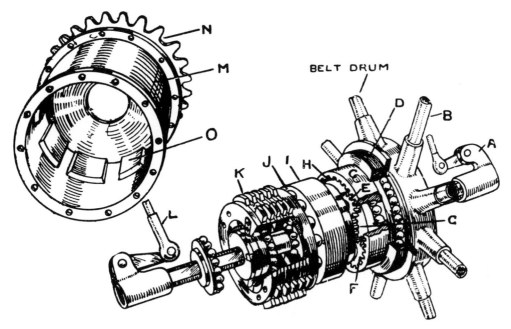

BELT DRUM

Figure 5 Some preferred to use the Armstrong-Triplex three- speed hub gear which, like the Sturmey Archer design works on the epicyclic principle. In the sectioned drawing A is the gear operating mechanism, found on the left-hand side of the rear wheel. B is the spokes of the belt rim, C the internally toothed lower gear ring and D the thread on to which the hub shell is screwed. E and F are the planet wheels; G the sun wheel. H is the carrier ring that holds the eight planet wheels. I is the top speed gear ring, J the clutch springs and K the disc clutch. The clutch operating mechanism L is located on the right-hand side of the rear wheel. M is the hub shell, N the free wheel sprocket, on the right-hand side of the rear wheel. O are the squares that engage with the driving discs of the plate clutch assembly K

A gearbox of the countershaft type is much easier to dismantle. If the end cover is removed, little difficulty should be experienced in extracting the internal gear pinions and shafts, which can be examined for signs of wear or damage. On gearboxes of the crossover drive type, it will be necessary to remove the final drive sprocket first. The sprocket retaining nut will be staked or have a tab washer to retain it in place; check that the nut itself does not have a left-hand thread. If necessary, use a sprocket puller to withdraw the sprocket from a tapered shaft without damage; it will probably be keyed into position. You may crack the end cover if you try to lever it off with a screwdriver.

When foot operated gear change came into almost universal adoption during the late thirties, gearboxes tended to be fitted with an inner and an outer end cover, so that the positive stop mechanism could be retained within a separate compartment. Unless wear has taken place, which is affecting the gear change or the manner in which the gears are selected, there is seldom need to dismantle the positive stop mechanism. Note, however, that in a great many cases the mechanism is 'timed' so that it will select the gears in the correct sequence. The parts concerned are normally marked in a manner similar to that used for the timing pinions of an engine, so that there is little risk of misalignment. It may be necessary to clean off all the old oil so that these marks are recognisable when reassembly commences.

Royal Enfield and Scott pinned their faith in the two-speed gear, which obviated the need for a conventional clutch. The design shown here is of P&M manufacture, simple in construction and efficient in operation

Veloce pioneered the positive stop footchange mechanism, which revolutionised motorcycle gearboxes in the early thirties when the Veloce patent coverage lapsed. The mechanism took the form of a circular box, bolted to the gearbox outer cover. It worked remarkably well

Scott later took over the Velocette design and built it into their own gearbox casting. It was still in use when production at the Scott works ceased during 1951

On most of the
earlier hand
change designs,
the notches in
the gearchange
gate acted as the
indexing
mechanism

If the gearbox is found to have a number of false neutrals after reassembly, this is invariably a sign that the timing of the foot change mechanism is not correct. Early foot change mechanisms are contained within a separate 'box' that bolts to the outside of the gearbox shell.

When the gearbox has been dismantled, it is advisable to renew the bearings, since they will almost certainly have developed some play, or perhaps rough spots as a result of exposure. Warm the gearbox shell to release the bearings; they will often fall out of position if the gearbox shell is warmed and then brought down smartly on to a table top. If they are a tight fit, they will have to be drifted out of position, after the shell is warm. Never drive the bearings out cold, or the bearing housings will suffer damage. Sometimes it is found the bearings have been spinning in their housings, with the result that the new replacements are a slack fit. It is here that modern ingenuity comes into play, for a special adhesive known as Bearing Loctite can be used, provided the surface of the bearing and that of the bearing housing is oil-free. Follow the adhesive manufacturer's recommendation and apply a thin coating to the outer surface of the bearing and to the inside of the bearing housing. If the bearing is now dropped into position the adhesive will harden after a set period of time so that there is no further risk of the bearing rotating. This technique can be used effectively to remedy an up to 0.005 in/0.13mm diameter clearance. If the housing is damaged, a different approach will have to be employed. In this case, it will be necessary to machine out the bearing housing to a greater diameter and fit a larger bearing that has the same diameter centre. Alternatively, some form of insert can be fitted, which will sleeve down the bearing housing to its original size. In either case a delicate machining operation is necessary, provided there is sufficient metal surround to make this practicable.

Apart from the prospect of chipped, broken or missing teeth, gearbox pinion wear is usually found on the dogs After a lengthy period of service, the edges of the dogs round off and in an extreme case, they may even wear to a wedge shape. This is one of the most frequent causes of jumping out of gear; when any loading is applied to the pinions

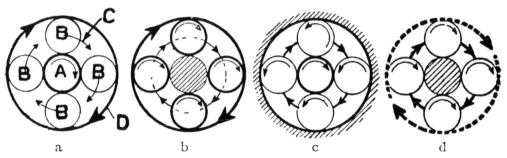

Figure 6 This diagram shows how a simple two speed epicyclic gear operates. In position a, the high gear direct drive is selected and in b, the low gear. c shows another method of securing a reduced motion. d represents a geared-up high speed

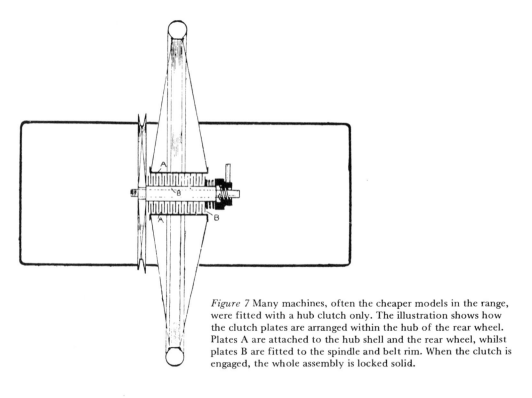

Figure 7 Many machines, often the cheaper models in the range, were fitted with a hub clutch only. The illustration shows how the clutch plates are arranged within the hub of the rear wheel. Plates A are attached to the hub shell and the rear wheel, whilst plates B are fitted to the spindle and belt rim. When the clutch is engaged, the whole assembly is locked solid.

concerned, the dogs ride up one another and force the pinions out of mesh. If new replacement pinions are not available, it may be possible to have the dogs reground to shape, which means they will be shallower and not quite so wide. In consequence, this operation is practicable only if they can be restored by the removal of a very small amount of metal. The alternative is to have the dogs built up by someone experienced in this type of work, after the pinion has been softened, and then have the built-up assembly ground to shape and rehardened. Worn splines are best built up by metal spraying, another operation that requires specialist attention. This also applies to splined gearbox shafts or places on these shafts where heavy wear may have occurred. Chipped gear pinion teeth can sometimes be built up successfully by the softening, welding, shaping and rehardening process, but this is about the limit to which a damaged pinion can be reclaimed. If a tooth is broken or missing altogether, a new pinion will have to be made, to the original design. Take careful note of the number and location of any thrust washers. They must be replaced IN THE SAME ORDER.

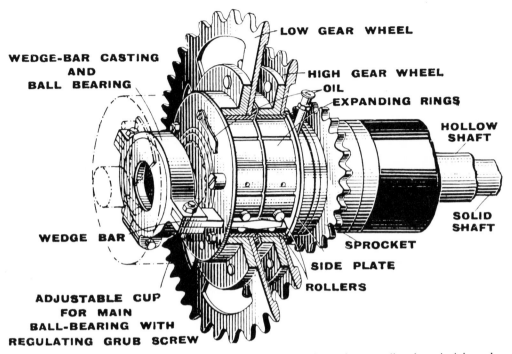

LOW GEAR WHEEL

WEDGE-BAR CASTING
AND
BALL BEARING

HIGH GEAR WHEEL
OIL
EXPANDING RINGS

HOLLOW
SHAFT

SOLID
SHAFT

WEDGE BAR

SPROCKET

SIDE PLATE

ROLLERS

ADJUSTABLE CUP
FOR MAIN
BALL-BEARING WITH
REGULATING GRUB SCREW

Figure 8 The two-speed gear of the type used by P and M. It works on the expanding ring principle, and can be likened to a manually-operated form of centrifugal clutch

The gear change mechanism rarely gives touble, unless the machine has covered a very considerable mileage or if the gearbox has been run low in oil content. Pawls are easily built-up for further service, or even remade, if necessary. Ratchets, on the other hand, will need to be renewed if badly worn because, like the gear pinion, there is no easy way of reclaiming the teeth. Do not omit to check the camplate, which will wear at the points where the profile abruptly changes direction. Care is needed if the profile is to be built-up and reshaped; it is advisable to have an accurate tracing of the original as a guide.

Selector forks tend to wear or distort; if the former occurs they can usually be reclaimed by building up the metal and grinding it to shape. No difficulty should be experienced in renewing the selector rods if the originals are bent or badly worn. They are readily machined from rod of the correct diameter and material specification, using the originals as a pattern. This applies to any linkages in the gear change system. Often, it is the yoke ends fitted to linkage rods that cause the most trouble, as the result of wear. If it is not possible to fit new replacements, the eye of the yoke ends can sometimes be opened out and an oversize clevis pin fitted.

If the gearbox shell or end cover suffers damage, it is best to entrust the repair to someone who is experienced in the welding of light alloys. There is always risk of the shell collapsing through embrittlement if special precautions are not taken. Generally speaking, the older the gearbox, the greater the risk. A repair of this nature should be effected only if a replacement is not available from some other source. Do not resort to metal stitching, which will effect a permanent repair but has the disadvantage of giving an unsightly appearance.

Before rebuilding the gearbox, check that all the internal threads are in good condition, for now is the time to fit Helicoil thread inserts if any have stripped. A coarse thread is normally used for studs or bolts that thread into aluminium alloy, but there are exceptions. Always check with a thread gauge first, if there is any reason for doubt.

Discoloured gearbox shells and end covers can often be cleaned up by giving them the treatment advised for crankcases in Chapter 3 — immersion in boiling detergent, after wire brushing. It is imperative, however, that all bushes and other inserts that may suffer damage are removed first, otherwise corrosion may occur, to their detriment. If the end cover was polished, it can be buffed-up with a mop fitted to an electric drill so that the original gleaming surface is restored. But do not adopt this finish if it was not part of the original specification. Whilst it may enhance the overall appearance of the finished machine, it may detract from the marks given to the machine if it is being prepared with concours events in mind. There is such a thing as gilding the lily and presenting a machine that is too good, as reference to Chapter 16 will explain. A good hand-applied polish that will help 'bring up' an alloy surface and at the same time provide some form of protection is Solvol Autosol, a product much used by motorcyclists who delight in keeping their machines in a presentable condition. Even a rough cast surface will respond reasonably well to this treatment.

When reassembling the gearbox, do not omit any oil throwers or oil seals, even if the latter are only of the felt seal type. They help reduce the level of oil leakage which is bound to occur with many of the older machines, no matter how carefully they are assembled. In most cases it will be necessary to make the gaskets, using an uncoated paper of the coarse wove type. For a number of years I have used quite successfully the covers from the magazine of a well known one-make club! The gasket is easily shaped by the old technique of tapping round the periphery with a hammer, whilst it is held against the face it is to seal. The ball end of the hammer, or a small punch, can be used for the holes through which any of the retaining bolts pass. Make sure the faces to be joined are perfectly clean; a rag soaked in methylated spirits will remove old gasket cement very effectively without having to resort to a scraper that may otherwise damage the surface. A thin smear of gasket cement should be used to make the perfect joint; use one of the non-setting variety so that no difficulty is encountered when the joint has to be broken on some future occasion. If distortion has taken place, which makes a good seal virtually impossible, the surface can be refaced by rubbing down on a sheet of flat glass wrapped around with fine emery cloth, using a rotary motion. In extreme cases, it may be necessary to get the surface machined, provided clearance problems do not arise as a result. Tighten the retaining screws in rotation, a little at a time until all are quite tight. Give the joint a final wipe over; nothing is worse than a joint oozing gasket cement, which quickly gets smeared all along the edge of the joint. At the same time, trim off any gasket that protrudes from the joint since this too is equally unsightly. A scalpel knife is good for this task.

Two-speed gears require more expert attention if they are of the internal expanding type like those fitted to certain of the Scott and P & M models. They work well provided they are adequately lubricated, but problems immediately occur if they have been allowed to run dry or are badly out of adjustment. If the take-up of the drive is exceptionally fierce, this is a sure sign that the clutch drum requires oil. A slipping clutch is caused by insufficient grip of the expanding ring on the drum. If pressure on the foot pedal causes the slipping to cease, all that is necessary is adjustment of the quick thread drum strap. The quick thread drum should be lubricated periodically with paraffin and NOT oil. Although the two speed gear is not difficult to dismantle, a certain amount of expertise is necessary if it is to be set

Most 'jumping out of gear' problems can be attributed to worn dogs on the gear pinions concerned. Here the rounded edges can be seen, a sure sign of advanced wear

These kickstarter ratchet components have been responsible for many a scraped shin! Once the edges have gone, slip is inevitable

Bevel gear pinions are used to transfer the movement of the gear lever to the belt and pulley system, via a chain, in the Zenith 'Gradua' gear

One of the chain drives is quite evident here, immediately below the magneto chain cover

Note the gear operating instructions (and warning) in the form of a special transfer on the petrol tank

Early Veloce gearboxes have a clutch that is actuated by a face cam. Here, the operating lever immediately behind the clutch can be seen

up correctly on reassembly. Do not dismantle it unless there is good need, and only then if advice is available from someone who is familiar with this type of gear. Apart from the breakage of some component part or the need to renew the cup and cone bearings, the gear should need only superficial attention in most cases, if it has not been abused.

Other variants, such as the friction drive used in the Ner-a-Car, are more of a rarity and in each case specialist attention will be required since the chance of obtaining any spare parts is virtually nil. The marque specialist is the one person to contact under these circumstances, since the problem in hand is likely to have been encountered by other owners in the past, including himself. Who you know is important when renovating a motorcycle and I can say that I have never been stumped on any particular requirement, once I have found the one-make specialist who knows the machine in question.

Mention was made earlier of the use of the engine pulley on belt drive models to raise or lower the gear ratio. Early models often have what is known as an adjustable pulley, in which the outer face of the pulley can be moved inwards or outwards so that the drive belt will either rise or fall within the pulley groove. Although this arrangement permits the gear ratio to be lowered at the roadside if, for example, a steep hill is encountered, it has one major disadvantage. The rider has to stop the engine and dismount so that the pulley can be adjusted. This entails slackening a domed locknut at the pulley boss, freeing the threaded outer face of the pulley for movement inwards or outwards, and then re-locking it in position. In practice, the rider found by trial and error the gear ratio that seemed to suit his machine best and thereafter left the pulley in the same fixed position. In consequence, the pulley tended to wear in one place only, since the revolving belt picked up grit and other materials from the road that acted as an abrasive. If a ridge develops, as it will ultimately, the belt no longer makes full contact with the pulley groove and slip sets in. This in turn necessitates removal of the complete pulley and its replacement with new parts, or the reconditioning of the originals.

If examination of the pulley shows evidence of a ridge or uneven wear of the internal faces, the pulley should be dismantled and refaced in a lathe by giving it a light skim. If the wear is more advanced, it may be necessary to build up the worn area first, using brazing metal, and then to grind or skim the surface again until the correct profile is obtained. When dismantling an adjustable pulley, note that the outer adjustable section will probably have a left-hand thread. After reconditioning, the inner faces of the pulley should have an angle that is identical to that of the sides of the driving belt, namely 28°.

One of the first significant advances in the adjustable pulley arrangement occurred with the introduction of the Phillipson pulley, a proprietary device that could be adapted to fit most belt driven motorcycles. It functions on the governor principle, so that as the speed of the machine drops on a hill, the outer pulley flange screws outwards quite automatically, or vice-versa, as engine speed rises. A friction brake, operating on the boss of the pulley, actuated by a handlebar control, assists the gear reduction process. Another means of providing a single gear machine with variable gear ratios was provided by the NSU two-speed gear, again of the engine shaft type. The gear, of the epicyclic type, is contained in an extension of the special engine pulley, controlled by a vertical spindle with a handle at the upper end. This type of gear permits a low gear reduction of the order of 30 - 40% and can be adapted by the manufacturer to fit most engine pulleys. Irrespective of the design, it is imperative that the inner faces of the pulley are angled at 28° and are not scored or ridged. The belt must make full contact with the sides as well as its base, if it is to provide an efficient drive.

Two ingenious methods of providing a belt drive machine with a variable gear should also be mentioned, the Zenith Gradua and the Rudge Multi. In the case of the former, belt tension is maintained by sliding the back wheel along the bottom stays of the frame, as the pulley flanges move apart and vice-versa. This is achieved by means of a handle mounted on the left-hand side of the petrol tank, having a bevel gear on the lower end. The bevel gear engages with a similar gear on the end of a revolving shaft, the rotation of the shaft being responsible for the movement of the rear wheel. A later refinement included a chain driven

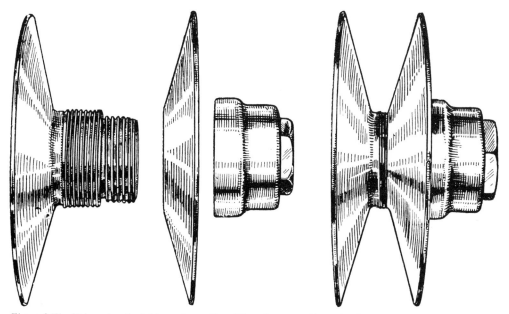

Figure 9 The Triumph adjustable engine pulley. When the outer flange has been screwed to the required position, it is retained there by the locknut. The flange moves on a left-hand thread

countershaft mounted forward of the engine that incorporated a clutch. On the original design, the belt was arranged to ride on a ring on the pulley shaft when the pulley was screwed as far out as possible, to provide a free engine. The clutch saved some of the strain that may otherwise have been placed on the belt. The design, either the original or the countershaft type, normally gives very little trouble and if the gear does not work, it is probable that the rear wheel sliding mechanism has seized up.

The Rudge Multi gear is also of the expanding pulley type, but by having moveable flanges on both the engine pulley and the rear wheel belt rim so that belt tension can remain constant, it is possible to obtain no less than 20 different ratios, between 3½:1 and 7:1. Gear changing is effected by means of a long lever mounted on the left-hand side of the petrol tank, which engages with a notched quadrant. A later refinement took the form of a small lever on the left-hand side of the rear hub, which permitted the belt rim to be moved inwards or outwards, independently of the gear changing arrangements. It will be appreciated that most of the variable pulley arrangements are simple in the extreme and are therefore unlikely to create any difficult problems as far as renovation is concerned. It is only the epicyclic arrangement that will cause headaches if any of the internal pinions are damaged.

Unit construction models were available much earlier than many suppose, for this form of engine and gearbox layout is by no means a modern innovation. At least one such model was available well before the first war, and many followed afterwards. Perhaps the best known of the post-vintage era are the New Imperial range, covering a 150cc single, right through to an upper capacity limit of 500cc as far as the road models were concerned. This type of engine layout demands a gear drive for the primary transmission and the need for the engine to run 'backwards'. As may be expected, the gear drive is responsible for a certain amount of mechanical noise, even though it is immersed in an oil bath. A certain amount of clearance has to be allowed for expansion purposes and this will only add to the noise level, even if helical cut gears are employed. As wear sets in, the noise will gradually increase, even though the oil content of the oil bath keeps this to a very low level. The New Imperial models could always be detected by the whirr of the primary transmission and if this increased beyond a tolerable level, renewal of the engine pinion and the clutch pinion with which it meshed provided the only satisfactory answer to the problem. It follows that maintenance of the correct oil level within the oil bath chaincase is of paramount importance.

Mention has already been made of the clutch incorporated in a hub gear of the epicyclic type. The introduction of the countershaft gearbox necessitated a quite different layout and it became necessary to attach the clutch to the gearbox mainshaft, using the sleeve gear that extended through the gearbox main bearing as the means of location. In most cases, final drive could then be transmitted to the rear wheel by means of a sprocket outboard of the clutch when chain drive was employed, assuming the gearbox was not of the crossover drive type.

Clutch operation is usually by means of a push rod inserted through the hollow gearbox mainshaft, which is actuated by a lever connected by a control cable to the clutch lever on the handlebars. There are, however, exceptions such as the early Velocette and Scott designs which rely upon a face cam arrangement, the later Velocette design that provides a form of servo action and the scissor type of mechanism adopted on some of the Triumph models of the late twenties and the more recent Royal Enfield twins. Dealing firstly with the push rod actuated clutch, problems will occur if the actuating lever is at a bad angle, if the push rod or rods are bent or have run dry from lack of lubrication, or if the hardened ends or the hardened insert in the clutch pressure plate have worn through. Often, poor operating angle of the actuating arm can be attributed to the omission of the vital ball bearing, which in many gearboxes, is interposed between the actuating arm and the end of the push rod or between the two push rods if this latter arrangement is used. The actuating arm must be arranged at an angle where it can provide good leverage. A bent or dry push rod will bind within its housing and cause heavy clutch action. But do not confuse this with a control cable that is dry or has tight bends along its run, which can give a similar impression. If the hardened ends of the push rod(s) or the pressure plate insert have worn through, usually because there has been no free play in the adjustment, the heat build up will cause the ends to soften and wear to take place at a quite rapid rate. This fault often proves difficult to locate, yet it is responsible for the need to adjust the clutch almost every time the machine is used.

Where the clutch is lifted by means of a face cam or quick thread arrangement (or a combination of both), under-lubrication will cause the mechanism to stick and possibly also to wear at a much more rapid rate. In an extreme case, heavy wear of the quick thread mechanism will cause the moving part to tilt and jam, rendering the clutch inoperative. Since it is not easy to reclaim the original parts, replacements will have to be sought or made to pattern from the originals. In this respect, it is always worth while making enquiries through the one-make club, because several of these clubs now have a rapidly developing spare parts service for the benefit of their members. Experience will have shown which parts are likely to need replacement more frequently, and these are the parts to which most attention will have been given.

The later-type Velocette clutch (and to some extent the earlier type) requires a very special adjustment procedure and any attempt to adjust it along conventional lines is bound to end in disaster. As a result, the clutch has to be adjusted by following a set routine, without any deviations or short cuts. It is also quite different from others in its construction and requires a special assembly technique, so in this case (and others where the clutch does not conform to conventional practice), it is imperative that the manufacturer's instructions and recommendations are read and understood. Fortunately, there is not too much difficulty in obtaining a copy of many of the older instruction manuals and parts lists as a result of the very good service offered to members by the Vintage MCC librarian or the various one-make specialists who operate under the auspices of that club.

Sooner or later the clutch will give trouble when the linings wear thin and the clutch commences to slip. Many of the older clutches are cork lined and although medicine bottle corks are somewhat rare today (they make ideal replacements!) cork table mats can often be used with equal success if the inserts are cut out to shape. It is important that the inserts should be a good fit and present a uniform surface. Beware of making them too thick to compensate for the amount of wear that has taken place on the originals, or it may not be possible to reassemble the clutch correctly. Linings of the friction material type are more difficult to renew. Modern epoxy adhesives permit bonded-on linings to be used, so that it may be possible to adapt clutch plates of this type from another, more modern type of machine. Sometimes a plate shaped from solid friction material offers another approach to the problem. Consult a clutch and brake lining specialist when such problems arise, for he will usually know a successful way round the problem.

Clutch slip can also be caused by weak clutch springs, which can be renewed. Always renew as a complete set, using springs of similar poundage. If the springs of a multi-spring assembly have unequal tension, it will not be possible to adjust the clutch correctly because the unequal pressure will cause the plates to tilt. Fortunately, this problem does not occur with a clutch that has one central spring. If the spring has weakened, it can often be retensioned by placing an extra washer or two under the retaining nut or cap, provided it does not become coil bound when the clutch is lifted. Some clutches contain a shock absorber in the centre — the clutch fitted to a gearbox of Norton manufacture is a good example. This should be dismantled and examined when the clutch has been taken apart since if the rubbers have commenced to crack or break up, they must be renewed. Little difficulty should be experienced when extracting the old rubbers, after the cover plate has been removed, but the new rubbers will prove quite difficult to fit unless they are lubricated to help them slip into position. Liquid detergent (washing-up liquid) is excellent for this purpose. Never use oil or any other liquid which may otherwise cause the rubbers to disintegrate prematurely.

The clutch centre bearing will probably also require attention, since if it is worn or has run dry, a noisy clutch will result. A worn centre bearing can often cause clutch drag too, as the inserted chainwheel and/or clutch plates will tilt more readily and rub together when the clutch is lifted. Hopefully, the bearing will not be of the uncaged type, since worn bearing tracks can give rise to problems that will require specialist attention. Check also the condition of the clutch splines and the projecting teeth of the clutch plates. After an extended period of service, the teeth will tend to indent the edges of any splines or cutaways so that a groove eventually forms which tends to retain the plate and prevent it from freeing. Unless the amount of wear is excessive, it is permissible to dress the splines or cutaways with a file until they are square once again and at the same time, to remove any burrs from the clutch plate tongues. A seemingly worn out clutch can often be given a new lease of life by such treatment.

Buckled or distorted clutch plates (usually the plain type) should be discarded and replaced wherever practicable, because it is difficult to straighten them with any success. The opportunity should also be taken to examine the profile of the teeth of the chainwheel sprocket, which will cause rapid wear of the primary chain if hooked or badly worn. If a new replacement is not available, it is often possible to retooth a sprocket, a relatively inexpensive task if handled by a specialist in this type of work. It is probable that the engine

The "Forward" Belt Fastener. Adjustable and Detachable.

Figure 10 Belt fasteners come in all manner of designs. These are a few of the designs that were at one time in common use.

The "Terry" Detachable Belt Fastener, with Key for Operating Locking Device.

The "Stanley" Detachable Belt Fastener, with Adjusting Links.

The "Simplex" Detachable Belt Fastener.

The post-war Douglas clutch is designed on car principles and forms an integral part of the engine flywheel

The Scott kickstarter return spring is of the clock spring type and can be changed without need to dismantle every part of the gearbox

The post-war Douglas kickstarter return spring is also readily accessible (and exposed!)

A typical engine shaft shock absorber. A sudden overload will cause the spring to compress and the cam to temporarily disconnect the drive to the engine sprocket

Sometimes, as in the post-war Douglas, the shock absorber is built into the final drive gearbox sprocket assembly

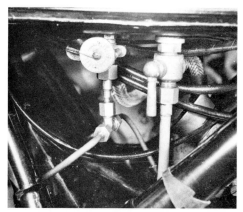

Exposed chains need regular lubrication. The Scott has an adjustable drip feed built into the bottom of the oil tank, to serve both the primary and magneto chains. The tap controls the main oil feed to the Pilgrim pump

sprocket will require attention too, in which case all worn parts of this nature can be sent away together.

If the clutch has a solid centre, it is probable that the shock absorber will be found on the end of the drive side of the crankshaft. A quite common design takes the form of a profiled spring-loaded collar fitted with internal splines that mates up with the splines on the end of the crankshaft. A matching profile is formed on the boss of the engine sprocket, which itself is free to rotate on the plain section of the crankshaft. Spring pressure forces together the collar and the engine sprocket, so that the profiles engage with each other and there is direct drive to the clutch, via the primary chain. Any surges will, however, tend to make the curved profiles run up one another, so that in an extreme case, the drive is momentarily disengaged and the surge is absorbed smoothly without placing strain on the transmission. It follows that the splines must be in good condition (they tend to wear as a result of the chattering action) and the spring sufficiently strong and correctly adjusted to prevent the drive from separating under normal load. If necessary, the spring can be packed out with washers to compensate for any weakening that has occurred, but never to the extent that it will prevent the drive from separating when fully compressed. If an adjusting nut is fitted, this should have either a locknut, tab washer or split pin through the crankshaft to prevent it from working loose.

On all but the very earliest machines, a belt of the rubber and canvas type was used to transmit the drive. Although prone to slip in the wet, it provided a very smooth drive because the material from which the belt was made was sufficiently flexible to cushion any transmission shocks and surges. A belt fastener was used to join the two ends of the belt, which was usually connected by a strongly made hook after each end of the belt had been drilled to accept the respective half of the fastener assembly. A special screw down belt 'punch' was supplied for drilling holes of the correct size, which was carried in the tool box or on the rider's person, so that repairs could be accomplished by the roadside if a belt happened to break or pull through. Unfortunately, drive belts of the original design are very difficult to obtain and many riders have been forced to use the Brammer belt as a substitute. Although it provides an effective drive, it is more unsightly and tends to detract from the general appearance of the machine. This is because it takes the form of small sections of rubber and canvas material, arranged in staggered form and pinned together with stout metal studs, to form a continuous loop. It has the advantage that it is possible to shorten or lengthen the run very easily, by either removing or adding sections. It was designed primarily as a machine drive and not for motorcycle transmission.

Chains are quite readily renewed since they are mostly of standard pitch. The so-called 'silent' chains used in some magneto drives may give rise to problems when replacement is necessary, but as they are usually enclosed within an aluminium chaincase, it would be relatively easy to convert to standard drive sprockets and chain without detracting from the outward appearance of the machine. Very small pitch chains were sometimes used for the magneto drive on some of the smaller lightweight two-strokes. Often a model shop can provide an adequate replacement. In some cases it is possible to use a standard bicycle chain, or the slightly larger width version that was designed for use on a tradesman's bicycle.

Mention of chains draws attention to the pedalling gear that was fitted to many of the older pre-1915 models, so that the efforts of the rider could be deployed to assist the not very powerful engine on steep gradients. In some cases they also provided a means of starting the machine, when it was placed on the rear stand, or by pedalling off from a halt. Although the chainwheel was often of distinctive design, it is not far removed from the type fitted to many bicycles and if the pedalling gear happens to be missing, bicycle parts can often be substituted. The drive was usually taken to a free wheel sprocket fitted to the right-hand side of the rear wheel hub, so that the pedalling gear would disengage immediately the engine started. When fitting chains of any kind, use a chain rivet extractor if the run has to be shortened. A spring link can be used to lengthen a chain by joining two lengths together, although it is generally considered bad practice to use two spring links in one run, especially if the machine is to be used at high speeds. Under these circumstances, the chain should be joined by rivetting and preferably the single spring link normally used for the final join dispensed with altogether. If a spring link is fitted, the closed end of the spring must face the direction of travel of the chain. Never join a worn length of chain with a length that is new, or it will prove virtually impossible to tension the chain correctly as the result of tight spots.

A few machines have shaft drive, including the BMW, Sunbeam S7 and S8 models and the Velocette LE and Valiant. On the larger capacity machines, a check must be made to find out whether solo or sidecar gearing applies, since it will be necessary to make adjustments to the final drive gear ratio if a change from one to the other is contemplated. Care has also to be exercised in the way in which the worm gear and pinion are meshed. It is worth noting that on the early Velocette LE models, where the drive shaft is enclosed within a steel frame tube that forms part of the swinging arm assembly, the tube itself is prone to fracture after lengthy service. This gives rise to peculiar handling characteristics that are difficult to diagnose immediately. The use of an alloy casting on the later models appears to have obviated the problem. On any shaft drive model, the shaft couplings should receive particular attention, since they are often the first components to give trouble as the result of wear.

Chapter Nine

Engines

As mentioned at the end of Chapter 3, it is quite probable that the engine will be in a seized condition because damp has entered it in one form or another. If the technique described has been applied whilst other work is being carried out, the chances are that it will have begun to free by the time the engine itself is due for attention. If not, more drastic action is required and it will be necessary to part-dismantle the engine first.

Work on the engine is greatly facilitated if some form of engine stand can be fabricated, so that the engine can be clamped rigidly to the bench. Apart from affording a means of holding the engine so that force can be applied to slacken the various nuts and bolts, it will also permit both hands to be used, since it will no longer be necessary to steady the engine. A large vice is not necessarily a good substitute since there is danger of marking the crankcase and even of cracking it, if too much pressure is applied. Remember that the grip of the vice is concentrated over only a very small area. Rusty nuts and bolts are always difficult to remove and it is virtually impossible to give any advice about the amount of pressure that can be applied without risk of shearing the parts concerned. It is only with experience that a certain amount of 'feel' can be gauged, which suggests when it is prudent to stop. The main essentials are copious application of a good penetrating oil, and spanners that are not only a good fit but also have good leverage. Use either a socket spanner or a ring spanner whenever possible.

Most engine seizures that occur during storage can be attributed to the piston rings rusting to the cylinder bore, which forms a remarkably good bond that is difficult to break. If the engine has a detachable cylinder head, the problem is eased, because once the head is removed, it is possible to flood the piston ring area with penetrating oil and then attempt to drive the piston down the bore by a series of sharp hammer blows applied to a block of wood placed on the piston crown. This somewhat drastic treatment will sometimes destroy the piston, especially if it is made of cast iron, so it is as well to ensure a replacement is available before letting fly! If, however, the cylinder is of the blockhead type or if the piston is already at the bottom of the stroke, such an approach is not practicable. The alternative is to apply heat to the cylinder barrel by means of a blowlamp, heating it evenly, to avoid local distortion. Sometimes the expansion that occurs will permit the penetrating oil around the piston rings to creep downwards and gradually break the bond. Patience is needed with this technique, since it may be necessary to heat and cool several times, with frequent applications of penetrating oil, before any signs of movement occur. If the piston is still immovable, the only remaining approach is to separate the crankcases by dismantling the bottom end of the engine so that the flywheel assembly can be extracted with the piston still in the cylinder bore. The penetrating oil approach can then be made at the base of the piston, if the assembly is inverted. This latter operation demands special care, since it is easy to chip or break the cylinder barrel fins. There is also the even greater risk of bending or twisting the connecting rod if the full weight of the flywheel assembly is not correctly supported.

The usual problem encountered when trying to separate the crankcases is removal of the crankshaft timing pinion, which quite often is keyed on to a taper and held in position with a left-hand thread nut. Generally speaking, all left-hand thread nuts should be stamped LH as a guide, but this method of marking is not infallible. If an unmarked nut proves almost impossible to move, try turning it in the opposite direction — it may be left-handed. The pinion itself is usually very difficult to extract without a puller and most pullers cannot be adapted to fit because the feet will prove too thick for insertion behind the pinion. If the crankcases are separated and someone else is available to hold the timing side crankcase whilst the flywheel assembly is held just above a folded sack on the workbench top, it is often possible to drive the end of the crankshaft through the pinion by striking it with a soft-faced mallet. Drastic action of this nature should be used only as a last resort since there is always risk of upsetting the flywheel alignment unless the greatest care is taken.

Make quite sure the timing pinions are marked before they are removed from the timing cover, which may mean cleaning them off first. If they are unmarked, mark them in a clear manner so that the correct valve timing can be achieved on reassembly. Some camwheels, such as those used on the Triumph twin cylinder models, have more than one keyway. It is advisable to mark the keyway in use, even though it is general practice to use the keyway that is directly in line with the timing mark. If there is any doubt whatsoever about the recommended valve and ignition timing setting, make careful note of the settings in use, before the engine is dismantled.

Removal of the valves from the cylinder head of an ohc model is easy if a valve spring compressor of the correct size is used. It is possible to dislodge the collets from the valve stems by other means, although they rarely prove quite so convenient. A valve spring compressor of a different design is needed for a side valve engine, so if you have to purchase a compressor, state the type you require. If the cylinder is of the blockhead type, the valves will have to be withdrawn through orifices in the cylinder head portion of the monobloc casting. These orifices are invariably sealed by large, threaded plugs, which may or may not have a finned cooling tower attached. The head is shaped in the form of a hexagon nut of very large diameter, so a special spanner will be required, usually of the cut-out type, that will fit the hexagon exactly. Needless to say these two plugs are screwed in very tightly, to prevent compression loss, and seat on copper or copper/asbestos washers. It is best to loosen them whilst the engine is still in the frame and is, therefore, held securely against the leverage applied. If the engine is dismantled first, a problem will immediately arise because there is no secure means of holding the cylinder barrel on its own without risk of damage. Under these circumstances, it is best to temporarily reassemble the two bare crankcase halves so that the cylinder barrel can be bolted back into position. If the whole assembly is now bolted into the engine stand, a reasonable amount of leverage can be applied to unscrew the plugs. The spanner must fit the hexagon all round, otherwise the edges will round off and make removal impossible. NEVER use a set spanner for this purpose.

Having dismantled the engine completely, the next stage is to clean each of the parts thoroughly, so that they can be closely examined for cracks, wear or damage of any kind. A 50/50 mixture of petrol and paraffin makes a suitable fluid in which to wash the parts, but has the disadvantage of being somewhat inflammable. The alternative is to use a cleaning fluid such as Gunk or Jizer which can be washed-off with water, carrying the grease and oil in an emulsified form. Parts treated in this manner will have to be dried thoroughly afterwards, otherwise they will very quickly rust.

Do not discard any parts at this stage, even if they are broken, worn or damaged beyond reclaim. They may be required to identify new parts that will replace them or may prove useful as a pattern from which to manufacture a new part. It will be necessary to save everything possible, the more so, the older the machine. The application of modern

This 1921 P&M engine had been left with the sparking plug removed. Although the piston was eventually freed, it was at the cost of the upper piston ring, which immediately caused replacement problems

Great care is necessary when removing the timing cover, as the pinions in the timing chest may not be marked. Make sure none come away with the cover or are pulled out of mesh

The timing pinions of the Triumph twin are clearly marked to aid replacement in their correct positions

techniques can often result in the reclamation of a part that only a few years ago would have been discarded. Splits and cracks found in castings can be repaired by welding, although this is hardly the job for the amateur welder. Very special treatment has to be given to parts that may have work hardened and become brittle with age, if they are not to distort badly or even shatter. Aluminium alloy and cast iron are notorious in this respect; specialist advice and attention should always be sought. Wear can be built up by metal spraying, stelliting, brazing and welding or electroplating, the technique to be used depending on the component concerned and the extent to which it will withstand heat without changing its characteristics. In each case a special finishing technique will be necessary, so that the correct tolerances are once again obtained. Often, these can be gauged only by examination of the worn part, in the hope that some portion still has the original contour. Even if the manufacturer's original handbook is available, it is very unusual to find wear limits listed, or the dimensions of the original part. Worn bearing housings will create problems if the amount of wear precludes a repair using Bearing Loctite. The option remains of boring out the housing to an oversize and fitting either a bearing of oversize outside diameter, or a specially-made sleeve to accommodate the original bearing. Blind bushes can be extracted by heating the casing and pulling them out of position after they have been threaded to accommodate a bolt that will provide the necessary leverage. Sometimes, immersing the crankcase half in a bowl of boiling water will suffice. In a few cases, it may be possible to drill a very small hole in the outside of the casting and use a pin punch to drive the bush out of location, sealing the hole afterwards. This same technique can be used to remove particularly stubborn outer races of roller bearings, without risk of damage to the housing. Oil seals should be renewed as a matter of routine, for in general they apply only to the more modern machines and should prove less difficult to obtain. Early models relied upon strips of felt to achieve the same effect, which are easily cut and shaped to fit. This does not apply to two-strokes, however, where a good crankcase seal is a vital necessity. If air leaks occur around the crankshaft, the engine is unlikely to run correctly, even if it can be persuaded to start!

One job that will certainly be beyond the capabilities of the enthusiast who does not possess a lathe, is renewal of the big-end bearing, unless the assembly happens to be one of the somewhat rare type that is used more extensively today. This latter type of bearing is of the shell type, with a split connecting rod and cap. It is most common on multi-cylinder machines and will be found on most of the Triumph twins. Because the connecting rod has a separate end cap, the assembly is easily dismantled for replacement of the bearing shells. Older types of big-end assembly are of the roller bearing type (caged or uncaged), or even a plain bush, and it will be necessary to separate the flywheels to gain access to the bearing. Unfortunately, this is not always as easy as it sounds, because the crankpin nuts (if fitted) will be very tight, whilst the crankpin itself may have tapers to locate with a tapered bore in the flywheels. Unless you are able to hold the flywheel assembly very rigidly so that considerable leverage can be applied to the nuts, work of this nature is best entrusted to someone who has the necessary facilities. Tapered crankpins that have a very slow taper, and no nuts, will cause even greater difficulties when the flywheels have to be parted, in view of the force needed to part them. NEVER drive wedges between the flywheels or use brute force without knowing exactly what you are doing. Many flywheel assemblies have been irreparably damaged in this fashion.

When the big-end bearing is accessible, it will probably be found that three components have to be renewed; the rollers, the crankpin and the sleeve pressed within the big-end eye of the connecting rod. On early engines, the roller bearings will probably be uncaged and possibly the connecting rod will not have a renewable sleeve. Whilst it may be possible to renew the rollers, and perhaps even obtain a new crankpin, it will not be so easy to recondition the connecting rod so that it is again fully serviceable. Under these circumstances, the problem is best handled by a bearing specialist, to whom the complete bearing assembly should be sent as a pattern. Although expensive, it is the only satisfactory solution if recurring big-end trouble is not to be experienced.

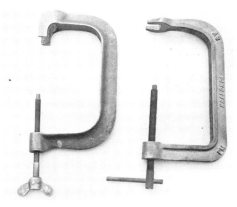

Valve spring compressors are needed to remove the valves. The design on the left is for ohv engines; that on the right for side valve engines

AMC Limited marketed this simple, but highly effective tool, for removing the hairpin valve springs from their ohv singles. A rocker box bolt was used to pass through the centre of the spring and the two 'ears' of the tool

A typical valve cap of the 'fir cone' type, fitted over the exhaust valve of a Sunbeam side valve single

Older type big end assemblies use uncaged rollers, in conjunction with a specially hardened crankpin and outer race for insertion in the connecting rod eye

The outer race will press into the connecting rod, when renewal is necessary. It can be used to press out the old race at the same time

Later big end assemblies are of the caged type, using a duralumin cage such as this to house the individual rollers

It has been suggested on numerous occasions that enthusiasts working in their own workshops can reassemble and realign their own flywheel assemblies without recourse to a lathe. The technique is based on the use of a set square; this is used to draw scribe lines across the outer rims of the flywheels before they are separated, and is then re-used as a means of realignment, during reassembly. Personally, I have never subscribed to this practice, which lends itself to errors and presumes the alignment was correct in the first instance. A badly aligned flywheel assembly will give a very rough engine, with noticeable vibration and general lack of performance due to the large amount of power absorbed by the misalignment. Bearing life is shortened too, especially the life of the main bearings. A well-aligned set of flywheels should have no more than $\pm$ 0.001 in/0.025mm runout at the extreme ends of the crankshaft. This is particularly important in the case of a bevel driven ohc engine, where any variations will affect the depth of mesh of the bevel pinions.

A one-piece or built-up crankshaft for a multi-cylinder machine will require specialist attention if wear problems are encountered; special tools will be needed to separate and realign the crankshaft in the latter case, if risk of damage is to be avoided. Some machines require very special attention, such as the Scott two-stroke twin, in which an unusual 'knocking-up' technique is required for assembly of the central flywheel and main bearings in the crankcase, all within the one operation. This is another area in which full use can be made of the manufacturer's original publications, assuming copies can be obtained. If not, ask the marque specialist. If you intend to tackle the job yourself, it must be right first time, and carried out in the correct sequence.

When rebuilding the bottom end of a bevel driven ohc engine, some experience will be necessary to ensure the bevels mesh together correctly. Ideally, they should mesh so that the teeth have full contact with each other, without the degree of mesh being too deep or too slack, to the extent that measurable backlash is only just detectable. Mesh is governed by raising or lowering the horizontal bevel and by moving the vertical bevel inwards or outwards on the crankshaft, by means of adding or subtracting shims of the appropriate thickness. Several attempts will prove necessary before the mesh appears to be correct — check that the flywheels revolve quite freely and silently without evidence of anything but the very slightest amount of backlash. If the mesh is correct, the bevels should give a slight whine when the engine is cold, which disappears as it warms up. If the engine is being built up from a host of parts where spares are included, it may be necessary to pair the bevels first, so that they will run quietly with each other. The need for selective assembly and meshing is one of the reasons why ohc engines are more costly to produce.

The timing pinions within the timing chest rarely give trouble, unless badly worn, in which case there will be considerable backlash between the teeth. Another source of mechanical noise is worn tappets (cam followers) and the guides in which they run. If excessive wear is present, as will often be evidenced by oil leaks, they should be renewed. Some machines have exceptionally quiet timing gear, such that any wear is soon noticeable through the increase in noise level. The Sunbeam singles are particularly good in this respect. It is assumed the cam wheel bushes will already have received attention, since they are easily removed and new replacements fitted. This also applies to the cams and the tappets (cam followers). Do not forget to check that the crankshaft pinion is fully home on the end of the crankshaft, keyed into position and secured with a nut and tab washer. Make sure the timing marks are aligned correctly too — sometimes the dot on the crankshaft pinion is masked by the tab washer.

As mentioned previously in this Chapter, an immediate problem will arise if the timing pinions are unmarked and no attempt was made to record the settings in use before the engine was dismantled. In the absence of the manufacturer's instructions or some form of reliable guide when looking through old magazines, a technique that will frequently get an engine running in reasonable fashion is to share the valve overlap equally between both valves. This will necessitate the use of a degree disc attached to the end of the crankshaft, so that the individual opening and closing points of the valves can be read off and compared. Insert the cams in approximately their correct positions and attach the degree disc to the

Crankshafts of the plain bearing type can cause problems, especially if the bearings are not of the split shell type. This was just saveable as most of the marks were due to local corrosion

Old and late-type Triumph twin crankshafts are not interchangeable, since later models have a crankshaft twin driven alternator

Threaded end of crankshaft is needed to retain the engine shock absorber assembly

107

end of the crankshaft, bolting it securely in position so that a pointer attached to some convenient place on the engine reads zero when the piston is **exactly** at top dead centre. Then turn the engine in the normal direction of rotation and note the reading when each valve commences to open and the point at which it has closed completely. From these readings, it will be apparent that both valves are open together during one phase of engine rotation — in other words, they overlap. The amount of overlap should be adjusted, assuming the timing is being set up from scratch, so that there is an equal amount of overlap either side of top dead centre.

Valve spring pressures often make it difficult to determine exactly when each valve opens and closes, so that if possible, one valve should be removed completely whilst the opening and closing of the other is being checked. Note that if the timing is being checked against known settings, it is often necessary to set the valve clearances at a special, temporary setting, to obtain accurate readings on the degree disc.

When using a degree disc, always turn the disc beyond the point of the reading desired, then turn back again to the correct setting in the normal direction of rotation of the engine. This will eliminate any backlash within the engine, and help ensure that a high degree of accuracy is achieved. The degree disc method is to be preferred in place of any other, since it will give the most accurate results. However, in the early days, it was more common practice to give readings in inches or fractions of an inch, related to the piston position at either top or bottom dead centre. In these instances, it will be necessary to use a graduated timing stick, inserted through the spark plug hole.

Quite a few engines have the oil pump contained within the timing cover, if the lubrication system is of the dry sump type. Other locations include an external mounting on the timing cover itself, in the base of the crankcase and even close to the magneto drive by means of an interconnecting peg. The oil pump is the heart of the lubrication system and should be checked to ensure it is functioning correctly, also that the drive is not in any way damaged. Pumps of the gear type are simple but efficient, although they rely on very small clearances if they are to function correctly. When wear sets in, they will still continue to function efficiently for a while, but will permit oil to seep past the gear pinions whilst the machine is stationary so that eventually the contents of the oil tank end up in the crankcase. This is one reason why it was customary to fit an oil tap in the main oil feed of the early ohc Velocettes and Nortons that had this type of pump. That is, until riders forgot to open the tap and ruined a perfectly good engine! Veloce Limited got around the problem by fitting a ball valve with a very light spring loading so that the ball was lifted off its seating, thus opening the oil flow, immediately the engine started. This, however, is a comparatively recent innovation. In the absence of any such device, renewal of the oil pump complete is the only satisfactory remedy. The plunger type of pump, used on the Triumph twins and some of the singles, as well as on some of the Ariel singles, does not often give trouble and is easily replaced if worn. Problems can occur if the spring-loaded ball valves at the base of each plunger stick open, but they are readily removed for cleaning.

Oil pumps attached to the exterior of the timing cover, such as the Best and Lloyd or Pilgrim, are virtually metering devices that permit gravity fed oil to enter the engine lubrication system at a controlled rate. Scott owners in particular will be well aware of the shortcomings of the Pilgrim pump, which will prove anything but reliable when wear sets in. The Achilles heel is the little cam that forms an integral part of the end cover. Made of the same zinc-based alloy as the remainder of the pump body, it does not possess good wear resisting qualities. At least one Scott specialist has a pump reclamation service in which the cam is machined off and replaced with one made from a much tougher metal. Earlier hand pumps deliver oil direct to the engine or to the engine and gearbox via a two-way tap. Provided the hand pump is in good order the only other problem that can occur is sticking of the one-way valve in the system — a necessary addition to prevent crankcase pressure blowing the oil in the reverse direction up the pipe. A simple disc valve is normally used for this purpose, which can be dismantled for access to the disc itself. Check the valve action by blowing through each end. Air should pass quite freely in one direction, but not in the other. The former would be in the direction of the oil flow.

Problems are likely to occur if the cylinder is badly worn or is damaged in some way. A rebore itself should cause little concern, provided the bore has not already reached the limit of plus 0.040 in/1.0mm, or in some cases plus 0.060 in/1.5mm. If it has, a new liner will have to be fitted, which will bring the bore down to standard size once again. It is the piston that will cause the trouble, because not many of the older designs are still available from stock. The problem becomes even more acute with early pistons of the cast iron type. It is here that the advice of a piston specialist should be sought, because it is often possible to use a piston designed for another quite different engine, provided the essential statistics are near identical. Note that if an aluminium alloy piston has to be used in place of a cast iron original, it will be necessary to have greater clearances, due to the higher rate of expansion of the alloy material. The engine may also have to be re-balanced. If only new piston rings are required and it is not possible to obtain replacements for the older type of very wide ring, the problem can be overcome by fitting two or even three rings of similar dimensions but narrower width, into the same groove. When refitting the piston, use new circlips even if the originals appear to be in good shape, assuming suitable replacements are available. If the gudgeon pin is of the older type that relies upon brass end pads, these will have to be specially made if the originals have worn thin, not forgetting the vent grooves or holes. On two-stroke engines, check the security of the piston ring pegs. If they work loose the rings may rotate and jam in one of the ports, causing considerable damage.

Gear-type oil pumps are inclined to let oil seep into the crankcase when the machine is standing, if wear or end float develops

Achilles heel of the Scott, the Pilgrim oil pump, was fitted to a number of other machines that have proprietary engines fitted. Problem lies in obtaining a small but reliable metered flow of oil at all times

This cylinder block will have to be scrapped. A previous, careless owner, has smashed the lower end of the liner whilst attempting to ease it off the crankcase

Many old cast iron pistons used soft end pads to retain the gudgeon pins, in place of circlips. Unlike circlips, they can be reused

Make sure a deflector-type two-stroke piston is fitted the correct way round. If unintentionally reversed, a mysterious loss of power will be experienced

The cylinder head must be the right way round too. This is a good example of the damage that occurs when a loose carburettor needle clip is sucked into the engine

The valves and guides will almost certainly need attention; at the very least the former will need grinding in, so that the seat is free of pit marks and other blemishes that may cause compression loss. After removing the valves by means of a spring compressor, clean the valve stems and the inside of the valve guides, using a pull-through in this latter case. Then check the clearance between the valve stem and the guide. It is hard to give any reliable figures for the limit that will decide whether renewal is necessary, because they will depend on the material from which the valve guide is made and whether the engine is of the sports or touring type. On an elderly engine with a valve head of approximately 1½ in/38.1mm diameter, renewal of the valve and/or guide would seem advisable if there is about 1/16th in/1.59mm play when the valve is in the normal full lift position. To remove the old guide, heat the cylinder head (or barrel in the case of a side valve engine) and drive the guide out of position with a double diameter drift, the smaller portion of which exactly fits the inside of the valve guide. Drift the new guide into position whilst the cylinder head is still warm and then have the valve seat recut. It is rarely possible to re-grind the valve seat effectively without excessive effort, unless a valve seat cutter is used.

These combustion chambers need a good clean up. One valve is stuck open in its guide, dampness having caused it to rust in this position

This valve seat will need to be reinserted as the valve itself is in danger of becoming pocketed

Make sure the valve springs have their correct seatings and the top cap is not cracked. If a valve drops in, it will cause extensive engine damage

A selection of valve collets, all for the single cylinder ohc Velocette. The lower item is a hardened end cap to go over the end of the valve stem — not of Velocette origin

After a lengthy period of service, the valves will tend to become pocketed, since continual grinding-in will gradually lower the valve seating so that the gas flow of the engine is interrupted and performance falls off. The only way in which the engine can be restored to its former efficiency is to have the valve seats reinserted, a highly skilled job that requires specialist attention. This will give the engine a new lease of life, especially one of the ohv or ohc type. When reassembling the engine, remember to replace the valves in their original positions if the heads are of the same size. Because the exhaust valve works at a much higher temperature, it is usually made from a different grade of steel that has imposed heat resisting properties. Quite often the head of the valve or the stem is marked EX to avoid confusion.

Many of the very early side valve engines are prone to break valves, because the special quality steel that is in common use today was unknown at that time. If the engine still has the original valves fitted, it is advisable to carry a spare since it is quite practicable to make a roadside replacement, if the head is pulled off one of the valves.

Valve springs should be renewed whenever the machine is decarbonised because they tend to weaken with use and eventually take on a permanent set. Weak valve springs cause sluggish performance and on the more sporting type of engine will encourage valve bounce to occur at much lower rpm than usual. On ohv and ohc engines, it is common practice to employ two sets of springs, an inner and an outer, which may or may not be a close fit within each other. They rest on special seatings around the valve guides, and in the case of the exhaust valve springs, the seating is usually raised a little from the cylinder head to interrupt the transmission of heat by conduction. Some machines employ the hairpin type of valve spring. The post-war AMC singles feature a cylinder head layout of this latter type and have the advantage that a very simple but effective tool can be used to remove and replace the springs without need for a spring compressor. Note that if coil springs of the variable rate type are used, they must be refitted so that the coils closest together are positioned nearest to the cylinder head. Always check the valve cap for cracks and make sure the collets seat correctly in undamaged grooves. After reassembly, it is good policy to give the end of the valve a smart tap with a hammer, to check that neither the collets nor the valve cap have failed to seat correctly.

Very early machines employed an automatic inlet valve, in which the opening and closing of the valve was initiated by suction from within the engine that would raise the valve off its seating. It will be appreciated that only a very light spring is required under these circumstances, since it must be sufficiently strong to return the valve to its seating after the induction stroke, but not strong enough to hinder the opening of the valve when it is required to lift off its seat by the suction effect. There cannot be many who are experienced in the art of setting up an automatic inlet valve correctly, for this valve arrangement became obsolete as far back as 1910 or thereabouts. The advice of the owner of a similar old machine is best sought under these circumstances, since adjustment by trial and error can prove both time consuming and extremely frustrating.

One of the more unsightly aspects of an otherwise mechanically perfect engine is chipped or broken fins on the cylinder barrel and/or cylinder head. This type of damage is often caused by a previous owner, who has resorted to the very questionable technique of using a screwdriver or other pointed instrument to break the joint between the cylinder barrel and the cylinder head. It is worth giving some attention to this point before the engine is reassembled, because it is easy to cut and shape the missing portions from another discarded component and braze them into position, cleaning up with a file afterwards to mask evidence of the joint. I have heard of silver solder or even epoxy resin used for the same purpose, but I doubt whether either alternative is really applicable on an early engine with scant finning, which would tend to run hot. When reassembling the engine, the problem of gaskets will arise, as mentioned earlier. Paper gaskets will cause no problems and if necessary, compressible gaskets, such as those used at the cylinder head joint, can be cut from sheet copper. It is, however, worth remembering that one or two gasket specialists offer a service that is of particular help. If they cannot supply gaskets of the correct type from stock, they will make them from the original patterns at reasonable cost. This is particularly helpful if the gaskets are of the composite copper and asbestos type. Make sure all the nuts and bolts used are undamaged — they are easily renewed unless of a special shape or thread. After reassembly, trim away any protruding portions of gasket which will otherwise look very untidy. A scalpel knife is very suitable for this purpose. Even more unsightly is gasket cement that has oozed from the newly-made joints. This too should be cleaned off. Methylated spirits is a good solvent in most cases, which will obviate the need to scrape the surface.

Hopefully, the cylinder head and barrel will have received a thorough cleaning prior to assembly, followed by a new coating of cylinder black (unless they are of aluminium alloy). Today's aerosol cans provide a particularly convenient means of giving a smooth, even coating, with a choice of an eggshell or matt finish that is really heat resistant.

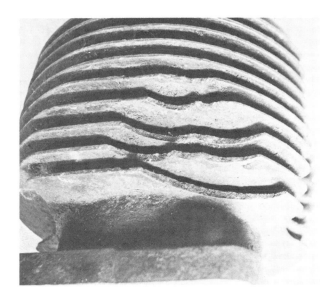

Broken cylinder barrel fins look unsightly, apart from preventing the full cooling effect from being achieved. They should be built up by brazing then smoothed off

Old cylinder head gaskets of the copper/asbestos type can often be reclaimed by annealing them, prior to refitting

A fine selection of machines outside one of the specialist suppliers of old motorcycles. Left to right is a Nimbus and sidecar, a Levis, an FN, an Ariel, a Vincent and a Triumph.

Chapter Ten

The ignition system

Early ignition systems used what is known as a trembler coil to generate the spark, a contact maker or wipe contact, driven from the engine, to determine when the spark should occur, and a battery to energise the circuit. There was no provision on the machine for keeping the battery charged; when it ran out, the ignition circuit ceased to function and the machine came to a halt. As may be expected, these primitive ignition systems were not very reliable, mainly because most of the component parts were of poor design or frail construction. Batteries shook to pieces from vibration. Wires would break or fray through, causing short circuits, because they passed through holes in metal panels without the protection of insulators or grommets. Even the spark plugs were not immune; they would crack and disintegrate through the use of inferior porcelain insulators, often with the risk of portions falling into the engine. The trembler coil alone escaped most of these types of problems because it was enclosed within a stout wooden box and contained external provision for adjusting the trembler arm to compensate for wear at the contacts.

As far as the owner of a very old machine is concerned, the enforced need to use modern replacements for the original battery and spark plug will automatically eliminate some of the above faults, whilst careful rearrangement of the wiring layout will account for most that remain. But there is no modern replacement for the trembler coil, if the original is damaged beyond repair. This is most likely to occur if the box itself is damaged, admitting moisture, or if the fine wire windings are broken and open circuited. A modern ignition coil can be hidden away in the same compartment as a convenient and easy way out, but if the trembler coil is substantially complete, it is quite feasible to have it rewound and restored to good working order. There are a number of specialists who handle the repair of scientific apparatus such as that used in schools. The trembler coil is only a miniaturised version of the 'shocking coil', often used to demonstrate electrical spark discharges. Some skill is necessary when adjusting the trembler arm. It should vibrate quite freely when the circuit is energised by the contact maker, to give a good spark at both high and low engine speeds. The difficulty lies in achieving the correct balance.

The ignition system was greatly simplified when the magneto superseded the trembler coil set-up. The magneto is a self-contained instrument that does not require any external means of energising - it operates on the electro-magnetic principle and generates its own HT current for the ignition circuit when driven from the engine. This eliminates the need for any wiring, apart from the HT lead(s) to the spark plug(s) and possibly a lead to a cut-out button, so that the magneto can be earthed in order to prevent the plugs from sparking and causing the engine to stop.

A magneto comprises three basic units; the magnet assembly, the rotating armature and the contact breaker, the latter mounted on the end of the armature. All three can develop their own particular faults, especially if the instrument has been exposed to the atmosphere for a long period without use, or worse still, has been left in a dismantled state. The magnet assembly tends to lose its magnetism as time progresses, especially if subjected to heat or strong vibration. Magnetism will also be lost if the armature is withdrawn without using 'keepers' to bridge the pole pieces of the magnets in its absence. These are usually off-cuts of mild steel strip or some similar magnetic material, that lodge between the pole pieces and are kept in place by the attraction of the magnets, to maintain the magnetic field. The best check is to rotate the armature by hand and note whether there is any 'pull' by the magnets, when the armature is in the position where the contact breaker points are about to separate. The contact breaker must be in place during this check, with the points clean and correctly gapped. Loss of magnetism can be corrected by having the magnet assembly remagnetised, a simple and quite cheap operation. It does, however, need specialised equipment.

The armature usually takes the form of windings encapsulated in shellac or a synthetic resin, and has a hollow taper on one end and a slip ring on the other. The condenser that forms part of the contact breaker circuit is also built into the armature. Exceptions occur in the case of some armatures where the magnets revolve and the windings remain stationary, although these, excluding the very last Lucas design, are very much in the minority. By far the most common magneto malady is 'shellactitis', a tendency for the shellac coating around the windings of the armature to absorb water from the atmosphere and become soft. Eventually the point is reached where the shellac begins to fling whilst the armature is revolving, interposing a thin layer of somewhat viscous shellac between the armature and the body and that the magneto virtually seizes. As this invariably happens when the rider is a long way from home, the problems are not easy to resolve! For this reason alone, it is often best to have an aged magneto checked over by a specialist in magneto repairs, who will rewind the armature and coat it with a synthetic resin, if the original shellac coating is showing signs of deterioration. It is worth adding, however, that the use of shellac to coat the armature windings seems to have ended when motorcycle production was resumed after the last war. In consequence, shellactitis is almost unheard of on post-1946 models, providing the magneto is the original. Whilst there is no permanent cure other than a rewind and re-impregnation with synthetic resin, it is worth while noting that a temporary 'get you home' repair can be effected by stripping the magneto and removing the armature. If the magnet pole pieces are scraped free of the shellac that has been flung, the magneto can be re-assembled after the armature has been liberally coated with French chalk to help solidify the sticky shellac coating. It is prudent, however, to keep the engine running until you reach home, or, if it is necessary to stop, to prevent the engine from cooling down. If the magneto siezes again, a further stripdown followed by similar treatment will prove necessary.

A rewind will also be necessary if the condenser has failed, a defect immediately noticeable by the sparking that occurs when the contact breaker points separate and the way in which the surface of the points burns away as a result. For obvious reasons, the condenser should always be checked when an armature has to be rewound.

The slip ring on the end of the armature can also create problems if it is defective in any way. A cracked or broken slip ring should be renewed without question or starting and misfiring problems are likely to occur. Moisture in a crack can lead to a dead short, since the HT current will take the line of least resistance and leak away along this path. The slip ring must be clean and free from any score marks or indentations, which will occur if the pick-up brush(es) are allowed to wear beyond the serviceable limit. It is difficult to remove and replace the slip ring without the appropriate equipment, since the inner race of the drive side armature bearing must be extracted first. Note that the magneto for a twin cylinder engine has a different type of slip ring from that used with a single cylinder engine, and that the angle of the cylinders has also to be taken into account. This also applies to the magneto itself if a change is contemplated. Quite apart from the need to ensure the direction of

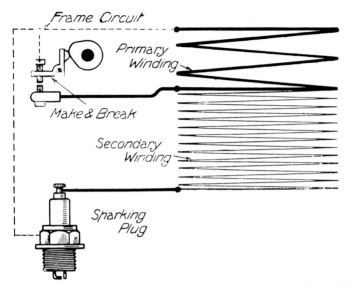

Frame Circuit

Primary Winding

Make & Break

Secondary Winding

Sparking Plug

Figure 11 This diagram shows the electrical connections for an early high tension magneto. The condenser across the ignition points has been omitted, even though it is a very necessary item that helps increase the intensity of the spark and also prevents the points from arcing as they separate

All manner of magnetos have been available over the years. This is the small ML type, suitable for two-strokes and similar machines of small capacity

The much sought-after square ML magneto, which is virtually a racing magneto and found on many machines with a sporting specification

117

rotation is the same, the number of cylinders and the firing interval must correspond. Note that the correct rotation of the magneto is always taken from the driving end.

If the armature bearings are worn, they must be renewed, since there is always risk of the revolving armature making contact with the magnet pole pieces if the amount of play is too great. The gap is only minimal and if the parts touch, extensive damage may result. Special tools are necessary to extract the inner and outer bearing races without risk of damage, and it is strongly recommended that this type of reconditioning is left to the repair specialist. If there is an oil seal fitted around the drive spindle, this should be renewed at the same time.

Various types of contact breaker are used, depending on the make of magneto to which they are fitted and the year of manufacture of the instrument. All rely on a set of points that separate when the spark is due to occur. It follows that the points must be clean and adjusted correctly at the correct gap, measured when they are fully open. Dirty points are best dealt with by removing them from the contact breaker base plate and cleaning them up with either emery paper or an oil stone. The main essential is a good, blemish free surface so that good electrical contact is made when they touch together. When dismantling the contact breaker assembly, take good note of the position of the various insulating washers. If they are not replaced in the correct order, the points will be short circuited and there will be no output from the magneto. If the points are very badly burnt or have deep pit marks, it is best to renew them, assuming the correct replacements are available. This also applies if there is very little metal left on their surfaces. Early magnetos have platinum points and as this is a very soft metal, care must be taken not to remove any excess when undertaking the cleaning operation. Later magnetos have points with a tungsten surface, a much harder metal that needs emery paper or an oil stone to make any appreciable impression.

It is usual to find the advance and retard mechanism close to the contact breaker assembly. This should be lightly greased when the contact breaker assembly is removed, so that it operates smoothly. A common location is in the end cover of the magneto body, operating the cam ring that surrounds the contact breaker assembly. Never over-grease, or there is risk of grease reaching the surface of the points, making electrical contact difficult. There is usually also a felt wick, to lubricate the surface of the contact breaker cam. This should receive one or two drops of light machine oil, again avoiding an excess. When replacing the contact breaker assembly, note that it keys into the end of the armature, so that it is always located in the correct position. Do not overtighten the central retaining bolt, since the shank is of small diameter and will shear easily if overstressed.

Apart from the pick-up brush(es) that bears on the slip ring, there is usually a somewhat larger diameter brush that bears on the edge of the armature, to make the earth contact. Both types of brush should make good contact and not be worn beyond the halfway point of their original length. It follows that the brush holders should also be in good condition and tightened fully. The pick-up brush holder is the one subject to most damage as it is usually made of a plastics material. It should have a gasket at the joint with the magneto body and a rubber cap around the joint where the HT lead is attached, to prevent the ingress of water. Beware of overtightening the retaining screws, if this method of attachment is used in place of a clip. The HT lead must make good electrical contact with the inner metal portion of the brush holder, a point where corrosion is likely to occur. Either a grub screw that pierces the cable inner or a screw cap that retains the belled out end of the exposed cable wires is the usual means of attachment.

It cannot be overstressed that the complete overhaul of a magneto is a task that requires a specialised knowledge and experience. It is a vital component that is today obsolete and if it ceases to function efficiently, the ultimate result will be the complete immobilisation of the machine. If it is decided to undertake a certain amount of renovation work, or perhaps only to check what repairs will prove necessary, do not overlook the fact that many magnetos have an earthing screw fitted, which locates between the flanges of the slip ring. If this is not removed together with the brush holders, the slip ring will be irreparably damaged when the armature is extracted after the end cover has been removed.

The more common type of contact breaker assembly, in which the opening and closing of the points is actuated by the outer cam ring. The cam ring is movable, to give advance/retard facilities

The face cam type of contact breaker, in which a short 'push rod' that bears on the face cam below, actuates the points. Note how the face cam is moved when there is need to advance or retard the ignition

This is, perhaps, the best example of the damage that can occur if a somewhat specialised repair job is tackled by a complete novice.

Coil ignition systems should not give rise to any undue problems. If the system does not function and the switch and battery are known to be in good condition, either the coil or the condenser are at fault, assuming there is no break or short circuit in the wiring and the contact breaker is known to be in working order. Without the appropriate test equipment, there is no really satisfactory way in which to test a condenser, other than by substitution. Fortunately, a new condenser is quite cheap and will always provide a handy spare, if not required. To check the coil, disconnect the electrical leads and remove it from the machine. Connect the HT lead to a spark plug that is known to be good, and wrap a bared wire around the metal base of the plug body and the coil itself, so that the two are interconnected. Touch a pair of battery leads across the two terminals of the coil and check whether a spark occurs across the plug points as this contact is made. If it does, the chances are that the coil is OK. If there is no response, do not discard the coil without first checking the HT lead for continuity. Coils cannot normally be repaired as they are manufactured as sealed units. Failure is most likely to occur if water has crept into the sealed container, or if the container has been dented, causing a break in the very fine gauge wire used for the coil windings.

119

Mention has been made earlier of the ignition cut-out, usually a push button mounted on the handlebars or on the end cover of the magneto. A cut-out is a convenient way of shorting out the primary windings of the magneto so that a spark will not occur at the plug(s). In consequence the engine can be stopped instantly. Instances have occurred where the cut-out button has jammed in the 'on' position, giving the impression that the magneto has packed up. Always check by removing the cut-out wire connection or the end cover of the magneto, before looking for the fault elsewhere.

The ignition system of any car or motorcycle creates interference with both radio and television when the vehicle is in close proximity, and for this reason it is customary to fit some form of ignition suppressor. The most common type is a special type of plug cap, in which the high value resistor needed to give the suppressor effect is incorporated. Occasionally, these suppressor caps develop a fault which will effectively prevent a spark from occurring across the points of the spark plug. Substitution or a check with the suppressor cap removed is the action recommended in this instance. Although a modern fitting may seem very much out of place on an elderly machine, the suppressor cap performs a very important social function and should be fitted in order to eliminate unnecessary radio and television interference on all occasions when it is not likely to detract from any concours

Old ignition coils are somewhat bulkier than today's counterparts. This Lucas coil is of a type generally available during 1930, in a sealed, protective can

The magneto cut-out button mounted close to the air control lever effectively earths the primary circuit of the magneto, when depressed. Under these circumstances, no spark can occur at the plug points

judging. Motorcyclists tend to have a bad image amongst those who know little about them, irrespective of what type of machine they ride. Some of the older magnetos deliver a very healthy spark and the range of the interference can prove surprisingly extensive. There are other ways of fitting a suppressor, by using an HT lead that has an internal carbon thread rather than the customary wire, or by means of a small resistor interposed between the brush holder and the HT lead. The former has the advantage of being particularly inconspicious. On an old machine, try and avoid the use of modern HT cable, which has a shiny plastic outer cover. It looks out of place and is immediately obvious. It should still be possible to obtain the original rubber type or the type covered with empire cloth.

Every so often the motoring and motorcycling magazines and newspapers carry advertisements about so-called spark intensifiers or 'superchargers', which are claimed to give an intensified spark across the plug points and improve the rate of fuel consumption through more efficient ignition. Some revealing tests, carried out by independent bodies, have shown that most of these claims cannot be substantiated. Much the same effect can be achieved by the old dodge of inserting a coat button in the HT lead, wrapping the wires around the adjacent thread holes so that a spark gap occurs between the two. This extra gap will create a more intense spark at the plug points and can be used effectively to clear a plug that has oiled up, or one that is subject to oiling up because the cylinder concerned is receiving too much oil. Occasionally, these proprietary devices are found on an old machine, no doubt fitted by a misguided owner of the past. They perform a doubtful function and should be discarded since if the machine is correctly overhauled, the fault they originally masked will have been eliminated.

It is seldom realised that the price of a good quality spark plug has remained remarkably stable over the years. The development of the spark plug is a complex topic, and all that can be said in brief, is that today's products represent a very considerable technological advance over the spark plugs that were available only a couple of decades ago. Unfortunately, a move towards the standardisation of the 14mm size commenced during the middle thirties, with the result that the 18mm size fitted to all the earlier models is now classified as obsolete. Until quite recently, some tractors and lawnmowers were fitted with 18mm spark plugs as standard, and these can be used on certain types of motorcycle, provided the engine is not of the high performance type. In this latter case, it is possible to fit a threaded adaptor which will effectively sleeve down the spark plug hold to accept a 14mm spark plug of grade equivalent to the original. But this may give rise to an added heat transfer problem, which will necessitate some experiments with grades differing from the original recommendation. However, this approach affords a way out where there is no other alternative. In most cases it will prove quite impracticable to renovate and re-use the old spark plug that was fitted when the machine was found, because pocketed electrodes or soiled insulators will result in inefficient combustion, with subsequent loss of performance. Nonetheless, an old spark plug should be kept and cleaned as far as its outward appearance is concerned. It can be substituted for the normal running plug during a concours contest, so that the machine specification appears to be utterly original.

It is probable that the owner of a two-stroke will have most problems with spark plugs, since this type of engine is more likely to give rise to oiling-up or whiskering problems. My own experiences with a 600cc Scott have shown that Japanese-made NGK spark plugs tolerate conditions under which all other plugs would have failed, seemingly because they have a much wider heat range. They compensate for the inadequacies of the Pilgrim pump lubrication system and will continue to fire when temporary over-lubrication creates a veritable smoke screen. The threaded adaptors fitted to the cylinder head enable standard, over-the-counter 14mm sizes to be fitted, the increased heat range of the plugs apparently coping with any heat transfer problems the inserts may have caused.

No mention has been made in this Chapter of magnetos that perform a dual ignition and lighting role, such as the Maglita, the combined magneto and dynamo units of the Lucas Magdyno or BTH Dynomag types, or the flywheel magneto. Information about these instruments will be found in Chapter 12, which deals with lighting and electrical equipment.

121

Protective caps are very necessary here, otherwise rainwater dripping from the radiator shell would quickly short out the spark plugs

The older, 18mm spark plug is on the right, a type that tended to be replaced by the 14mm type in the mid-thirties. The 14mm type shown on the left has a taper seating, and does not require a sealing washer

This simple, but ingenious, spring clip was supplied with all KLG spark plugs during the late forties. It helped make quick plug changes possible

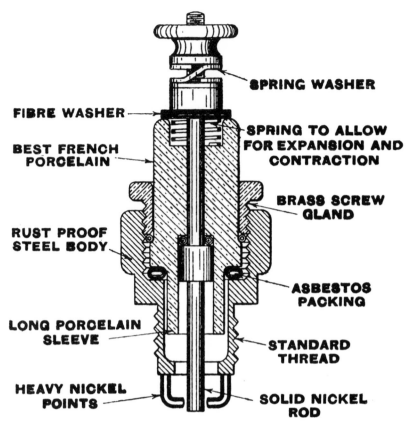

Figure 12 A cross-section of an early spark plug. Modern plugs are of more sophisticated design as the result of improved insulators and better metal/ceramic seals

It should be mentioned, however, that a flywheel magneto of the type fitted to many of the popular, low cost two-strokes does not necessarily carry lighting coils to provide a dual ignition and lighting function. Most ignition troubles with this type of generator can be traced to either a cracked pick-up brush assembly that allows the high tension current to earth itself, or to the flywheel having moved on the mainshaft taper, to which it is normally locked. The remedy for the first type of fault is renewal of the defective parts; refer to Chapter 12 in the case of the second. Should it prove necessary to gain access to the contact breaker points other than through the 'windows' in the flywheel rotor, it will be necessary to draw the flywheel off the mainshaft taper first. The centre nut acts as a self-extractor. When a spanner is applied, it will slacken, then tighten again as it commences to draw the flywheel off the taper. Usually, a keyway is provided so that the flywheel will realign in approximately the same position - an important factor since apart from retaining the accuracy of the ignition timing, the position of the flywheel magnets in relation to the ignition coil is critical. Unless they are in close proximity to each other when the points separate, the high tension voltage generated will be greatly weakened and may not even initiate the desired spark.

Above all else, it must be emphasised that the reconditioning of an old magneto or one that is broken down, is not a matter to be taken lightly, especially in view of the risk of causing further damage to an instrument that may prove irreplaceable. There are a small number of repair specialists who are prepared to accept magnetos for repair at very competitive prices, many of them working in a retired or semi-retired capacity. They have the know-how and many of the very scarce parts that may be needed in the rebuild. It is in your interests to make use of these services, whilst they still exist.

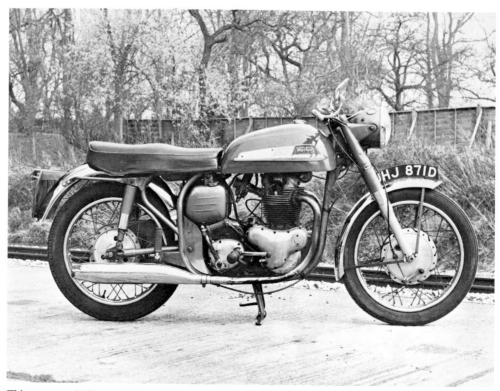

This ten year old Norton Atlas is typical of the type of machine now being hunted down by today's restorers. Although somewhat eclipsed by the later Commando models, the Atlas enjoyed a very fine reputation in its day. This example needs only a general tidy up and the substitution of twin carburettors to restore it to original specification

Still in active service (with the Yeovil Learner Trainer Scheme) this early D1 plunger-spring Bantam is now eligible for certain events organised by the Vintage MCC. It has remained remarkably original in specification and requires only superficial attention to bring it to full concours presentation. At one time, the Bantam was Britain's largest selling motorcycle

Chapter Eleven

Carburettor and exhaust systems

One of the items likely to suffer the most wear and prove the most difficult to replace is the carburettor. In the very early 'pioneer' days, a device known as a surface carburettor was used to supply the correct ratio of petrol vapour and air to the engine, for ignition. Crude in the extreme, these instruments depended on vaporisation from the surface of a pool of petrol contained in the base, using various adjustable flaps and similar devices to control the admission of air. The chances of obtaining a replacement surface carburettor are remote, to say the very least. If the original instrument is damaged or has parts missing, a professional repair specialist, used to this type of work, is the only answer.

When the jet carburettor came into fashion during the early 1900s, the change in design made possible the replacement of parts that were likely to be subjected to wear, such as slides, jets and needles — all used to meter the flow of petrol or air. There have been a great many different types of jet carburettor available over the years, so that it is virtually impossible to cover even the main types individually. There are, however, certain areas in which wear is likely to occur and give rise to problems, which can be discussed in general terms.

Early carburettors are usually made of brass, a relatively soft metal that will split or shear if excessive force is applied. Furthermore, the exterior surface will corrode quite badly, due to the combined effects of heat, the atmosphere and petrol, to form a dark, crusty layer that completely masks the true identity of the base metal. From about the mid-thirties onwards, a change was made to the use of zinc-based alloy die-castings, an even more difficult metal to handle. Although much lighter in weight, these castings will shatter without warning if over-stressed, and are then beyond repair. They do not, however, corrode so readily and are more easily cleaned. Up until 1930 or thereabouts, the three most common makes of carburettor were the Amac, Brown and Barlow (often abbreviated to B & B) and Binks. Then all three companies merged to produce the Amal carburettor, the type of carburettor found on most machines of British manufacture.

In carburettors that use a slide alone or a combination of slide and needle as a form of control, the carburettor body itself will begin to wear as mileage increases, although not at such a high rate as the slide, which is a replaceable item. The older the carburettor, the more sensitive it is to this form of wear, since air leaks will occur around the slide which will upset the carburation and may even make it impossible to obtain satisfactory slow speed running. Because wear does not occur in an even pattern there is not any satisfactory method of reclaiming a worn carburettor body. A modern carburettor can be used as a temporary expedient to get the machine running and perhaps on the road, but it is immediately obvious to one and all that a major departure from the original specification has been made. The

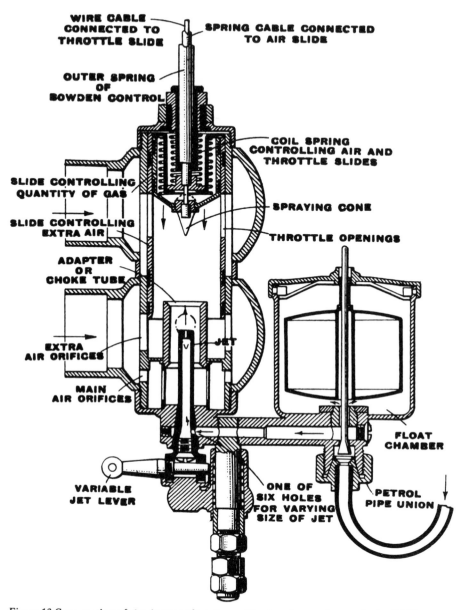

Figure 13 Cross-section of the Amac carburettor, of the type in popular use during 1910

only alternative is to advertise, in the hope that someone will have a carburettor body of the correct type that is less worn, or to visit some of the 'flea markets' or 'autojumbles' where such items are often found. Always take the original as a pattern since superficial differences can often make it difficult to restore the carburettor to its original working order. I once encountered some carburation problems that made a vintage two-stroke virtually unusable and it took weeks of frustrated effort before the cause was eventually traced. Someone had unwittingly fitted the jet block from a late-type Amal carburettor into a body of the earlier type that has the air holes in a different location. Perhaps this is why I obtained the bike cheaply!

The other problem with the carburettor body is likely to be stripped threads at the

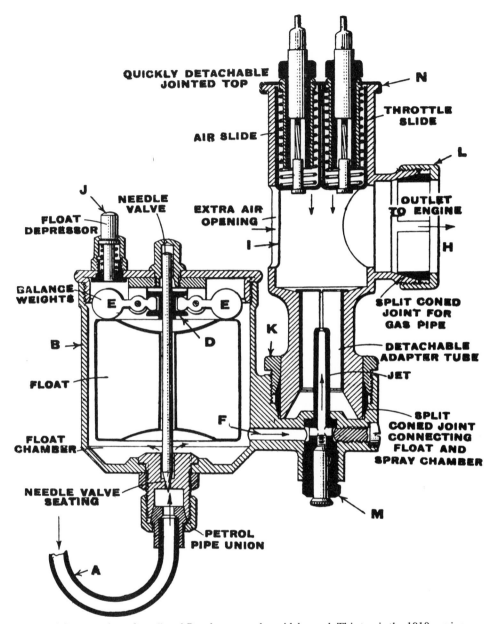

QUICKLY DETACHABLE
JOINTED TOP

N

THROTTLE
SLIDE

AIR SLIDE

L

OUTLET
TO ENGINE

J

NEEDLE
VALVE

EXTRA AIR
OPENING

FLOAT
DEPRESSOR

I

H

BALANCE
WEIGHTS

E

E

SPLIT CONED
JOINT FOR
GAS PIPE

B

D

K

DETACHABLE
ADAPTER TUBE

FLOAT

JET

F

SPLIT
CONED JOINT
CONNECTING
FLOAT AND
SPRAY CHAMBER

FLOAT
CHAMBER

NEEDLE VALVE
SEATING

M

PETROL
PIPE UNION

A

Figure 14 Cross-section of the B and B carburettor, also widely used. This too is the 1910 version

top, where the locking ring threads on to secure the carburettor top. This is another point at which a serious air leak can occur, and if the top works really loose, the slide can stick in the throttle wide open position, with no means of shutting off. Competition riders will know this problem only too well, since it is more likely to occur under conditions of vibration and dust. Because it is not possible to reclaim the stripped or worn thread without becoming involved in a major operation, a satisfactory compromise can be effected by slitting the knurled locking ring and then using a worm drive clip to clamp the two ends together firmly, after the top and locking ring have been positioned correctly. Although not aesthetically pleasing, this modification will effect a permanent repair and enable the machine to be used with safety, until such time as a more acceptable arrangement can be found.

Early carburettors will have suffered from wear and can create very serious problems if satisfactory performance is to be achieved

Stripped threads in other parts of the carburettor body can probably be reclaimed by means of a Helicoil thread insert, which necessitates the use of special equipment. Many dealers operate a Helicoil thread reclamation service for a quite nominal fee. Problems will occur if it is not possible to fit a thread insert that has the same thread form as the original. However, since most of the parts to be fitted take the form of screws or plugs, it is not too difficult to remake them with a matching thread as brass is a very easy metal to machine.

Throttle slides are usually made of brass and tend to wear at a greater rate than the inside of the carburettor body, in which they constantly move upwards and downwards. Wear is usually found in the portion of the slide that abuts against the carburettor outlet to the engine induction pipe or passage. It also occurs to a lesser extent around the portion with the cutaway, in the vicinity of the carburettor intake. This type of wear is often responsible for the audible clicking noise heard when the engine is running at tickover speeds. It is caused by the slide vibrating backwards and forwards within the carburettor body, as it is attracted by the suction of the induction stroke. There is, unfortunately, no easy remedy, apart from renewal of the slide itself, which is rarely possible in the case of an old model. Since it is not often possible to adapt the slide from another type or make of carburettor, due to differences in diameter, the only option is to have one specially made or to locate a spare which is still serviceable.

The jet block fitted inside most carburettor bodies may also be subject to wear in the small areas where the throttle slide makes contact. It may be possible to build up the affected areas with solder, a very delicate task that requires some skill with a soldering iron and the subsequent reshaping. At the best this will provide only a temporary expedient, since solder is a very soft metal with a correspondingly high rate of wear. The long term answer is a jet block that is less worn, preferably with a matching slide, assuming the carburettor is an early type for which new replacement parts are out of the question. If the carburettor is of Amal origin, the problem is likely to prove less acute. Although replacement parts for some of the early pre-Monobloc instruments are becoming increasingly difficult to obtain, it is still possible to acquire new spares from some of the more out of the way dealers, who may still hold small stocks.

If corroded, the jet block should be cleaned as much as is practicable, without removing any of the base metal. Avoid the use of harsh abrasives such as emery cloth. Although it will take longer to achieve the same effect, metal polish is a better substitute, provided it is used sparingly. After cleaning, be sure to give each of the small internal air passageways a blow-through with compressed air, to make sure they are unobstructed. Never use wire or any pointed object to clear them, otherwise there is risk of enlarging them and upsetting the carburation. This advice also applies to removable jets.

If the carburettor is of the needle and jet type, both the needle and the jet in which it slides are likely to have worn. The usual symptoms are high petrol consumption, a tendency for the engine to run with an over-rich mixture (as defined by general sluggishness and black smoke from the exhaust), and difficulty in starting when the engine is warm. The same problem with replacement parts will again occur for it is unlikely that the jet and needle from another make of carburettor can be used as a substitute. Fixed jets, which usually screw into the jet block or some part that extends therefrom, are not likely to suffer so badly. Care should, however, be exercised when removing or tightening them as they will shear very easily if overstressed. Always check for a bent needle before final reassembly, by rolling it on a sheet of glass.

In most carburettors the float chamber takes the form of a separate attachment, containing the float and needle which keeps the petrol at a constant level. Occasionally, a punctured float is encountered. This is an easy repair to effect, since most floats are made of either brass or copper that will solder very easily. Make sure the float is empty before soldering the leak, and use the smallest quantity of solder possible. Solder is a heavy metal and too much will weight the float, causing the petrol level to alter. A dented or crushed float can often be repaired by drilling a small hole and injecting a little water. If the hole is then sealed off and the float heated, the steam given off by the water will often push the float out again to its original shape. Needless to say this is a delicate and somewhat dangerous operation. If the pressure within builds up too high, the float will explode into a series of shrapnel-like fragments. The water will have to be drained off, and the float re-sealed, afterwards.

The float needle is the component most likely to wear, together with its seating, which is often an integral part of the float chamber body. Wear usually takes the form of a ridge around the pointed section of the needle, causing the needle to seat over only a very narrow surface. Engine vibration breaks the seal quite readily, and petrol is admitted to the float chamber without any control. In consequence, petrol constantly drips from the float chamber and the engine has a permanently over-rich mixture. It is possible to regrind the point of the needle and its seating by using very fine grinding compound, but this is recommended only if both the needle and the seating (or the float chamber of which it is part) are obsolete parts. In all other cases, the worn parts should be renewed.

No mention has been made of the air slide assembly, which is rarely subjected to wear, except on a very early machine where the air control has constantly to be varied to match road conditions. Here again, the replacement problem will occur. Some carburettors use 'butterfly' flap valves as a means of controlling the admission of air, which will show most wear at the points where the flap pivots. Drilling out and bushing seems to be the only really satisfactory means of repair, after the parts have been dismantled. This is a very skilled operation, well suited to a model maker or someone experienced in the use of a small lathe.

It cannot be overstressed that an enormous amount of ingenuity has to be used to keep an old carburettor in reasonable working order. This is one of the few ancillary components on the machine that is subject to slow but constant wear which, if allowed to continue, will make the machine difficult to control. Even at its best, a carburettor of this type has to be operated intelligently, making full use of both the throttle and air controls all the time the machine is being ridden. A badly worn carburettor can transform a journey that could normally be a pleasure, into a nightmare.

The controls that operate the carburettor and the cables that act as the link between them have been discussed more fully in Chapter 4. It is essential the complete system is in good working order and is well maintained, otherwise it will prove virtually impossible to obtain any sensitivity of control over the carburettor. If anything, an elderly carburettor should perform much better than it did originally, due to the better quality petrol that is available today.

Another vital part of the machine is the exhaust system, which quite often is missing in its entirety. This will create special problems, especially if the machine has a two-stroke engine or happens to prove particularly sensitive to changes made in the original system. In a

The Amac carburettor, favoured by
many during the late twenties, looks
like the later Amal TT carburettor at
first glance. Compare to the following
illustration. It is of the slide and
needle type, suitable for road use

The track racing Amac carburettor,
forerunner of the famous Amal racing
carburettor used on JAP-engined
speedway bikes. It has no needle and
should be used with alcohol-type fuel

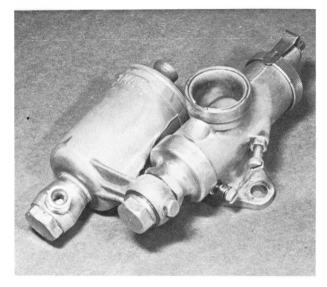

The Amal type 6 carburettor, used
successfully on most 500 singles and
twins during the post-vintage and
early post-war period

Smaller capacity machines used the Amal type 4 carburettor. The type fitted to the post-war Douglas twins has a top feed float chamber

For racing purposes and when alcohol fuel is used, twin float chambers ensure there is an adequate flow of fuel at all times

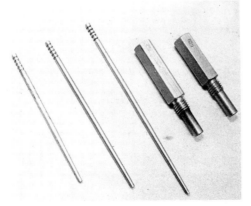

There is a variety of needle and needle jet sizes, each specified for a particular type of carburettor. The type number or size, is stamped on each. Obscure carburation problems will occur if parts are interchanged that do not correspond

The component parts of a bottom feed type 6 float chamber. The float chamber tickler and securing bolt for the top cover are not shown. Note the notch on the float needle, to ensure correct float level

great many cases, the exhaust system is designed to 'blend in' with the engine characteristics, so that the maximum amount of silencing can be obtained with minimum loss in performance. With a two-stroke engine, correctness of design is even more important as the complete exhaust system performs an extractor function, removing all burnt gas from the cylinder. Changes made unwittingly (or somtimes intentionally!) will only reduce this planned efficiency, resulting in overall loss of performance and higher petrol consumption. The classic example of removing the baffles from a two-stroke silencer is a significant example. Although the louder exhaust note gives the illusion of speed, the machine is nearly always very much slower and petrol is consumed at a greater rate. Even a change of silencer will often have much the same effect, if the replacement differs in design from the original. And it can affect a four stoke as well as a two-stroke. The Velocette singles provide an outstanding example, where even a change to a 'pattern' silencer will bring about a marked fall-off in performance. This can usually be traced to differences in the design of the silencer baffles. The original takes the form of louvres cut in the side of the baffle tube, which deflect the exhaust gases outwards at an angle. In the pattern type of silencer, several rows of holes serve the same function, in theory only. There is no longer any attempt to direct the exhaust gases outwards and the pattern of the gas flow is changed as a result. This is sufficient to alter the flow characteristics and affect engine scavenging. Even the exhaust note differs to the practiced ear.

Where the exhaust system is missing altogether, the first stage is to obtain a photograph or a drawing of the original set-up so that a replica can be constructed. The latter is a task for the expert, since tube bending is a highly skilled art. Fortunately, there are still one or two specialists in this field who are willing to undertake this type of work for motorcycles. It is, however, imperative to take and leave the machine whilst the system is being constructed, so that it is a perfect fit. A minute error in the angle of any of the bends will render the system useless, if it is made separately, to be fitted at a later stage to an unseen machine.

As may be imagined from earlier comment, it is the design of the silencer that will create the greatest problems, assuming it is no longer possible to obtain one of the originals. With a two-stroke engine, a certain amount of experimentation may prove necessary, using a silencer from another make of two-stroke. With no knowledge of the machine's original characteristics and no guide to the construction of the original exhaust system, other than by means of a photograph or illustration, there is, unfortunately, a high degree of hit and miss. There are not many enthusiasts with a similar model who will be prepared to remove and lend the exhaust system from their own machine, for a pattern to be made.

If the original system is available, the problem is much less acute, even if it is in an advanced stage of deterioration. Do not on any account discard any of the parts, since they will prove invaluable to the pattern maker. Corrosion will occur from both the exterior and the interior, often leaving parts that are wafer thin. A two-stroke exhaust system is likely to deteriorate much less rapidly than a four-stroke system, due to the oily nature of the exhaust gases. In most cases, the covering of oil will prove sufficient to deter interior corrosion unless water has entered and caused the oil to emulsify. Avoid using copper pipes, even if they do have a nice appearance initially and are much easier to bend. Copper tarnishes very rapidly and work hardens with use, so that eventually the pipe may become quite brittle and shear off. Polished copper looks out of place in any case; most exhaust systems were plated in either nickel or chrome.

One of the most frequent problems to be encountered is the fit of the exhaust pipe in the cylinder head or barrel. If the pipe is a loose fit, air leaks will occur, causing the engine to backfire on the over-run. If the pipe is a push fit into a recess, the end can be belled-out slightly by driving a tapered wooden plug into the end. This should 'stretch' the pipe the required amount. If a flange fitting is employed, with a union nut of some kind, a broken flange will have to be brazed or welded back into position and cleaned up, or a new flange formed by making a series of small saw cuts and bending the end of the pipe over the required amount. In this latter example, a thin copper sealing ring may prove necessary to

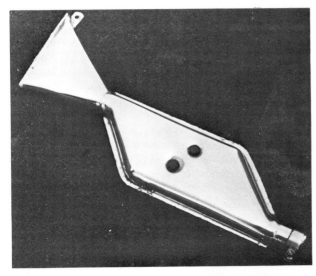

A Brooklands can is probably the most suitable wear for a racing machine of the thirties that originally had a straight through exhaust pipe. This is a pattern type — original Brooklands cans are very rare and correspondingly expensive. It will reduce performance, but will make the machine roadworthy

Two-strokes (and some four-strokes) are most susceptible to changes in silencer specification. The post-war Scotts favoured a Burgess straight-through silencer, unfortunately no longer obtainable. A glassfibre lining is used to absorb noise, without creating unwanted back pressure

obviate the risk of air leaks. Often, the flange is perfect, but the union nut thread either around or inside the exhaust port has stripped. Fortunately, there are still one or two specialists in this type of repair who will make and fit a form of insert (internal) or restore the original thread (external), a task that requires special equipment and a good knowledge of the problems involved. As a last resort, it is possible to bore out the port opening and fit a stub, which can be locked into position. This may necessitate a different end to the exhaust pipe, a problem that can be surmounted without too much difficulty.

The exhaust system must be suspended rigidly, without strain, along its entire run. The junction between the exhaust pipe and the silencer (or expansion chamber or box if the machine is of an early type) must be a good fit, since this is another point at which an air leak can occur. Clamps should pull up tightly before their ends meet and without bending the clamping screw or bolt. Union nuts are often of the finned variety and require a special 'C' spanner to tighten them fully, without risk of breaking off one of the small fins. Do not succumb to the temptation of fitting one of the finned clamps at the point where the exhaust pipe enters the cylinder head. Although they may enhance the appearance of the machine, they look out of place on an early model and should not be fitted unless they formed part of the original specification.

The temptation to redesign the exhaust system should be resisted, even if the characteristics are left substantially unchanged. I once owned a Coventry Eagle Flying Eight that had separate exhaust pipes and silencers fitted, one on each side of the machine. Although they gave the machine a more balanced look and seemed to have no effect on either the performance or the carburation, the machine looked out of place when lined up with other machines from a similar era. It was a major departure from the original specification and in a concours event would have been sufficient to exclude the machine from any possibility of appearing on the awards list.

Mention has been made earlier of the use of 'pattern' parts and the effect they may have on an engine that is particularly sensitive to changes in the exhaust system. It can be argued that a system made up from pattern parts is better than no system at all, especially if the pattern parts are reasonably good facsimilies of the originals. A certain degree of compromise will have to be accepted when any machine is restored, particularly if it is necessary to keep to a tight budget. In some instances, a pattern part may provide the only practicable solution - for example, the Brooklands can on a machine that has associations with this historic venue or on a machine that has a decidedly sporting nature. If a racing machine is to be rebuilt for use on the road, a silencer may never have formed part of the original specification, in which case the choice of silencer to be fitted is at the discretion of the rebuilder. The Brooklands can is probably the best choice under these circumstances - with the proviso that it should be used only on machines manufactured *after* the date when it became a compulsory fitting for all users of the Brooklands race track. Older machines should follow the practice of the day and use a bolt on, detachable fishtail.

Chapter Twelve

Handlebars and handlebar controls

Handlebars are one of the items on any motorcycle most subject to change from the original specification, since the rider will fit a pair that give him the riding position he desires most, if the originals prove unsuitable. Over the years, all manner of designs have been available, the manufacturer himself often providing a choice. They range from the 'sit up and beg' type to the TT or 'dropped' type. Handlebars come in two sizes - 1 inch diameter as used by most manufacturers in the early days, and 7/8 inch diameter, which is still the size most commonly found on machines of British origin. Only one manufacturer proved to be the exception - Triumph - who used a size in between these two limits. Early handlebars are usually constructed like those fitted to a bicycle, having an integral centre stem that passes through the steering head assembly and is held firmly by means of an internal, expanding sleeve. They are usually nickel plated or covered with a black celluloid composition rather like the steering wheel in a car. Often the handlebars are drilled either side, so that the various control cables can be led through the centre, to give a 'clean' effect. From the late twenties onwards, many manufacturers reverted to a handlebar bend that was clamp arrangement although there are instances where the main pivot takes the form of a lug, In this instance, a chromium plated finish is more likely to be employed. On some of the cheaper or smaller capacity models, the main control lever pivots may be welded on, so that their position cannot be changed. As always there are exceptions. Some manufacturers, such as Veloce Limited, preferred a black enamel finish and there are a few others that followed suit. The celluloid covering had become much rarer at this time. Some of the very late machines have what is known as 'clip-ons' - two short and usually straight sections of handlebar that terminate in a welded-on clamp so that they can be bolted around the exposed stanchions of telescopic forks. These will generally be found only on machines of a 'clubman's' or racing type, where they give a riding position best suited to road racing events.

A crash will often cause the handlebars to bend and great care has to be taken when straightening them, so that they do not 'neck' and fracture at the place where the bend commences. It is best to apply local heat to the area of the bend whilst straightening, to help offset the risk of fracture or fatigue failure. Clip-on handlebars can give trouble if the welding on the clamp is poor, especially if it has been weakened by rusting.

The preparation of handlebars for either plating or enamelling should follow the procedure described earlier in this Book for the frame and forks, and all old plating removed. If, however, the celluloid covering is damaged and has to be replaced, it should be stripped off completely and the metal underneath cleaned up in similar manner. Although it is no longer fashionable to apply a celluloid coating, the same effect can be achieved by

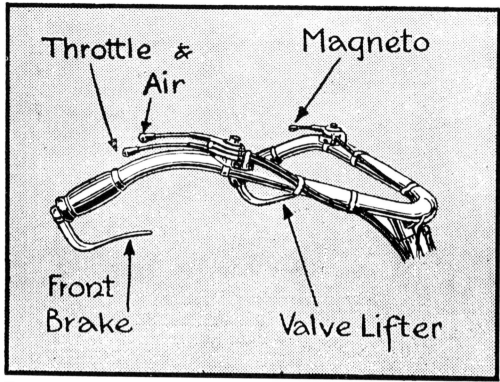

Figure 15 The layout of the handlebar controls tended to form a set pattern. This is a typical example, found on a veteran Triumph

Figure 16 The control system fitted to a Rudge. Note the tank mounted ignition advance lever

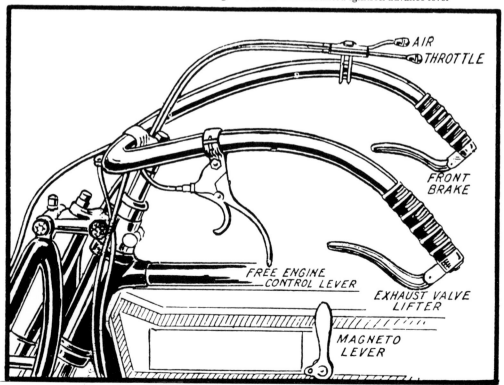

The handlebars fitted to this KTT Velocette are not far removed from the once popular touring style

Douglas preferred to fit the flat type of handlebar, with only a very slight bend at each end

These Scott handlebars are of a type that was once very popular. They give a comfortable riding position and permit the controls to be located where they are in their most natural position

137

means of another plastic, usually pvc. A firm specialising in dip coating plastics can often help in this respect, as the technique is widely used today for the protective covering of many domestic articles such as vegetable racks, the legs of kitchen stools and a variety of decorative wirework.

Handlebar controls can be sub-divided into four main categories, levers of the type used to operate the clutch or front brake, push-pull controls with a limited range of movement such as those used for ignition advance and air control, a rotating drum used on later models for the throttle and occasionally, ignition advance, and electrical controls, usually of the switch or push button type. Most are attached to the handlebars by means of a split clamp arrangement although there are instances where the main pivot takes the form of a lug permanently welded to the handlebars or, in the case of the so-called inverted lever, an insertion into the open ends of the handlebars.

After the initial clean up, lever controls should be examined for wear, which is most likely to occur at the pivot and in the pivot bolt itself. The lever pivot can be filled up with brazing metal and redrilled to the correct size, or drilled oversize and bushed. At the same time, a check should be made to ensure the lever blade is straight. Levers of the more recent type are still comparatively easy to renew, but earlier controls will have to be bent straight, a task which often necessitates very careful manipulation if they are made of brass. The clamps should give little trouble, provided they are of the correct size. It is amazing how often 1 inch clamps are fitted to controls mounted on 7/8 inch handlebars, necessitating the use of a packing piece and little chance of securing the control with any rigidity. On a brake or clutch lever, the extended portion of the pivot must run parallel to, and up against, the handlebars, or the whole lever assembly will flex badly when the lever is squeezed with any force. This will give the control a spongy feel, which will mask some of the positive action. When renewing 'modern' levers, avoid the use of the ball-ended type, which will immediately look out of place. Although they are a necessity on a machine that is used for competitive events, other than rallies, it is still possible to purchase the older straight blade type, which was a standard fitting on most pre- and post-war machines.

Controls of the push-pull type, such as those used for manual operation of the ignition advance, should be dismantled by unscrewing the screw or bolt in the centre. This will release the top of the control, the push-pull lever and the circular diaphragm spring that provides the frictional loading. Modern controls are characterised by the stubbiness of the operating arm; generally speaking, the longer the arm, the older the control. In the early days, twin controls were quite common. These are constructed on the same principle, except that the lower operating arm has its own adjusting nut in the centre, so that it can be tightened or loosened independently of the upper arm. The lower arm, which is usually the longest, is the throttle control, in lieu of the twist grip that has since replaced it. The upper arm is used for the carburettor air control. One manufacturer (Ariel) used for a period, a twin lever set-up to operate the ignition advance and the valve lifter, a somewhat unusual combination. Invariably, the controls operate in an inwards direction, so that they are pulled towards the rider. There are exceptions, however, such as the round tank BSA of the mid-twenties, where the controls work in the opposite direction. Some controls are held to the handlebars by the customary split clamp arrangement, others by means of two hinged clamps that are tightened by a single screw through their extremities.

From the late twenties onwards the twist grip came into vogue, even though some very early machines, such as the Indian, had used it much earlier. There are three main types of twist grip, the internal type in which the control cable is contained within the handlebars, the standard rotating drum type and the competition type, which provides quick action. The internal type takes the form of a sleeve that fits over the handlebars with a helix cut into its internal surface. A specially-shaped brass slide that engages with the nipple on the end of the throttle cable is arranged to move within a slot cut in the handlebars. A raised portion of the brass slide engages with the helix in the twist grip sleeve so that as the sleeve is rotated, the slide moves along the handlebar slot and opens the throttle. This type of twist grip is

Do not discard old control cables, even if they are no longer usable. They can be used to ensure the replacement cable is of the correct length, or as a means of making up a new cable to pattern. Sometimes, the nipples and ferrules can be reused

The controls fitted to this old P&M are unusual in so far as they bolt through the handlebars and do not clamp around them

Some levers clamp around the handlebars and have a ball end

Others have a flat end and bolt to the front brake lever

A special long bolt is needed for the combined lever clamping arrangement

Generally speaking, the older the lever, the longer its length

The dismantled lever assembly. The dished spring provides the tension to prevent the lever from closing of its own accord, after the centre bolt is tightened the desired amount

For maximum efficiency, the lever pivot must press against the handlebar

The small gap shown here will give the control a 'spongy' feel, as the pivot can flex when the control is operated

This control was designed for an inch diameter handlebar. Note the packing piece necessary, when fitted to handlebars of 7/8 inch diameter

Some controls have a built-in adjuster for the cable. They are of recent origin and should not be used on old machines

Early clutch operating levers are of quite distinctive shape and sometimes referred to as an 'open' lever

This early throttle and air control has a barrel-shaped housing, against which the cables abut

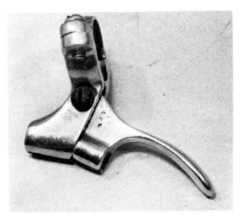

Not often seen today — the tiny 'trigger' lever usually fitted to operate a valve lifter or decompressor

normally fitted to machines of the touring type, since the throttle opening action is somewhat slow. Furthermore, it is often quite difficult to remove any backlash from the throttle cable itself. A rotating drum to which the end of the throttle cable is anchored forms the working principle of the more common type of twist grip. This provides a quicker action and makes throttle cable adjustment easier. The only disadvantage is that there is no longer a straight pull on the cable, as it is bent around the drum. The competition 'quick action' twist grip is a variant of this approach, using a larger diameter drum to provide a quicker throttle opening action.

All twist grips (with the exception of the competition types, which must be self-closing) are fitted with a friction damper, in the form of a metal shoe which can be made to press on to the surface of the drum by means of an external adjuster screw and locknut. It is thus possible to prevent the twist grip from closing of its own accord, if so desired, when the hand is lifted off, as may occur when giving road signals. At one time, Triumph used a variation of this arrangement by cutting ratchet teeth on the edge of the drum and having a small spring-loaded 'wedge' in contact with these teeth so that the grip would not return of its own accord. Instances of throttle sticking caused this method to be abandoned and it is recommended that if your machine has one of these twist grips, it should be replaced by one of the more conventional type, in the interests of safety.

It follows that a twist grip will operate freely only if it is well greased and there are not flats or imperfections in the end of the handlebars that will cause it to bind. A heavy twist grip will give the illusion of poor performance and can make the wrist ache on a long run. Note that a twist grip control is sometimes provided for the ignition advance or headlamp dip, on the left-hand end of the handlebars.

Handlebar-mounted electrical controls are usually of the switch or push button type, depending on whether they are used to provide a dip facility for the headlamp, or to operate the horn or ignition cut-out. It is seldom practicable to make an effective repair to a broken dipswitch and for this reason, a new replacement should always be obtained. Cut-out or horn buttons should not give rise to any problems, provided they are not rusty at the point where the clamp makes contact with the handlebars. This is usually the earth return of the system. Care should also be taken to ensure the bared wire does not contact the metal surround or the handlebars, at the point where it enters the inner insulator. Whilst this will be obvious in the case of the horn, when the battery is re-connected, it will not be so in the case of the ignition cut-out. If there is a permanent short to earth, the magneto will be immobilised very effectively.

This very useful Miller control combines the horn button with the dip switch

Pre-war handlebar grips tended to be longer than their modern counterparts

The type of control cable most commonly used is Bowden or standard wire in which the cable is made up from a number of strands of flexible steel wire, twisted together. This inner cable, which performs the actual control function, is contained within an outer sheath of square section steel wire, rolled into a continuous coil so that it is flexible and can be taken around curves. It has an outer covering of black cotton-based Empire Cloth, to give the required weather protection and improved appearance. Small metal ferrules at each end form the seating for the outer sheath in the various cable stops and adjusters; brass nipples of the desired shape are soft soldered to the ends of the inner cable, to connect with the actual controls.

Old cables can rarely be reclaimed, especially if the outer covering is cracked and frayed. It is necessary to make up new cables from a length of inner wire and outer sheathing cut to size - many accessory stockists and motorcycle dealers can still supply cable in this form. Use the old cable to give the correct lengths of the inner cable and outer sheathing so that the initial make-up results in a cable that will fit and operate correctly. It is usually possible to salvage the original nipples, ferrules and any adjusters, although even these are still not too difficult to obtain today. There is an art in soldering and some experience is needed before the best results can be obtained. The main essentials are to have the soldering iron at the correct temperature and the wire clean and free from grease, so that it can be tinned as a preliminary, at both ends. There is also less risk of the wire unstranding if it is tinned at the point where it is to be cut. Heat both the wire and the brass nipple with the soldering iron, then insert the wire into the nipple so that it protrudes about 1/16th in/1.59 mm above the surface of the nipple. Flood the nipple with solder, allow it to cool, then clamp the wire in a vice so that the nipple rests on top of the vice jaws. Now clench the end of the wire over, so that it cannot pull back through the nipple. Re-heat the nipple until the solder flows, pull the cable back through the nipple until the clenched over part seats firmly, and refill with solder. When the solder has solidified and the nipple has cooled down, clean up with a file to remove any excess solder, so that the nipple will fit back into its control, without difficulty. Oil or grease the cable, except at the outer extremity, insert it through the outer sheathing which has been cut to the right length and fitted with ferrules, add any adjusters or spacers that may be necessary, then solder the nipple on the other end, using the same technique. The new cable is now complete.

Figure 17 How to make up control cables

a

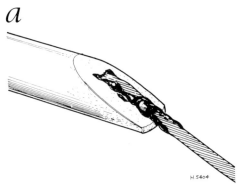

a) Tin the cable, using plenty of flux, until the solder runs freely through the cable strands. Do not allow the cable strands to fan out

b

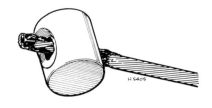

b) Position the nipple so that the solder holds it in place with about 1/8 inch of cable protruding. Allow to cool, without the position moving

c

c) Peen over the cable strands, using a light, ball-ended hammer. The cable should be held in a vice fitted with soft clamps and the cable ends peened over sufficiently to stop the cable pulling through

d

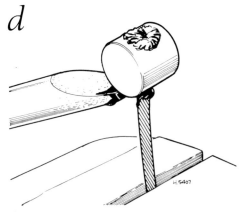

d) Heat the cable nipple until the solder melts and raise it upwards so that the cable end seats in the recess provided. Maintain the upward pull until the solder has cooled and set

e

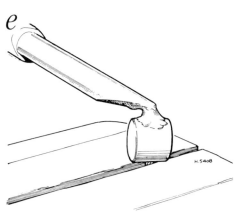

e) Fill the recess with solder, holding the nipple in the vice clamps so that it cannot slide down the cable as the solder melts. Maintain a pull on the cable, if possible, throughout this operation

f

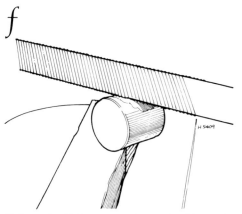

f) Smooth off the excess solder with a file, so that the original profile of the nipple is restored and it will move freely in the control into which it is inserted

143

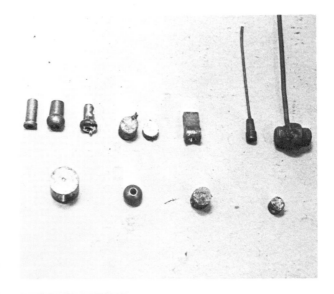

Just a few examples of the many
different types of cable nipple
available. Make sure the correct type
is used

Never use a solderless nipple, except in
a roadside emergency. The ferrule on
the right is sometimes used in a
carburettor top, in lieu of an adjuster,
mainly on ex-WD models

Much of the outer sheathing sold today has a black plastic covering in place of the
Empire Cloth used in the past, which was prone to crack and split in service. Whilst the
plastic-covered sheathing is more desirable on a number of counts, it will detract from the
presentation of the machine during a concours contest and result in loss of marks. It is the
smaller attentions to detail that often have the most effect on the outcome of a concours
contest.

Cables should always be arranged so that they have even sweeps and no tight bends,
otherwise control action will become unnecessarily heavy. They should be lightly clipped to
the frame or other near-by components with black rubber clips of the type sold by most
bicycle shops. Don't forget that control cables need regular lubrication, as mentioned again
in greater detail, later in this book.

Whilst dealing with the handlebars and controls, mention should be made of handlebar
grips, another small but nonetheless important item than can give rise to loss of marks during
a concours contest. Today, plastic grips are in common use, which are completely out of

context with an old machine. A hunt can quite often produce a pair of their rubber counterparts which will look much better, even if you cannot trace a pair embossed with the manufacturer's name. Unfortunately the old 'long' rubbers are no longer available, or the somewhat bulbous Shockstop rubbers that were at one time very popular. The owner of a very old machine will have even greater problems, unless he is able to use a pair of celluloid bicycle handlebar grips as a substitute, which are also becoming very rare. The ever increasing use of synthetic materials is one of the greatest headaches of anyone hoping to restore to original specification.

Don't forget that parts to be plated must be polished to a very fine finish if high quality plating is to result; as mentioned earlier, the quality of the finished plating can only be as good as the surface preparation, As far as rough parts are concerned, they should be smoothed down initially with a fine file and then all surface marks removed with 120 emery cloth. Finish off with 240, 360 and 500 wet and dry paper in this order, applied dry. If sufficient care is taken with the preparation, the results will be very rewarding.

Not just another photograph of a Velocette - this machine illustrates well the result of one person's desire to build a thoroughbred special. This is supposed to be a Velocette 500 Scrambler, a competition machine, of about 1959; obviously it has been made safe for the road, and is taxed. Although it uses about 90% Velocette parts it is really a 1953 MAC fitted with a Thruxtonised Venom engine and many genuine Scrambler parts. Builder Tim Parker intended it to be fun, which it is, rather than exhibitable

Restored before its time? Although this is a 1967 Velocette Venom the owner John Parker has made sure that it will never need to be restored, as such, by keeping it well fettled and regularly ridden. Once in a good condition no old motorcycle should just be left in the expectation that it will always remain so. Constant attention continues to be necessary

Chapter Thirteen

Lighting sets and electrical equipment

Although electrical lighting equipment has been fitted to motorcycles for so long that it is difficult to remember any alternatives, it was not until the early nineteen thirties that it became anything like universally adopted. Until then, acetylene lighting had reigned supreme, mainly on account of the extreme simplicity of a gas lighting system which was self-generating and had no dependence whatsoever on the mechanical functions of the machine to which it was fitted. Yet electrical lighting was not completely unknown, even in the days prior to the 1914-18 war. Never in widespread use, complete lighting systems existed that drew their current from rechargeable batteries, which had to be removed from the machine at regular intervals and be recharged in order to keep pace with the electrical demand. A few manufacturers, with commendable foresight, incorporated a dynamo in their electrical system, to keep the battery charged whilst the engine was running; the American Indian and the Swiss Motosacoche were two such makes. But in the main, these early systems were somewhat primitive and of flimsy construction compared to those that were to be much more widely accepted a couple of decades or so later. Until then, acetylene lighting had the edge in terms of simplicity, lower cost and, to a point, overall reliability. In consequence, if a newly discovered pre-1927 model is found to have lighting equipment fitted, it will almost certainly be of the acetylene type.

Acetylene lighting depends upon the generation of highly inflammable acetylene gas within a generator, which may or may not form an integral part of the headlamp, by dropping water on to granules of calcium carbide. The top half of the cylindrical generator takes the form of a water container, with a screw-type needle valve that will admit water into the lower half, at a controlled rate. The lower half of the generator contains the calcium carbide granules and there is provision for piping off the gas to the burner jets in both the headlamp and rear lamp. To an extent, the height and intenseness of the flame can be controlled by the rate at which water drops on to the carbide granules. In the case of the headlamp, a mirror placed behind the burner helps to concentrate the ensuing beam of light in much the same way as the reflector in an electrical headlamp. The action of the water converts the carbide granules to slaked lime, a quite harmless product that is easily emptied out when the generator has to be recharged. The lights are extinguished by pinching the tubing or blowing out the flame. Although turning off the water will have the same long-term effect, it is not advisable to resort to this technique, unless the machine is stopped for a while.

Over a period of time, generators suffer from the effects of corrosion. They are made of brass, usually black enamelled and sometimes nickel plated, to give them a more pleasing and lasting appearance. Provided the effects of corrosion are not too bad, repairs can be

Most acetylene generators are black enamelled. The screw cap is the water filler, the needle valve for controlling water flow, in the centre, operates on the notched ring

The lower portion of the generator, which contains the calcium carbide, detaches with a simple twisting motion. It can be emptied and refilled by the roadside, without need to detach the generator

Figure 18 Cross-section of a typical acetylene headlamp and separate generator. The gas is generated by dripping water at a controlled rate on to the dry calcium carbide in the bottom of the generator

A Burner   B Lens Mirror   C Front Lens   D Rubber piping
E Water Compartment of Generator   F Carbide Container of Generator
G Needle Valve Adjuster   H Water Filler Cap   I Gas Outlet Pipe

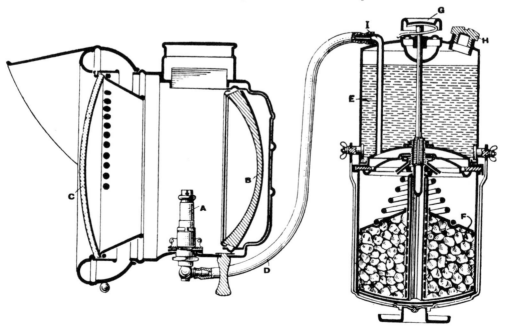

effected by skillful use of a soldering iron and fine emery cloth, before the whole assembly is replated. Splits and cracks may also occur as a result of the brass work hardening. Here again, the soldering iron can be used to good effect — solder takes to brass very readily, provided the surface is clean and bright. Unfortunately, it is not too easy to obtain a replacement for a badly corroded or damaged original. Acetylene lights and generators have tended to become collector's pieces and can often be seen in antique shops, where a high price is asked. Surprisingly, calcium carbide is not as difficult to obtain as one may imagine. It is still used for the high intensity lights employed by railway workers, who need to make track and other repairs during the night, and in the helmet lamps often used by potholers and other cave explorers. For obvious reasons it has to be stored in very clean, dry conditions, out of contact with the air. A tin with a tight fitting lid, like the original in which the carbide is supplied, seems to be the best proposition. If the carbide gets damp, acetylene gas will be generated, which can present a fire or an explosion hazard, in a confined place.

The headlamp will most probably be clamped to the handlebars of the machine and held on long, slender arms. The clamps must be tight to prevent the lamp tilting with its own weight or working loose with vibration; they should have a pair of split clamps within, shaped to fit the handlebar curvature, so that an even grip is obtained. The headlamp will also most probably be made of brass, in which case repairs can be effected in much the same manner as those used for repairs to the generator. Difficulty may be experienced in replacing the mirror, which more often than not is broken. Replacement of the headlamp glass is easier, because a clock or watch repairer will usually have a domed clock glass of identical size. It may be possible to have one of these silvered and used as a mirror, provided the radius of curvature is not too great.

Often, the question arises as to whether the age of the lighting set is equivalent to that of the machine to which it is fitted, or whether it is a much later fitting. This is a question that is very difficult to answer. Perhaps the best guide is to check with a lampmaker's catalogue, or with the periodicals of the period.

The rear lamp is usually cylindrical in shape and arranged to bolt direct to the rear number plate, which it must illuminate, by law. The rear lamp is the one likely to give most trouble as it is the lamp furthest from the generator, and will often go out if the machine hits a severe bump in the road. Because it is not too easy to check whether the lamp is still lit whilst the machine is in motion, 'old timers' concocted an ingenious method that ensured the burner would re-light promptly if it happened to go out momentarily. A needle or a strand of Bowden wire was arranged so that it projected into the burner flame and the tip became red hot. If the flame suddenly went out, the glow from the needle tip was sufficient to re-light the gas. It worked too, provided there was not too long an interval and the needle cooled down.

Most lighting problems with acetylene gas stem from water in the rubber tubing that connects the lamps with the generator, or through blocked burner jets. In the case of the former, the tubing should be detached at regular intervals and blown out with a blast of compressed air. A blocked burner is easy to clean, using a thin strand of wire. Often, a cleaner of this nature is clipped inside the main headlamp shell. To avoid blocked burners, keep the system clean, especially with regard to the contents of the generator, and do not run with a flame that is too low. Do not forget, incidentally, that the water in the generator will freeze in cold weather and may even cause the generator shell to burst. The addition of a small quantity of methylated spirits or anti-freeze will prevent this from happening. Many amusing stories have been told about ways of topping up the generator when the water supply has exhausted itself! If a sidecar is fitted, there will be a sidecar lamp to look after too. This can be regarded as similar to the tail lamp in construction and mode of operation. A check valve is often incorporated in the system, so that most gas can be directed to the headlamp. It has to be set on a trial and error basis.

Red rubber tubing may prove very difficult to obtain these days, but do not resort to plastic tubing, no matter how well disguised. Avoid using black rubber tubing of the type that was at one time fitted to cars using suction operated windscreen wipers. This type of tubing has longitudinal ribs along the outside surface and seems to split very readily along these ribs, rendering the lighting system useless in a very short time. It is usually too small to readily accept the union connections.

Not all acetylene lighting systems rely upon a water and carbide generator. As the design of lighting systems progressed it was possible to obtain what was known as dissolved acetylene (DA), in effect, acetylene gas compressed into a small cylinder and dissolved into a porous substance. The supply of gas was thus regulated by the simple expedient of turning on or off the main tap. Another innovation that gave a much brighter headlight without the need to use a greater supply of gas was the Fallolight pastille — in effect, a mantle around the burner flame which glowed with a much more intense light. This was the gas light at its best, for it utilised a DA cylinder too.

The question arises about the legality of driving with acetylene lighting during the hours of darkness. Like so many other legal points, it seems almost impossible to obtain a hard and fast decision. Certainly late type tail lamps are legal, but earlier ones — mainly veteran cylindrical ones, are illegal because their red lens is too small. However, no one has been prosecuted (to the best of my knowledge) for using a lighting system of this type, and it may be assumed that provided the equipment is fitted to a period machine, no problems are likely to arise. From the rider's point of view, however, it is questionable whether acetylene lighting will provide sufficiently good illumination in the dark, especially if a long distance has to be covered, and/or it is raining. Today's high intensity quartz halogen lights can have a very strong dazzle effect under certain conditions and an acetylene light, no matter how good, will not prove a suitable match. In terms of personal safety alone, it would be best to keep off unknown roads during the hours of darkness if acetylene lighting equipment has to be retained in order to maintain the originality of the machine.

It is possible to convert an acetylene lighting system to electrical operation by skillfully replacing the burners with electric bulbs and leading the wires through the original rubber tubing. The battery can be carried in some inconspicuous position, such as the toolbox. Although this makes a very effective and practicable compromise, it will none the less offend the purists and give rise to marks against the machine in a concours judging competition. The practical considerations and the fact that you may have just arrived from Auchtermuchty will count for little in the judge's final analysis.

The battery lighting systems, briefly mentioned earlier, are simple in the extreme and once they are wired correctly, there is very little to go wrong provided the battery is kept charged. In the early days, when systems such as these were available, the main problem was the poor construction of the battery itself, which promptly fell to pieces as a result of vibration. It was not appreciated that a special, more robust, type of battery was a necessity for this type of use. Furthermore, there was a definite limit to the life of the battery and the number of times it could be recharged. Fortunately, battery technology has advanced a pace or two since then, to the extent that most of today's rechargeable batteries would give an old system a new lease of life. The battery is usually mounted in a form of carrier attached to a convenient frame tube, often the one immediately below the saddle, but it may also be carried in a metal box, attached by brackets to the rear of the headlamp. A few designs of battery lighting system used dry batteries, but in practice these had even more limitations. The most obvious one was the fact that they were not rechargeable, necessitating the use of new replacements, provided the shops were still open! The light they gave was generally poor, too; the light would dim quite rapidly as the voltage dropped. And, if the exhausted batteries were left in situ, they would corrode very badly and sometimes destroy the carrier or container in which they were mounted, if it were made of ferrous metal.

Early dynamos (and magnetos, in which the LT circuit is utilised for battery charging purposes), generally had a somewhat low output so that they had great difficulty in keeping pace with electrical demand. So it was still necessary to remove and recharge the battery if the lights were used to any extent, albeit not quite so frequently. At the other end of the scale, if the lights were not used at all, some charging systems would overcharge the battery, causing the electrolyte to overheat, expand and overflow, with consequent severe

A typical acetylene headlamp. The front hinges, so that it can be opened with ease to light the burner within

Some early acetylene headlamps have a cowl over the front, rather like an eyeshade

The rear lamp also has a hinged front to permit ready access to the burner. It is the lamp most likely to give trouble, as the result of road shocks which tend to extinguish the flame

A long run of tubing will be necessary to reach the sidecar lamp. Attach it firmly, so that it cannot scuff or abrade

Even on a vintage machine, a reflector is now a legal requirement

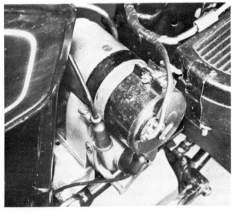

The Lucas 'Magdyno' took the form of a magneto and dynamo combined, with a single drive. The design was arranged so that the dynamo could be detached, leaving the magneto to perform its usual ignition function

151

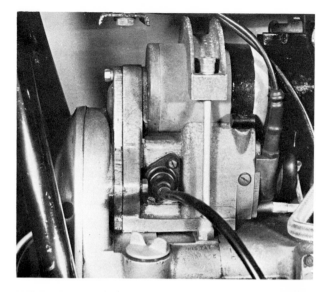

This side view of a Lucas 'Magdyno' shows how the dynamo can be detached, after removing the end nut and slackening the clamp around the dynamo body

Lucas dynamos are available in two lengths and are usually interchangeable. The longer dynamo is the E3L 60 watt version, which superseded the earlier E3HM and similar 45 watt types

Some machines, such as this post war model S8 Sunbeam, utilise a Lucas 'pancake' dynamo, which fits over the end of the crankshaft

corrosion problems. These defects applied mainly to the equipment made before the first war or during the early twenties. From about 1930 onwards, electrical equipment as a whole became much more reliable and was capable of providing a much higher output. Even so, some manufacturers were prone to overstate their virtues. Veloce Limited claimed their GTP two-stroke had an emergency start system, so that if the battery was fully discharged, the machine could still be started by placing it in gear and running alongside until the output from the dynamo was sufficient to provide a spark in the coil ignition circuit. They conveniently forgot to mention that you needed to be something of an athlete and run up to a speed of 20mph before anything happened! They were not alone either, as reference to other instruction manuals will show. The strangest of all the generators was the Maglita, originally made by ML and later taken over by Lucas. It was virtually a combined magneto and dynamo, using a single rotating armature. This arrangement gave a somewhat low output and in consequence it was necessary to run the generator at normal engine speed. This in turn brought its wake of problems, the most serious being the generation of a second, unwanted spark during the engine's operating cycle. Worse still, the spark would occur when the Maglita was turned either way, quite unlike the conventional magneto. If a somewhat careless starting technique was used, there would be more than a fair chance that a Maglita-equipped machine would catch fire. If the ignition was a shade over-advanced, the engine would kick back and this would initiate a second spark, enough to ignite the mixture that now blew back through the carburettor. And if the carburettor happened to be quite liberally flooded ... ! Another curious feature of the Maglita was the centrifugal cut-out, to prevent the battery discharging through the armature when the instrument was stationary. Often this would jam in position, hence the wise rider usually took the precaution of temporarily disconnecting one of the battery leads if he left the machine unattended for any period of time. Other generators had their own peculiarities and shortcomings.

Two-strokes, particularly those of Villiers origin, relied on a flywheel magneto to supply the ignition requirements, and it was found that the addition of a couple of extra coils to the fixed stator plate would provide ac current that could be utilised for the lighting system. Because ac current was used, there was no means of charging a battery unless a rectifier was added to convert the current to dc, an addition that was made only at a later date to all but the cheaper models.

Unless this addition had been made, the lighting system worked on the direct principle, which meant that lights were available only whilst the engine was running. The effect was rather like that of a bicycle equipped with a dynamo that pressed on the side wall of the rear tyre. All the time the wheel was turning at a reasonable pace, the lights were reasonably good. But at low rpm, the rider was in danger of running over the headlamp beam! For parking requirements, a small dry battery was clipped to the inside of the headlamp shell.

As the machine aged and had been dismantled several times, there was an increasing tendency for the flywheel magneto to slip on its taper, especially if it had not been tightened fully in the first instance. In consequence, the ignition timing slipped badly, the engine stopped and the lights went out. Villiers introduced their special Hammertight spanner to obviate risk of this happening — a spanner with a cut-out that fitted the nut in the flywheel centre and the end shaped like a small anvil to withstand hammer blows. Many riders carried one in their pockets. Often when refurbishing an old machine the flywheel slipping problem becomes prevalent, no matter how tightly the centre nut is drawn up. In cases such as these, it is worth while investigating the state of the tapers, both external and internal. Usually, a series of ridges will be found, which means that the flywheel is seating over a very small area only. Provided the damage is not too great, the ridges can be ground away to give a smooth surface once more, by the careful use of grinding paste. Great care is needed, however, because excessive grinding will move the flywheel boss further along the engine mainshaft and cause it to jam against either the crankcase or the end of the main bearing. The Wico Pacy generator, a familiar fitting on many BSA Bantams, is another variant on a similar theme.

When electric lighting became more reliable and enjoyed more widespread use, manufacturers of electrical equipment recognised the need for a more compact generator and the thought occurred that it could be combined with the magneto, even though both retained their separate functions and were capable of working on their own. The two best examples are the Lucas Magdyno and the BTH Dynomag, in which the dynamo is mounted immediately above the magneto, taking its drive from a secondary pinion mounted on the magneto drive shaft. This arrangement permits the necessary speed-up of the dynamo drive by means of a suitable gear ratio (the magneto has to run at half engine speed on a four stroke) whilst at the same time enabling a pre-loaded clutch to be incorporated in the drive so that if the dynamo happens to seize, there is no risk of shearing the magneto drive. Early Lucas Magdyno designs have the dynamo an integral part of the main body of the instrument, even though it functions as a separate, self-contained unit. On later examples, the dynamo is quickly detachable as a complete unit, after slackening a retaining strap and removing the nut from a projecting end stud.

Dynamos were also available as separate units. Some manufacturers, such as AJS and Matchless, preferred to fit a dynamo and magneto separately, not necessarily in the same location. One version had a contact breaker assembly contained in a special compartment next to the end cover, so that it was suitable for use in conjunction with a coil ignition system.

As far as British machines are concerned, dynamos were either of Lucas or Miller manufacture, both designs having a 45 watt output, direct current, and operating at six volts. Externally, there was very little to differentiate between them, apart from the manufacturer's name stamped on the case. Since the drive was often by chain or belt, the drive shaft was deliberately arranged in an off-centre position, so that the chain or belt could be tensioned correctly by rotating the dynamo body. Of the two forms of drive, the belt is much preferred because it is sufficiently resilient to act as a simple shock absorber and in consequence is much kinder to the armature bearings. Should the dynamo seize, a comparatively rare occurrence but one that has to be taken into account, the drive will slip, unlike that of a chain. On the other hand, if the belt tension is too slack, slip around the pulleys will occur quite readily, giving the impression that the dynamo is not charging. Many a Velocette owner will be aware of this possibility. When charging, a dynamo absorbs a surprising amount of power, which will certainly initiate slip with a slack belt. Irrespective of the type of machine to which the dynamo is fitted, always check the drive first in the event of the dynamo failing to show a charge. Some machines, such as the early Norton Dominator twin, used a fibre pinion to take up the drive inside the timing cover. It is by no means unknown for pinion teeth to shear quite unexpectedly, completely immobilising the dynamo.

If the instrument revolves in a satisfactory manner, yet still fails to show a charge, run the engine slowly so that the dynamo cut-out points do not close, and momentarily touch them together. Sometimes the polarity of a dynamo will temporarily reverse itself, especially if the machine has been standing for a long while. This technique should reverse the polarity back to the original direction, in which case a charge will be registered. If this technique has no effect after several attempts, the dynamo must be removed after the engine has stopped. If not already detached, take off the end cover or the cork-lined strap around the brush gear. Check that all the brushes are making contact with the armature, that they have not worn so short that the spring contact is too weak and that they are free to slide in their holders when the spring pressure is temporarily released. If in doubt, fit new brushes, remaking the original connections. Note that the brush tips are curved to conform to the curvature of the armature; if the old brushes are replaced, they must be inserted in their original positions as they will have bedded down correctly.

The armature itself may have a dirty commutator — the copper segments at the end on to which the brushes bear. Clean with very fine emery cloth and then wash with a rag moistened in petrol, to remove any traces of grease. Each copper segment is separated from the next by a mica insulator. If the mica is standing proud as the result of commutator wear, it can be undercut until it is just below the surface by using a thin section of hacksaw blade. This is a very skilled job, since the mica must be only just undercut. Sometimes overheating of the dynamo will cause the ends of the armature windings to 'fling' from their connections with the alternator segments. This can be seen from the band of solder that has flung from the connections when the connections parted. It is permissible to clean off the solder, then remake the connections, using as little solder as possible. The other item likely to fail is the field coil, which is bolted very tightly to the shell of the dynamo, around its pole piece. The two ends of the field coil can be seen protruding through the insulated base plate of the brush gear end, and if they are temporarily disconnected, a continuity check can be made. Attach a battery and 6 volt bulb, in series, across the two ends of the field coil. If the lamp lights, the field coil is intact. If it does not, the coil has either burnt out or has an open circuit. Note that the bulb may not light very brightly, due to the resistance of the many turns of fine wire used in the coil winding. Replacing a defective coil is a job for the expert. It must be tightened correctly so that the pole piece only just misses the revolving armature. If the screws work loose and the clearance disappears, the resultant damage will destroy the dynamo and possibly the whole drive system.

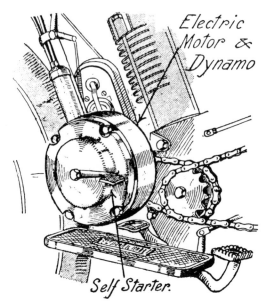

Figure 19 The American Indian was unique in having a combined self-starter and generator well before the first world war

A good check, prior to dismantling, is to see whether the separate unit type of dynamo can be made to motor. Although this is not an infallible test, it will show there is little wrong with the dynamo, if it can be made to rotate by means of a simple electrical hook up. Remove the dynamo from the machine and join together the two dynamo terminals with a lead that runs to the positive terminal of a 6 volt battery. Then connect the negative lead from the battery to the outside of the dynamo case. This should convert the dynamo into an electric motor, with the result that the dynamo will rotate at slow speed. If the dynamo has a cut-out fitted alongside the brush gear, it will be necessary to close this manually to make the test work. This test is obviously best suited to a Lucas or Miller dynamo of the early type with two separate connections. Do make sure, however, that the negative lead from the battery makes good contact with the dynamo case, which is often rusty or covered with a layer of oxide that acts as an efficient insulator.

If it is necessary to renew the dynamo, this can present a problem because the dynamo is now an obsolete instrument. It may be possible to replace it by an ex-WD type, some of which still exist, but check to ensure the direction of rotation is identical — it is marked by an arrow stamped on the outside of the case. A dynamo is a unipolar instrument and will charge in one direction only. It is possible to reverse the rotation characteristic by swapping over the brush leads and their associated connections, however. Also make sure the output is the same. Dynamos of the Lucas E3HM type have a 45 watt output, whereas the later E3L version has a 60 watt output and a longer body. This latter factor can prove important, where space limitations exist. In all other respects, the dynamos are completely interchangeable, provided their direction of rotation is the same and they are used in conjunction with the correct type of voltage regulator unit. In only very rare instances is the drive pinion a different size. The Scott provides one such example. Because the Magdyno has to be driven at engine speed (for the two-stroke engine), a larger than standard drive pinion is fitted, to prevent the dynamo from turning too fast.

Occasionally, pancake dynamos are fitted. During the twenties, BTH manufactured a very good design that was fitted to many of the Douglas marque, amongst others. More recently, dynamos of this type, of Lucas manufacture, have been fitted as standard to the Sunbeam in-line twins and to the post-1948 Scott range. Now the trend is to fit an alternator, which is capable of giving a much higher output and enables a 12 volt system to be used for the first time. The first widespread use of alternators occurred when they were introduced to the BSA and Triumph ranges during the fifties.

155

One way of checking whether the electrical equipment on an old machine is the original, is to take a close look at the dynamo. Up until about 1936, the three brush system was used as a convenient means of controlling the level of output. In practice, this meant the addition of a third and often thinner section brush approximately mid-way between the two main brushes of the commutator. By moving this additional brush one way or the other, the dynamo output could be either increased or reduced. Lucas dynamos of this period also had the cut-out built in with the brush gear section. From 1936 or thereabouts, onwards, Lucas employed a voltage regulator unit in the form of a small oblong shaped black box that clamped to some convenient part of the frame. Now the dynamo had only two brushes; the output was controlled by a solenoid and a set of vibrating contact points mounted inside the black box, alongside the cut-out, which had also been transferred to this new location. On manufacture, the regulator unit was correctly adjusted and then sealed with a wire and a lead seal, so that only a qualified Lucas agent could make adjustments without invalidating the guarantee. In many respects this was advisable, for it is far from easy to re-set either the cut-out or voltage regulator with any real accuracy unless a sensitive moving coil voltmeter is available and the detailed adjustment procedure is followed closely. In short, unless you are an electrical expert and have the appropriate equipment, entrust this type of work to the specialist. Miller went about the problem their own way and abandoned the third brush system in place of a cylindrical carbon pile regulator, usually mounted immediately above the dynamo. Although adjustable by a set routine, the latter had one major advantage. If the unit went wrong the regulator cartridge could be removed for repair and by a very simple rearrangement of the connections, the dynamo would still give output, although somewhat reduced. The cut-out, however, still remained attached to the base plate that held the brush gear, with the result that the only way in which to distinguish a late-type Miller dynamo from an early pattern is to count the number of brushes and observe whether the dynamo has one output socket or two. Several fancy names have been attached to these systems. The Lucas voltage regulator system is commonly referred to by the initials avc or cvc, which respectively stand for automatic voltage control and compensated voltage control — they both refer to the same system. The earlier three brush Miller system masqueraded under the initials SUS, this being the descriptive coding they used in their period advertisements. It should be added that Miller had their own dynamo coding, the early three-brush design being stamped DM3G. The later two-brush dynamo is the type DVR. Both types of instrument have a 45 watt output; although Miller did eventually manufacture a dynamo with a 60 watt output, that appeared much later than the Lucas equivalent.

Lighting, and in particular headlamp switches, have appeared in so many variations that it is virtually impossible to give anything but the briefest description. When electric lighting made a serious comeback in the mid-twenties, the switch was not incorporated in the headlamp shell. Instead, it was mounted on one side of the 'between tubes' petrol tank, which was considered to be the most convenient place from the rider's point of view. But as tank designs changed, a new location in the headlamp shell itself was arranged and this has remained by far the most popular location. However, some machines had an instrument panel in the centre of the petrol tank, for an interim period.

Generally speaking, lighting switches seldom give rise to more serious problems than dirty contacts, assuming the switch is not of the multi-contact type that also contains an ignition control function. The types in most popular use throughout the late vintage, post-vintage and post-war eras can be dismantled and reassembled with ease, so that the roller or plunger that makes the actual contacts can be removed and cleaned. The switch is held on the underside by a shaped wire clip in the case of the Lucas design, and by means of two small BA nuts and washers in the equivalent Miller counterpart. Once removed from the headlamp shell, the centre screw that retains the switch should be removed, so that the lever can be detached. The rotating part of the switch will now press downwards, out of position. In the Lucas design, great care is necessary during this operation, since the plunger or roller is very small and is easily lost. Because it is spring loaded, it will jump out of position very readily.

The Lucas MCR1 was the original regulator unit designed for use in conjunction with their 45 watt two-brush dynamo. This is the type that clamps around a frame tube

A later version, the MCR2, is larger in size and identified by the 'blisters' on the cover. Designed for use in conjunction with the 60 watt dynamos, it will also replace the earlier MCR1 type, without need for any wiring modifications

The 'blisters' on the MCR2 cover protect the carbon resistance fitted to this type of unit

The coil on the right controls the dynamo cut-out; that on the left, the output voltage from the dynamo

The Lucas lighting switch is part of a small panel, attached to the headlamp, complete with ammeter, for access to the wiring connections

Some early three-brush dynamo systems utilise this half charge resistance to convert excess current into heat. Although somewhat primitive, it none the less lessened the risk of overcharging the battery

157

Modern techniques can often be used to good advantage, and it is useful to note that dirty contacts can often be cleaned in a very satisfactory manner, without need to dismantle the switch. A number of aerosol type cleaners are available in the radio and TV repair business, which can be sprayed on to both clean and lubricate the switch.

All wiring connections to the switch should be tight and make good contact. The ends of the connecting wires should be bared and then rolled into a tight ball, so that the wire cannot pass out through the slot in the side of the switch connector. If the pointed grub screw is then tightened fully, a good, permanent contact must result. Miller went one step further with their equipment. They soldered a shaped connector to the end of each wire, which slips into the switch connector and is held firm by a similar grub screw.

Switches that also include an ignition function seem much more prone to internal troubles and, being of more complicated design, are virtually impossible to repair with any satisfaction. Some are sealed, so that they cannot be repaired at all. Unless you happen to be a watchmaker by profession and can cope with the dismantling and reassembly of a whole host of tiny parts, it is best to scrap the switch and try and find an identical replacement — with key included. Fortunately, this type of switch has appeared mostly on machines of more recent origin. The earlier the design of switch, the easier it is to take apart; built-in obsolescence was almost unheard of in the early days.

A somewhat curious attachment often found clamped to a headlamp switch is what is known as a half charge resistance, basically a few turns of resistance wire wound around a ceramic former. Its function is to reduce the output from the dynamo when there is little or no demand on the electrical system as a whole. A half charge resistance is used mainly on the systems that incorporate a three brush dynamo, since this forms an additional means of regulating the dynamo output. It comes into use when the headlamp switch is in the 'off' position and is over-ridden when the switch is moved to one of the lighting positions (Lucas) or to the extra 'Charge' position on the Miller switch. In this latter case, there is the option of a full charge during daylight running, if so required. Keep wires within the headlamp shell well away from the resistance wire, since it becomes quite hot when it is live. I have never seen a figure published for the actual resistance value in ohms.

An instrument that has to withstand a fair amount of abuse is the ammeter, an instrument that was once regarded as an essential fitment on all machines fitted with electric lighting, to show whether the battery was being charged by the dynamo. Exposed to the weather and subject to all manner of vibration, this little instrument needs to be exceptionally robust. Unfortunately, it is not practicable to repair a faulty ammeter and it has to be replaced with a new one or cut out of the circuit altogether by bridging the terminals across the back. If an ammeter develops an open circuit, it will give the impression of a general fault in the wiring system, the exact effect depending on the way in which the circuitry has been arranged. Most troubles are caused by water entering the instrument and causing the needle pivots to rust, or a complete break up of the internals, as the result of machine vibration. A burn out, through an electrical short or overload, is almost invariably accompanied by some visual evidence, such as burning or discolouration of the scale.

Without doubt, the component that suffers most from the combined effects of neglect and vibration is the battery — a component which, even under the best of circumstances, normally has a useful working life of approximately two years. So if the machine has been standing for a very long while with the battery still attached, it can be taken for granted that a new one will be required. But do not discard the original, no matter how bad it may appear, provided the case is sound. The reason will be apparent after reading further.

Ignoring their physical size, which is generally related to the battery's capacity, batteries of the lead-acid type can be sub-divided into one of four main types. The standard battery has a black, hard-rubber case and is normally held in a specially-constructed carrier which is clamped to almost any convenient part of the machine — most frequently on the nearside, below the saddle. Unless the battery carrier has anti-vibration mountings, which is rarely the case, the battery is not protected from road shocks or from the vibrations of the machine itself — conditions that can lead to a more rapid breakdown of the battery due to

Instrument panels mounted in the petrol tank were very popular during the late thirties. The item immediately above the two instruments is a detachable inspection lamp, with its own lead wire

The pre-war and early post-war Lucas ammeter has a fully marked scale, as shown

Commencing during the early fifties, a new type of scale was used by Lucas, having no figures

Later still, the figures reappeared, but only part of the ammeter needle is now visible. A typical Miller ammeter is shown on the left. A transparent 'window' in the base permits the dial to be illuminated by diffused light from the headlamp itself, during the hours of darkness

disintegration of the plates or displacement of the paste contained within their framework. In consequence, a special type of battery, known generally as the 'T' battery on account of its shape, was made available for use on some of the more expensive machines. In effect, this battery contained its own anti-vibration mountings, built into each of the extending ears of the 'T'. Alas, the 'T' battery has long since disappeared, along with the hard-rubber casing used for all the older batteries. It needed a special type of carrier since it was suspended, rather than clamped.

A third design of battery that proved very popular was the Varley, a lead-acid battery in which the sulphuric acid electrolyte is absorbed in glass wool. In consequence, the battery could be inverted without any of the electrolyte escaping, a great advantage on any motorcycle, where there is always risk of spillage. For reasons unknown, this type of battery never achieved the degree of popularity it deserved.

The fourth type is the one that is in general use today — the battery with a translucent or transparent plastic case. Although the design represents a considerable advance in battery technology, (the electrolyte level is more easily checked and it is also possible to inspect the plates and their paste content), this type of battery looks completely out of place on an elderly machine and the eye is attracted to it immediately. Unfortunately, it is probably the only design that can now be purchased over the counter, unless a dealer has a small number of the 'old' style batteries hidden away. They are usually dry charged and will store for very long periods without need of attention, but it is not often that such luck will abound. It is here that an old battery can be used to good effect, when an alternative way round is needed. If the old battery is washed out to remove all traces of any acid that remain, it is comparatively easy to cut the whole centre from the battery, so that the complete plate assembly can be lifted out with the soft pitch covering. It is then easy to sink the new plastic cased battery into the space now vacant so that it is completely camouflaged by its new surroundings. Even a concours judge would have difficulty in spotting the conversion, provided the plastic-covered leads can be disguised!

If a new battery has to be purchased, make sure you obtain one with a well-known brand name and that it has the same amp hour capacity as the original. Cheap batteries are available, even some with a black, hard rubber case. But they represent a bad purchase on at least two major counts. Firstly, the lead content of the plates will be much less, with the result that the plates will be thinner in section and will buckle more easily. This also means reduced capacity. Hold a good quality battery and one of the lesser known makes in each hand — you will immediately notice the difference in weight. Secondly, many cheap batteries use a plastic sealing strip in place of the usual screw-in vent plugs or moulded plastic former. This sometimes makes a very poor seal, with the result that acid can leak on to the surrounding area of the machine, causing severe corrosion.

Other types of battery exist, such as the Nife type, which has an alkali and not an acid electrolyte. These batteries are, however, in the minority, their greatest disadvantage being their loss of capacity in very cold weather. Always check the type of battery fitted and what its contents are likely to be, before topping up. The addition of acid to an alkali content or vice-versa could prove quite lively, to say the least!

Electric headlamps have been manufactured in all manner of designs, although the designs in most common use, usually of either Lucas or Miller origin, conformed to a general pattern. Originally, the reflector was attached to the headlamp rim and glass by means of wire clips, with a rubber or cork seal to prevent the ingress of water. When the need arose to change any of the bulbs, the wire clips had to be removed and the assembly dismantled, that is, in the Lucas designs. Although the Miller headlamp used an almost identical form of construction, a specially-shaped bulb holder fitted on the back of the reflector and was held in position by a stout wire clasp. With this design, the bulbs could be removed without having to disturb the reflector. In both cases, however, the reflector rarely had a perfect seal and sooner or later would tarnish from the effects of the atmosphere or the ingress of water.

During the early fifties, a new type of reflector unit made its debut, the so-called sealed beam type — an unfortunate misnomer which conflicts with the even more up to date

The most commonly used type of battery in the post-war era has a black, hard rubber case. Pre-war models used a battery that was virtually identical

The 'T' battery, a more expensive version of the standard Lucas type that has in-built anti-vibration mountings

design that is in general use today and has been given the same name. In the original design, the reflector and headlamp were made as one, sealed together. It was therefore necessary to use a special type of headlamp bulb which could be inserted from the back of the reflector, to locate in a pre-arranged position. The bulb was of the pre-focus type, this latter phrase being a better and more accurate description of the headlamp arrangement. The reflector unit was not hermetically sealed because provision had to be made for the renewal of the main bulb, whenever needed. Now lighting has gone one stage further, with a true sealed beam unit in which the bulb is an integral part of the reflector unit. If a filament goes, the complete unit has to be renewed.

For the sake of originality, the old lighting arrangement should be retained, provided it is intact, for it is easy to have the reflector re-silvered by either electroplating or vacuum coating. On the older systems, a good reflector is a must, if a good, usable headlamp is to result. Note that pre-war and very early post-war headlamps had a flat glass, whereas from about 1947 onwards. a domed glass was fitted. If the machine is to be used for commuting, which includes riding in the dark, it is advisable to make use of one of the latest sealed beam units, provided one can be obtained that is the correct size and has provision for the inclusion of a pilot light. Although such a fitment will mitigate heavily against a concours bike, the rider will have reasonably good lights, even with the lower wattage dynamo — a very important consideration in terms of personal safety. It is as well to remember, too, that good lights depend on good electrical connections and a good earth return. The latter point is frequently overlooked when overhauling any lighting system, especially where new paint may act as a very effective insulator. Remember the bulb contacts oxidise and that after extensive use, the bulb filaments will lose some of their lighting brilliance.

The lighting regulations stipulate that the lighting system must be powered by a minimum of 6 volts and that no bulb should have a wattage of less than 6 watts, that is, as far as the bulbs used for illuminating the front and rear of the machine are concerned. The headlamp must be arranged so that it does not dazzle oncoming traffic too, and all machines registered after 1931 must be fitted with provision for dipping the headlamp beam. To check

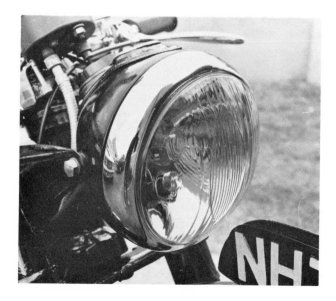

The domed headlamp glass came into fashion about 1948/9. This is the very early version, with a separate reflector unit clipped to the rim

The older pattern of rear lamp is no longer legal, because the area of the red lens is not large enough. On a dark, wet night, it is very difficult indeed to pick out one of these light units

It is easy to accommodate a stop lamp switch in a quite inconspicuous manner

This sidecar lamp is of ingenious design since it also acts as a grab handle. A rear lamp is an integral part of the unit

163

whether the headlamp is correctly aligned, position the machine so that it is 25 feet away from a wall, standing on level ground. The main beam should be aligned so that it is concentrated at the same height as the distance from the centre of the headlamp to the ground, with the rider seated normally. If the machine has a spring frame and a pillion passenger is carried, this passenger should be seated too. Adjustments are easily made by tilting the headlamp, after the two fixing bolts at each side have been slackened a trifle. After re-tightening, re-check the accuracy of the setting. On older machines having a headlamp with a separate reflector, the main bulb has provision for focussing, without need to detach the reflector from the headlamp glass. Remove the front of the lamp, loosen the screw around the clamp that retains the main bulb holder, and slide the bulb holder inwards or outwards until the desired intensity of beam is obtained, before re-tightening the clamp and replacing the front of the headlamp.

Unless the machine is of quite recent origin or has been modified in accordance with changes in the lighting regulations, the rear light will almost certainly have to be renewed. The old type is no longer acceptable if the red lens has a diameter less than two inches. It must also illuminate the rear number plate (as before) and must have a reflector moulded into the lens if a separate reflector is not mounted elsewhere. This latter requirement is a sensible and obvious safeguard since the rider himself will rarely know if his rear lamp bulb has failed whilst he is on the road. Unfortunately, it does mean that if electric lighting is fitted, a more modern rear lamp has to be used, containing a bulb rated at not less than 6 watts. This is a statutory requirement and will destroy originality, if the rider is to remain within the law. The fact that the lighting equipment is in full working order but is never used is no excuse. If the equipment is fitted to the machine, it must conform to the statutory requirements in every respect. Some take a chance and hope they will never get caught — and they may well get away with it. But it needs only an after dark accident to produce a test case, which could cost the rider a great deal of money in legal fees. With acetylene lighting, the situation is even more complex, as mentioned earlier. A loophole may exist in this case, however, since the lighting system is not electric.

A further requirement on some machines is a stop light, to indicate when the rear brake has been applied. This requirement applies to all machines registered after 1935. Fortunately, the stop lamp can be combined with the rear lamp, using a bulb of the double filament type with offset pins, and the switch mounted in the most convenient place for it to be actuated by the brake pedal or rod.

If a sidecar is fitted, this too must have its own lamp, showing white to the front and red to the rear. It must be mounted on the nearside of the sidecar, the mudguard being the favourite position. One design was particularly attractive. It was made like a handle, with the white and red lamp at either end, to form a useful grab rail for the passenger when entering or climbing out of a single seater sports sidecar.

When involved with electrical systems, by far the greatest problem is likely to be the condition of the wiring itself. Plastic-covered wire did not come into general use until some while after world war 2, the usual covering being rubber, with sometimes an outer layer of cotton braiding. The rubber would eventually crack and perish through the combined effects of sunlight and heat, or would swell and deteriorate rapidly through the effects of petrol and/or oil. The cotton braiding tended to slow down the rate of deterioration, but even this extra covering would eventually fray and rot. In most cases, this means that the wiring system on any old machine will almost certainly have to be renewed, especially if a previous owner has replaced part of it with the inevitable odd sections of flex and miscellaneous pieces of wire that are quite unsuitable for their present role. But before you strip off the whole untidy mass, make an accurate drawing of all the connections, along with their colour code markings, if any. This will save hours of time later, especially if it proves impossible to obtain a copy of the original wiring diagram.

When rewiring, it is obviously preferable to use plastic-covered cable of the correct current carrying capacity, preferably with each separate wire colour coded to make reconnections easy. But a moment's reflection will show that the wiring will then become far

The Lucas Altette horn was at one time a standard fitting on most British motorcycles

A more modern horn can sometimes be adapted to fit, without looking too out of place. A horn in working condition is a legal requirement

too predominant, especially against the traditional black frame and cycle parts of a newly reconditioned machine. The wiring can be hidden with black sleeving, but even so, it will still be obvious where it emerges. In consequence, it is preferable to use black coloured wire and slip a small colour coded ring around each end. Despite this precaution, plastic covered wire will be frowned upon heavily by a concours judge, who is not over-concerned with the more practical aspects. If you use rubber-covered wire like the original, be prepared to cover it with sleeving as much as you can and for the need to renew it from time to time. Never make joins along the wire, since this is one of the best ways in which to cultivate high resistance joints. Avoid the use of unsightly insulating tape too. Arrange the cables neatly, and clamp them into position, using rubber clips of the type used for bicycle control cables. An untidy looking wiring system will spoil the overall look of an otherwise presentable machine and may even create a hazard if loose wires can touch hot components or become trapped between moving parts.

165

Mention has yet to be made of two electrical components that will have to be renewed if they malfunction, since neither is repairable. The first of these is the rectifier, a component that is fitted to an ac generator system in order to convert the current into dc, for charging the battery. Avoid over-tightening the rectifier or scratching any of the vanes. If the rectifier appears to malfunction, first check that the earthing connection is good — usually made through the mounting bolt. If there is no improvement, this is the time to seek the aid of an electrical specialist, since sensitive measuring equipment is necessary to conduct a full test. Many rectifiers are inadvertently destroyed by connecting the battery the wrong way round — watch out for this. The other component is the electric horn. Most of the better quality horns have provision for adjusting the note, by turning a small screw in the back of the instrument. Move it only a fraction at a time and re-check. Only slight adjustment should prove necessary, at infrequent intervals, to compensate for wear of the internal vibrating points. On no account remove the centre nut and change the setting of the screw that is held by a locknut. If this is badly set, the horn may function quite well, but take an excessive current from the battery. Note that a dc horn will not work with an ac circuit, or vice-versa. A horn in working condition is, of course, a legal requirement. If acetylene lighting is fitted, or if the machine has no lighting set, a horn of the bulb variety is an essential fitment. The only problems these latter fittings are subject to is a perished or split rubber bulb, or a broken or missing reed. Occasionally, a Klaxon-type horn is encountered, which is mechanical in function, or even a bell or exhaust whistle — the latter one-time alternatives that were permissible by law.

A peculiar fault that often manifests itself in some of the older two-strokes is a tendency for light bulbs to fail after only a very short period of service. In many cases, this can be attributed to a poor earth return and when completing the rebuild of a machine, it is wise to ensure good earth contact with the frame, mudguards or other cycle parts is made, if necessary by scraping away a small portion of the paint film at the point of contact. It should also be noted that two-strokes having a direct lighting system (no lead acid battery) are fitted with a special type of headlamp dip switch, in which electrical contact is not broken, even momentarily, when the lamp is dipped. If a standard dip switch is fitted in error, there will be a break in continuity whilst switching and small though this may be, the sudden electrical surge resulting from a nil electrical load, will be sufficient to blow the bulbs.

Perhaps the most confusing aspect of all is the interpretation of the regulations that relate to lighting equipment and the DOE test, to which every vehicle more than three years old must be subjected before a test certificate can be obtained and a road tax licence issued. The official interpretation is that if a machine has any part of the lighting equipment fitted, including the wiring loom (and presumably the lighting coils in a flywheel magneto) a test certificate will be issued only if the complete assembly is there, and the equipment, as a whole, is in full working order. Alternatively, if the machine has no lighting equipment at all (as in the case of a trials machine, for example), a test certificate can still be issued because the machine will then be exempt from the lighting requirements. This interpretation has been confirmed recently by the Department of the Environment, in view of the many test cases that have come to their attention, especially those where a trials machine rider has been warned of prosecution for not having a stop light on his machine. It follows, of course, that the above ruling about exemption applies only if the machine is not used during lighting up time. If in doubt, always enquire. No one can ever be 100% sure of the full implications of a legal definition, other than by bringing a test case.

Chapter Fourteen

Accessories

Accessories is a particularly vague description that covers a multitude of fittings forming part of the specification of any motorcycle. Here, in this chapter, the description refers to parts which, if not fitted, would not necessarily prevent the motorcycle from being used, although in some instances they are a statutory requirement. Unfortunately some of these parts are often removed at an early stage during an overhaul and may be easily lost, if the owner loses heart and never proceeds further. Other parts are sometimes removed to give the machine a more sporty appearance; chaincases and chainguards are especially susceptible to this. The main problem is that if the originals are missing, there is no pattern to work from, and even a part that looks right, may not necessarily fit. The Triumph alloy chaincase is a typical example. A number of versions are available, of quite different dimensions, which look similar at a quick glance. If the wrong one is obtained, it will prove extremely difficult or perhaps impossible to fit. Fortunately, many of the older machines, and especially those in the lower price bracket, use pressed steel chaincases and it is comparatively easy to make a replica or to adapt another design that is not too different. It is only the cast alloy 'oilbath' chaincases that cause the greatest headaches. There is really only one answer - to try and find another of similar design to the original, or to make up some form of protection for the primary chain until such time as the original can be located. It is obligatory by law to have the primary and secondary chains covered, along their uppermost run at the very least. Do not forget, however, that if a previously enclosed primary chain has to run exposed, some provision for a chain oiler will have to be made. Obviously a chain cannot be run in this fashion if the clutch is one designed to work in oil.

The secondary chainguard, normally, is more easy to fabricate if it is missing, unless the chain is fully enclosed like that of many of the vintage Sunbeams. Often, the chain guard from a bicycle can be modified and adapted to fit - or one from another make of machine. It is easy to cut off the original fixing brackets, or to reposition them. The chainguard must, however, be rigidly mounted. If it works loose and becomes tangled with the chain, a nasty accident can result from the locked rear wheel. A good tinsmith could make a replica of an original, without too much difficulty, even if the design is of the full enclosure type.

Footrests do not usually cause much of a problem because even if they are missing, they are not too difficult to fabricate. If you have the originals, they are rarely anything like straight, and can be restored to their original shape by removing them from the machine, peeling off the rubber grip and applying heat from a blowlamp whilst pressure is applied. It is best to use a long, large diameter tube, that will slip over the end of the footrest, to provide the leverage, the footrest itself being clamped firmly in a vice. This is generally more effective than a hammer, with less risk of causing damage. Never bend a footrest, brake pedal or gear change pedal without the use of heat, or there is good risk of it snapping off. Older footrests need special care, especially if they are of the type that has a 'D' shaped rubber and two outrigger bolts - like those found on most Nortons and veteran Triumphs etc. It may also be good policy to save the original rubbers, no matter how badly they are worn or split. They may come in useful as a pattern at the very least, and could conceivably be built-up in an extreme case with the compound that can be used for repairing wellington boots. A few one-make enthusiasts and specialists are having footrest rubbers and handlebar grips made to original designs, which is a fact worth knowing. Although somewhat expensive, due to the very limited production run, they can make all the difference to a really well renovated machine and may even swing the balance in a tightly fought concours final.

Footboards can prove more of a problem, because often they will have almost completely rotted away. A new base can be shaped from wood without too much difficulty; the problem lies in applying the metal surround and the metal or rubber top. Frequently, the originals are too far gone to save. As a temporary expedient, a car mat of the moulded rubber type can be cut up and used for the top surface; alternatively, the footboards can be dispensed with altogether and footrests substituted - they were often available as an optional extra in any case. Some footboards were sprung, as on some of the early Scotts.

Brake pedals and gear change levers can be straightened in a similar manner to that suggested for the footrests. Often the pivot bearing will require attention, which may, or may not, have been bushed and will have worn badly as the result of lack of lubrication. If the metal itself has been bored out, the hole can be drilled oversize and a bush made and inserted to bring the bearing down to its original size. If there is a bush already, it is mainly a case of substitution. If there is room, fit a grease nipple to aid future greasing. Check also for wear in the clevis pins and yoke ends that form the linkage from the pedal. A small amount of wear here and there will add up to a considerable amount of lost motion, if left unattended.

Machines made prior to the first world war, including autocycles, will be fitted with pedalling gear, which may also need attention. Soon, the pedal cranks will bend, through contact with the kerb or if the machine has fallen over. To straighten them, knock out the cotter pins that hold them to the pedalling gear shaft and withdraw both cranks, so that they can be clamped in a vice, heated and straightened. Usually, it will be necessary to remove the actual pedals first, so that the straightening tube can be slid over the crank. Note that the right-hand pedal will have a left-hand thread, to prevent it from working loose. If the pedals and cranks are missing altogether from a veteran machine, bicycle parts can often be substituted to good effect, until such time as the originals may come along.

Quite a few manufacturers had their name moulded into kickstart and footrest rubbers

Footboards are not too difficult to
make up, using rubber mat for the
top covering

Difficulties will arise when the
original design had a complex pattern
and the manufacturer's name in
embossed letters. This example has
both!

If pedalling gear is fitted, there will be need for a freewheel at the hub of the rear
wheel and this is another component that can give trouble. If the original is broken and
beyond repair, a problem will immediately occur because it is unlikely that a bicycle freewheel can be substituted on account of the hub size and a difference in chain pitch. Most
pedalling gear uses the type of heavyweight chain that was originally designed for use on
tradesman's bicycles. Inject paraffin to free a seized freewheel, or penetrating oil. If the
wheel can be freed, it can almost certainly be saved. Broken teeth can be repaired by a
sprocket specialist. The entire freewheel assembly threads on to the rear wheel hub and has a
left-hand thread in most cases. It is quite easily dismantled and reassembled after removal
from the hub, although the internal ball bearings and springs are of small dimensions.

Number plates have been necessary almost since the inception of the motorcycle, although changes have been made since then in both the statutory size of plates and the dimensions and spacing of the letters and index numbers thereon. The essential requirements are that the number plates are permanently mounted and easily read, and that the rear one is illuminated by the rear lamp during the hours of darkness. Before making up new number plates or renovating the existing ones, it is as well to acquaint yourself with the regulations - even the spacing of the numbers and letters is specified. If an old machine is used occasionally on the road, the rider may not be able to get away with the original small number plates that were part of the original specification. But here again, this is one of the twilight areas of the law, where no one can be really sure whether failure to comply with the later regulations constitutes an offence.

Early number plates had the letters and numbers hand painted and many a really good machine renovation has been spoilt by poorly painted number plates. It is well worth the effort (and expense) to have them painted by a signwriter, after giving him the essential dimensions. Never resort to today's self-adhesive letters and numbers. Even if they are expertly applied, the overall effect is never the same and they look out of place. Later machines can be fitted with embossed aluminium number plates, bolted or rivetted to the original unlettered plates that were supplied with the machine. Unfortunately, it is becoming increasingly more difficult to find a supplier who produces anything other than the black and yellow reflective plates in common use today - strictly taboo on any old machine. As a last resort, reflective plates can be purchased and repainted aluminium and black. Embossed plates will enhance the appearance of the machine, but should be reserved mainly for machines of the post-vintage era. Current legislation has conceded that it is no longer necessary to fit a front number plate, but presumably there is no reason why it should not remain attached to an old machine, if only for the sake of authenticity.

Another of today's legal requirements is a speedometer, which must be fitted to any machine of over 100cc capacity, registered after January 1, 1937. It must, of course, be in working order whilst the machine is on the road and must also have a defined degree of accuracy. Even if not a legal requirement on the older machine, it is a very useful fitment to have. Apart from the registering speed, the odometer that is usually incorporated in the dial will provide a useful indication of the total mileage covered and can be used as a reliable guide to the interval between routine maintenance schedules.

As far as possible, the instrument and its drive should conform with the year of manufacture of the machine, and care should be taken to ensure the drive ratio is correct, so that indicated readings are accurate. On older machines, the drive was taken from a sprocket attached to the spokes of either the front or the rear wheel. This meshed with a smaller fibre pinion attached to a gearbox, which in turn transmitted the drive via a flexible cable to the speedometer head. The gearbox was bolted rigidly to the front or rear forks, so that the correct depth of mesh was achieved. Later, the drive was transferred to the inside of the brake drum (when this type of brake was in widespread use) so that the mechanism was no longer exposed to the elements. Later still, with the advent of the telescopic front fork, a gearbox was devised that slid over the rear wheel spindle and picked-up the drive from the rotating hub. That is, unless the manufacturer elected to take the drive direct from the gearbox, like BSA and Triumph.

Although the flexible drive cable was, and still is, the method used in transmitting the drive to the speedometer head, cables were by no means identical or interchangeable. For this reason it is always advisable to keep the remains of an old, broken cable. At the very least, the end connections can be saved and used to make up a new cable, because it is the ends that differ in their mode of attachment. Usually, the inner cable can be removed quite easily by withdrawing it from one end of the outer cable. This is necessary because the cable will require periodic greasing with graphite or high melting point grease. Never grease the last six inches at the speedometer head end, however, otherwise grease will eventually work its way into the head and immobilise the movement. When greasing an inner cable or replacing one that has broken, always check to ensure the outer cable is not compressed or damaged at

Old number plates have distinctive shapes, which should be preserved. A neatly signwritten finish gives a pleasing effect, often overlooked in the anxiety to get the machine on the road

The use of two index letters and four numbers permits this rear number plate to have a particularly pleasing shape that is quite distinctive

A speedometer in working order is a legal requirement on all machines registered after October 1st 1937 and of more than 100cc capacity. The Smith chronometric speedometer shown was used almost exclusively on most post-vintage and early post-war models

Drive take off is usually from the rear wheel, when telescopic front forks are fitted. Machines fitted with girder forks usually take the drive from within the front brake assembly

Early speedometers, such as this Cowey type, are much sought after. They will add bonus points to any well prepared concours machine

171

any point along its run. If it is, it must be renewed too, otherwise the new inner cable will break in the same place very quickly. Whilst greasing the cable, do not omit to grease the gearbox too. Remember that if the cable has to be renewed, or perhaps only the inner cable, the replacement must be of identical length. Furthermore, the cable should be routed so that it is not subjected to tight bends or stands a chance of being trapped between moving parts.

A damaged or broken speedometer head, no matter how old, can often be repaired or even restored by one of a handful of instrument repair specialists who are highly skilled in this type of work. This also applies to drive cables. Provided the dimensions of the original are available, along with the broken parts, a new cable can be constructed that is a replica of the original. Work such as this is, of necessity, somewhat expensive in view of the need to use highly skilled hands. Most speedometer heads are of either the chronometric (clock mechanism) or centrifugal type, for it was not until the middle-to-late fifties that the magnetic speedometer came into general use, using similar drive mechanism. It should not be overlooked, however, that the Cooper Stewart speedometer of the late twenties operated on the magnetic principle and was one of the originators of this design.

A change in tyre sizes will affect the accuracy of a speedometer reading, as will a change in gear ratios, when the speedometer drive is taken from the machine's gearbox. In this latter case, alternative drive ratio pinions were originally available from the manufacturer of the machine, especially if the machine was being converted for use in conjunction with a sidecar. With exposed drive pinions of the older type, it was relatively easy to make changes in the drive ratio. The older pinions will need periodic inspection to make sure the depth of mesh is correct and that none of the fixings is working loose.

Tachometers are usually found on racing machines and were not in widespread use until the post-vintage era. In most respects, the tachometer can be considered similar to the speedometer, in the sense that the general design of the instrument head, the cable drive and the gearbox take-off are similar in construction. As a result, similar maintenance and repair techniques will apply. The drive is taken from some convenient engine pick-up point, often from one of the valve timing pinions, by the simple expedient of having a close fitting shaped cup that fits over the flats of the nut retaining the timing pinion on its shaft. A slot cut in the end of the cup locates with the protruding tongue of the drive gearbox, which bolts direct to a machined flange and cut-out in the standard timing cover. Another convenient drive take-off point is from the slotted end of the camshaft, assuming the engine is of the ohc type. Tachometer gearboxes are usually available in two ratios: 1:2 or 1:4, so it is important to have the matching head. Legally, a tachometer is not acceptable as a substitute for a speedometer, as several cases have shown.

An unusual instrument sometimes found on older machines is a combined speedometer and average speed indicator, a somewhat sophisticated instrument originally marketed by Bonniksen. It is instantly recognisable on account of the two separate pointers, which sweep around the dial at timed intervals to record their separate functions. The Bonniksen now has a collector's value, so if you are fortunate enough to have one, take care that it is not easily removed if the machine is likely to be left unattended. Also, often found as a handlebar fitting, is a clock or watch - a useful addition for the rider who rides in long distance road trials. Several manufacturers, including Terrys, marketed a shaped clip that would bolt to the handlebars and carry a standard pocket watch of the 'turnip' variety. Vibration is the enemy of most clock or watch mechanisms and it may be necessary to devise a special anti-shock mounting if the clock or watch itself is not shockproof.

A fitting not often seen these days is the tyre pump, a hand pump of the plunger type that resembles the average bicycle pump but has a folding attachment at the base, so that the pump barrel can be retained by the foot. Punctures were much more prevalent in the early days and a tyre pump, along with a puncture repair outfit in the toolbox, was a more or less essential requirement. The pump is normally retained by a pair of shaped clips, as on a bicycle, that form an integral part of a frame tube or a chainguard. If the clips are missing, it is possible to purchase free-mounting clips that clamp around a tube with their own screw clip. Many veteran machines have the pump in a very prominent position - clamped to the

This watch holder dates back to the 1914 era and is a very rare fitment these days. A standard pocket watch fits within, of the type that once graced many a waistcoat front

Almost unknown today is the tyre pump, which was at one time supplied with every new machine. A favourite location is by clips over the rear chainguard

If the machine has acetylene lights or no lighting at all, a bulb horn is necessary to satisfy the requirements of the law. This early design, of the 'curly' type has the rubber bulb removed, to show the reed

A somewhat later type of bulb horn, typical of that used in the twenties. It helps complete the specification of this concour-winning AJS

top frame tube, immediately above the flat petrol tank. Some manufacturers actually had their name specially stamped on the pump; needless to say, these pumps are extremely rare these days.

Another fitment often carried on very old machines is an oil syringe. On veteran Triumphs, for example, there is a short tube attached to the main saddle tube into which one of these syringes will fit. Made of brass, the syringe was charged with oil and used for any part that required lubrication whilst the machine was on the road. It in no way acted as an auxiliary oil pump; if the latter was needed, it was invariably built into the main oil tank, as a permanent fixture.

Sometimes, a real touch of authenticity can be added to a superbly renovated machine by adding a period RAC or AA members badge, which may itself have been restored in keeping. The older badges are difficult to obtain, although they do sometimes turn up in antique shops or during auction sales. It is advisable, however, to be a member of the motoring organisation concerned if you sport their badge, since a roadside break-down could lead to an embarrassing situation! I have known a local RAC or AA man to produce a much desired badge, if advised well in advance of the need. The old badges are very occasionally handed in and you may be lucky in obtaining one by this backdoor approach, which undoubtedly would be frowned upon officially! Legally, the badge is the property of the motoring organisation who originally issued it - the badge will most likely have a serial number stamped on it. Hence the advisability of being a paid-up member. Club badges can be used with similar effect too, provided they are 'period' or not too modern looking. The original bronze Vintage MCC badge is a particularly good example. Mascots, although at one time popular, are generally out, since they tend to detract from the overall appearance of a machine. They can constitute an accident hazard too, if bolted to the front mudguard or clamped to the handlebars.

This type of RAC badge was in current use immediately after world war 2

Club badges, especially those of national or one-make clubs, do not look out of place if mounted in a sensible position

Old AA and RAC badges are becoming more difficult to find, as they have a collectors value on their own

Local club badges are not quite so common on older machines, and should be used with discretion

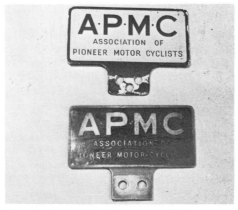

Some badges, such as these, are made for handlebar mounting, using a clip. This type of badge would look fine on a really old machine — provided the rider is a member

This mascot could only be on a Scott. At one time there was quite a craze for mascots such as this, but they are now very rare. Make sure they are firmly secured

Period licence holders should be used whenever possible. Fortunately there is no problem with the post-war Douglas, which makes ingenious use of the nearside headlamp mounting bracket

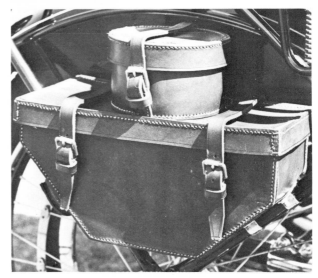

The round leather box above the tool box is used to carry a spare, coiled-up, inner tube. Once a common fitting, it is not often seen today

Chapter Fifteen

Sidecars

Often, a machine is found with a period sidecar still attached, or if the owner of an old, large capacity mount, is able to obtain a matching sidecar, he will have a convenient means of taking his family with him. In many respects, the sidecar can be regarded as a somewhat anti-social form of transportation, because the occupants of the sidecar are isolated from the rider of the machine and virtually incommunicado. Furthermore, the standard of comfort and the attendant difficulties in entering or leaving the sidecar may not be all that is desired. However, against this, the big sidecar outfit is unquestionably a very cheap form of transportation and because a well-aligned outfit has quite remarkable handling qualities, it can prove very good fun to use in conditions where most other forms of road transport find the going difficult. It must be stressed, however, that sidecar driving demands skill and it is necessary to develop a special technique that is quite different from that used when riding solo. Once the technique is mastered, the probability is that the sidecar drivers' ranks will be swelled by another convert.

All manner of designs have been manufactured, ranging from the woven wickerwork sidecars that were so popular in the early days to the huge double-adult sidecars that can still be seen occasionally today. The development of the sidecar and the extent of its popularity probably reached a peak during 1924, then a gradual decline set in following the advent of the cheap, mass produced small car. The ubiquitous Austin 7 of the early twenties struck the first blow against the sidecar outfit and soon there were many other makes available that offered an even greater challenge. Today, the sidecar outfit is a comparatively rare sight.

Anyone about to restore a sidecar will immediately realise that extra problems now exist, over and above those which have already been encountered when tackling the machine itself. Familiarity with woodworking, glazing, trim and upholstery now have to be added to the list of skills, and perhaps panel beating. In other words, the restoration of a sidecar becomes a project on its very own.

The first task is to separate the bodywork from the chassis, and tackle each as separate units. If the bodywork is too far gone, or requires expert attention that is beyond the capacity of the restorer, now is a good time to get this part of the work under way. Wickerwork bodies often present the most difficulty, but there may be a local basketmaker or perhaps a training school for the blind, where restoration work can be undertaken relatively cheaply, especially if it helps to provide training facilities. Alternatively, a complete replica body can be made, using the remains of the original design as a pattern; the original wickerwork may have deteriorated to such an extent that repairs are no longer practicable. Anyone experienced in coach building or trimming should be able to handle the repair or restoration of a later and more conventional type of sidecar body — at a price. It is always

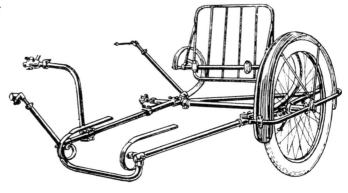

Figure 20 Top A simple sidecar chassis, showing the four points of attachment to the machine

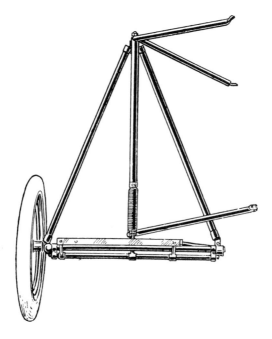

Bottom Scott enthusiasts will appreciate the advantages of this triangulated chassis

A very nice example of an early wickerwork sidecar. Definitely a fine weather attachment, it provides no protection for the passenger in the cold or wet

wise to obtain a written estimate in advance because work of this nature, which demands skilled operatives, is of necessity somewhat expensive. The alternative, especially if the budget is tight, is to carry out the renovation work yourself. This is not quite as difficult as it may sound, unless the whole outfit has deteriorated very badly.

Having stripped the body from the sidecar chassis, the very first requirement is to check the chassis for alignment. Any buckled or badly dented tubes should be obvious. Remove the sidecar wheel and check the stub axle. Often this is bent as the result of lengthy service and will require straightening or possibly even replacement, if the sidecar wheel is to be in track after reassembly. Check the suspension springs, too, and replace any damaged or broken leaves. Many sidecars favoured semi-elliptical springs as a means of mounting the body, but just about every variation of springing has been tried at one time or another — each manufacturer having his own individual ideas on the subject. The sidecar wheel may not be rigidly mounted either, even though this is the more usual arrangement. Here again, all manner of arrangements have been used, ranging from a floating axle to a form of swinging arm suspension.

An unusual type of sidecar chassis not often encountered these days is the folding chassis, designed to permit a sidecar outfit to be wheeled down a narrow passage or through a narrow gateway without need to detach the sidecar — a lengthy and somewhat tedious task. The body, of course, has to be removed before the chassis can be folded, but this, too, is readily detachable due to the use of quick release fastenings. In the folded position, the complete outfit can be wheeled through a gateway 28 inches wide or a passageway that is a minimum of only 5 inches wider. There are several such designs, such as the Dorway, Paragon and Hopley which rely upon a unique system of pivots and locking devices.

The straightening of a bent sidecar chassis or one having a bent stub axle, is best entrusted to a frame repair specialist, who will have the required experience, together with all the necessary jigs and mandrels. If the outfit is to handle properly, the chassis itself, and the wheel, must be in perfect alignment.

Other important factors are the manner in which the sidecar chassis is attached to the machine and the way in which it is aligned. Dealing with the first point, at least three separate connections are necessary, and perhaps four — the attachment to the machine should be as rigid as possible. Most machines suitable for sidecar work will have built-in lugs on the frame, which make the attachment of the sidecar much easier. The three most common points of attachment are by means of a swan neck to the front down tube, immediately below the steering head of the machine; to the saddle tube, usually high up, and in the vicinity of the rear wheel spindle or rear fork ends, using a ball and socket joint. If a fourth fitting is used, this can be made to whatever other firm anchorage point happens to be available. The various fittings will have provision for adjustment, necessary when aligning the sidecar with the machine. They are often supplied by the sidecar manufacturer or the dealer who attaches the sidecar to the machine. Alternative fittings of the clamp type are available in cases where the frame of the machine has no built-in sidecar lugs. But before using them, it is advisable to check whether the machine is recommended for use in conjunction with a sidecar. Not every manufacturer is in favour of fitting a sidecar, especially if the machine has a somewhat unorthodox form of rear suspension. Generally speaking, 500cc is considered to be the minimum capacity for any sidecar machine, and even then the overall gear ratios must be lowered by the use of a different engine or final drive sprocket. It is sometimes possible to fit a lightweight sidecar to a much lower powered machine, especially if the local area is quite flat, with no steep hills. But in a strong headwind, there will be little or no reserve of power, making forward progress quite difficult! Other requirements when fitting a sidecar for the first time will be a steering damper and a heavier fork spring, possibly also a need to change the trail of the forks by using different links. It is here that specialist advice is needed.

To align the sidecar with the machine to which it is to be attached, first make sure the floor is level, then loosely fit the various points of attachment so that the sidecar wheel is parallel to the track of the two wheels of the motorcycle. This can be checked by using a

Another excellent example of an early sidecar, complete with detachable windscreen. One hopes it is glazed with toughened glass and not plate glass that was at one time considered acceptable

The sidecar attached to this side valve Norton looks exceptionally comfortable and has been extremely well renovated. The lining of the panels and the transfer on the door help to break up the monotony of an otherwise large painted surface

Yet another old sidecar, showing the method of attaching the body to the chassis. One may presume the customary 'C' springs provide the form of attachment at the rear

You need to be both slim and agile to climb into this one! It is in keeping with the American X in-line four, to which it is attached

Of more modern design, this small wheeled sidecar looks a little out of place attached to the Rudge

A sidecar mounted on the right indicates a machine of foreign manufacture, as indeed proved to be the case with this Danish Nimbus outfit. The finish is exceptionally good and quite dramatic in effect

A swan-neck fitting is invariably used for the attachment to the front down tube of the frame. Most machines have a built-in lug here

Equally popular is the rear ball-joint attachment, which permits a wide range of adjustment when lining-up

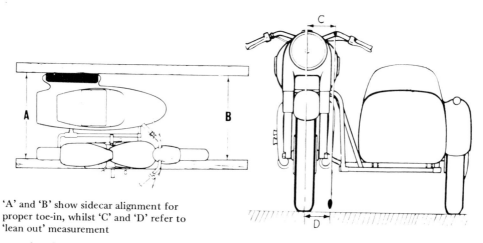

'A' and 'B' show sidecar alignment for
proper toe-in, whilst 'C' and 'D' refer to
'lean out' measurement

couple of straight planks resting on bricks to ensure they touch two points on each wheel.
Then make adjustments so that the sidecar wheel 'toes in' towards the front wheel of the
motorcycle from 3/8 to 3/4 in/9.5 to 19mm (see accompanying diagram). Another adjustment should be made to ensure the machine leans away from the sidecar. Using a plumb line
to set the machine so that it is completely vertical, adjust so that the distance 'C' in the
accompanying diagram is approximately 1 in/25.5mm greater than that at 'D'. With regard to
the position of the sidecar wheel, this should be at least 2 in/50.8mm in front of the rear
wheel of the motorcycle, this measurement being from the respective wheel centres. Note,
however, that the various measurements given serve only as an approximate guide to correct
alignment. There are many differing views on what the exact measurements should be and it
is best to heed the advice of someone skilled in sidecar fitting. The difference in handling
between a poorly aligned outfit and one that has been carefully set up has to be experienced
to be believed. Much will, of course, depend on the type of sidecar fitted. For example, for a
single seat sports sidecar a 6 in/152mm lead of the sidecar wheel can be employed to
advantage, whereas a 2 in/50.8mm lead would be preferable in the case of what is best
termed a family outfit. Too much lead causes the sidecar wheel to lift on left-handers, but
will tend to hold it down on right-handers. Correspondingly, a small lead will tend to make
the outfit more stable, at the expense of tight, right-hand turns. A point not previously
mentioned is the need to ensure the back of the sidecar body does extend behind the rear
of the machine.

The repair of damaged or rotting bodywork is not one to be taken light heartedly and
in the majority of cases expert attention will be required, since this type of repair is beyond
the capabilities of most amateur enthusiasts. This is especially so in the case of a wickerwork
sidecar, or one of the coachbuilt type, having metal panelling on a wooden frame. The latter
will need to have the panelling removed and the damaged portions of the woodwork cut out
so that new wood can be inserted in their place. A good working knowledge of joinery is
more or less essential, if a strong, durable repair is to result. Panel beating is an art that is not
easily acquired either, for when removing dents it is only too easy to spread the metal,
leaving a permanent buckle. Often, aluminium is used for the panelling, as it is easily worked
and will show a significant saving in weight. It is held in place with gimp pins and the joins at
the edges concealed by means of beading.

The windscreen, or windows, depending on the type of sidecar, must be made of
toughened glass and not ordinary window glass, for reasons that are quite obvious. The
older, soft top used non-flammable celluloid, a necessity when a detachable or folding cover
is fitted which can be stowed away during fine weather. Fortunately, this type of material
has been superseded by other, more modern plastics, that are much more suitable for the
job. The chief disadvantage with celluloid is its tendency to yellow with age and crack or
split. Toughened glass can be used only where the surrounding area is permanently in place.

Perspex is another ideal material for a windscreen. A heavy duty grade of transparent pvc, polythene or some similar flexible material can be used in detachable hoods and similar weatherproof fittings, where folding and stowage problems have to be encountered.

If the sidecar is of the folding top variety, it is almost certain that the hood will require renewal, either because it has worn badly or because it is no longer waterproof. The chances of finding a new hood in usable condition are very remote, but it is not too difficult (or expensive) to have a new hood made to the original pattern by a firm that specialises in trimming work for sports cars and the like. A double texture material is commonly used for this purpose, resembling a sandwich in cross-section. It is arranged so that a layer of rubber is enclosed between two layers of fabric, so that the material looks like a thick sheet of fabric from both sides. More modern materials of the pvc leathercloth type have tended to supersede the sandwich type of covering, because sooner or later the rubber layer in the centre of the sandwich will perish and lose its waterproofing properties. PVC leathercloth is itself waterproof, but its appearance may outweigh the practicalities on an old sidecar that is being restored.

Another factor to be considered is the internal trim of the sidecar and the upholstery of the seat or seats. Modern, plastic-based fabrics, some of which are self-adhesive or can be firmly attached with an impact adhesive of the Evo-Stik type, offer the most obvious advantages after the old material has been stripped and cleaned off. The most serious problem likely to arise is matching the previous covering, an important consideration if originality is to be retained. The older coverings were often in very sombre colours and it may prove almost impossible to get anything that makes even a reasonable match. The upholstery may possibly be in Pegamoid or Rexide, in which case restoration is not feasible, if the covering has deteriorated too far or worn thin. Where leathercloth has been used, it is probably better to recover the seat with a more durable, modern equivalent — assuming the colour matching problem can be overcome. Sometimes, a Bedford cord type of material is encountered. Provided it is not faded or badly abraided, a household cleaner such as 1001 or a carpet shampoo can often be used to good effect in restoring the finish. Although a specialised job, like many of the others mentioned in this Chapter, it is much easier to find an expert in upholstery who will undertake the necessary renovation work.

From the foregoing, it will be realised that the complete restoration of a sidecar calls upon many additional skills not normally encountered when rebuilding the average motorcycle. Indeed, the restorer will find himself having much in common with those who make a hobby or a living in restoring old cars.

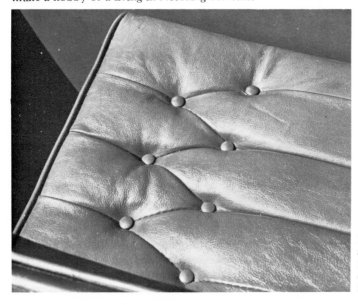

Fine attention to detail, such as this buttoned seat, makes the interior of a sidecar especially attractive. In this instance, the colour is green

The last and most important task is the painting of the sidecar, a task that demands great care and attention because the large surface areas will tend to show up any surface defects. Careful preparation of the surfaces to be painted and absolute cleanliness are both essential requirements; the techniques described earlier for the painting of the motorcycle itself can be used to good effect. Often, large areas painted in black or some other dark colour are relieved by a thin white line or some other decorative effect. If you have a shaky hand it is best to rely on carefully positioned masking tape or to have a professional signwriter complete the task. It is only too easy to spoil the effect with a line of varying thickness or one that is not straight — two defects that will be immediately obvious to the eye.

Retain as much as possible of the original sidecar because some of the smaller fittings, such as the turnbuckle releases for the hood and various press studs will no longer be available without a very protracted search. Even more ingenuity will have to be used in the case of a launch sidecar with a body that looks like a ship's deck — very popular at one time! Simulated deck planking, a rail and even tiny ship's ventilators make up the overall effect and may have to be fabricated from scratch, if the originals are too far gone.

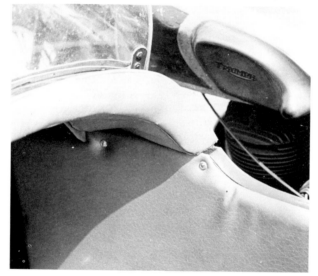

There is quite an art in trimming the interior so that it has a professional appearance. Note the use of special washers under each of the screw heads, used extensively by the upholstery trade

Some sidecars have an external luggage grid on top of the boot, to which camping gear and similar items can be strapped. Aero elastics come in handy here

Chapter Sixteen

Assembly notes and tips

Having arrived at the assembly stage, with each of the major units reconditioned and complete, the most interesting stage of the whole project has been reached. Gone are the dreary, uninteresting tasks, such as rubbing down, filling, cleaning and degreasing and such is the relief that one is tempted to plunge into the reassembly of the now clean and gleaming parts with a hitherto unknown zest. But take heed and pause for a while before you get carried away. Rush tactics will end in disaster, with the consequent risk of damage to some vital and irreplaceable part. Inevitably, something important will be overlooked whilst striving to get the machine completed in the shortest possible time. This is the stage, precisely, where things start to go wrong.

Before reassembly commences, plan the actual sequence in which it is to take place. For example, does the gearbox have to be fitted into the frame before the engine and is it possible to insert the complete engine without having to remove either the rocker box or cylinder head? By far the greatest problem will be the protection of the newly painted surfaces of the various components, especially the frame. Touching in the damage afterwards is rarely very successful, even if it is easy to gain access to the damaged areas. Apart from the use of extreme care and the help of a second person to steady various parts as they are fitted together, some damage can be prevented by wrapping rag around the areas most likely to be damaged. If the earlier stripdown of the machine was carried out in a methodical manner by yourself, you will have some knowledge of the most appropriate assembly sequence. If, on the other hand, you bought the machine in a fully dismantled state, a look through the manufacturer's handbook may give some guidance — assuming, of course, that a copy of the original can be obtained. Use only good quality tools that fit the various nuts, bolts and screws, and never resort to adjustable spanners, slip-nose pliers or similar 'general purpose' tools that are beloved by the home handyman. Nothing looks worse than nuts with rounded corners, or screws with ragged slots.

It follows, of course, that the original nuts, bolts, screws and washers should be used as much as possible, provided they are still serviceable and have replated successfully. Metric nuts and bolts, cross-head screws, allen screws and the like will look completely out of place on an old machine, unless they are original fitments, and should be avoided like the plague. Usually, someone can come up with some matching nuts, bolts or screws to replace the originals, even if it means renewing the whole set so that they all look alike. The set of taps and dies mentioned in an earlier Chapter can now be used to good effect; if the various screw threads are cleaned up prior to assembly, the whole task will be very much easier.

Although everyone has their own working plan, which to an extent must depend on the ease with which parts go together, I usually start with the bare frame, then add the forks, followed by the engine and gearbox. If the wheels are then added, it is comparatively easy to move the machine around in order to gain access to some of the more inaccessible spots. This method is particularly advantageous if you are working in a confined space or in a lock-up used to garage a car. The bike can be wheeled out of harms way at the conclusion of each assembly session. Use plenty of clean oil to lubricate the working parts throughout assembly, and if you have to break off in the middle of a task, cover-up any parts that may be exposed. As far as possible, it is best to keep to the practice adopted by professional race mechanics. Never break off until a complete assembly sequence has been completed in all respects. This is the only sure way that nothing is overlooked.

Do not be tempted to try and start the machine before everything is complete. I have always made it a golden rule that no attempt will be made to start the engine until the machine is complete in every respect, even to the final grease-up and tyre pressures check. I once witnessed a disastrous fire that started because the person who was reassembling his newly reconditioned machine could not wait to hear the engine run. With no top on the float chamber the carburettor spat back due to over-advanced ignition and the resultant fire not only destroyed the machine but the garage in which it stood. Moral: if you must indulge in these tactics, make sure a working fire extinguisher is near to hand. Far better, however, not to run the risk at all.

When reassembly is complete, grease all the various greasing points, check the tyre pressures and then add petrol and oil. Make sure all the controls are working, as they should, then place the machine on its stand, so that is is standing firmly on level ground. Each machine demands its own starting technique and if the machine is new to you, you will have to work it out the hard way, by trial and error. When the engine starts, keep it running at a fast tickover, so that the oil will get a chance to circulate, and the new parts can start to settle down. Do not let the engine get too hot — only a short running time should be necessary to ensure that everything is in order and there are no serious oil leaks. If the engine has a dry sump lubrication system, check that oil is returning to the oil tank. This may take a short while because the oil has first to build up as it works its way around the newly rebuilt engine. If it shows no signs of returning, stop the engine and investigate the cause. Irreparable harm will be caused if the engine is run for any length of time with a malfunctioning lubrication system of any kind.

Before taking the machine on to the road for the first time, check that the brakes are correctly adjusted and work efficiently. All legal requirements must be fully met, such as speedometer, horn, lighting and tyre tread depth. If the machine is to be taken for its DOE test, book the appointment first and make sure insurance cover is operative before you venture on the road. You must wear a helmet, and even if the weather is so warm that ordinary clothes will suffice, make sure you wear a pair of gloves.

The question of what grade of petrol to select is one that frequently arises, since petrol did not have a star grading in the old days, or such high octane ratings. A side valve or two-stroke should run quite well on 2-star fuel, and an ohv or ohc model on the higher 3-star rating. With older machines, it is rarely necessary to go into the higher star (or octane) ratings unless the engine has been extensively tuned or has a higher compression ratio than the original specification. Even greater problems can be encountered when selecting oils, since today's multigrades are a comparatively recent innovation. Wherever possible, it would seem preferable to adhere to the viscosities originally recommended by the manufacturer, often stamped on the filler cap. Some monograde oils are still available which are well-suited to the older type of machine; often, an oil manufacturer can give advice on the most suitable grade to use from his current range. Two-strokes have a special requirement, since an oil not specifically designed for this type of engine will contain additives that will ash within the engine and cause plug whiskering or fouling. A number of oil manufacturers sell oils specially designed for two-stroke use. NEVER, however, use an oil of the self-mix type as anything other than a direct additive to the fuel. An oil of this type does not have sufficient 'body' to act as a lubricating medium when the oil feed is separate. Above all, never mix a vegetable-base oil of the 'R' type with one of the normal mineral oils. Although a very nice smell will

Most damage to paintwork occurs when the engine is replaced in the frame. Note how masking tape has been used to protect the paintwork; it is easily removed immediately the engine is in its correct position

Don't forget the cylinder head steady, if fitted. Some machines, like this KTT Velocette, vibrate very badly if this all important attachment is left off, or not fully tightened

Chain alignment is important if undue wear of both chain and sprockets is to be avoided. The Scott shown here uses drawbolt adjusters of the cycle type

Cable adjustments are equally important. A mid-way adjuster sometimes saves a great deal of work in getting to a more inaccessible adjuster, as on a gearbox

Make sure the whole of the suspension system is well greased. On the post-war Douglas, the unique torsion bar rear suspension has numerous greasing points on the links that connect the swinging arm to the torsion bars themselves

result when the engine is running, sooner or later there will be a complete lubrication breakdown. Vegetable and mineral based oils do not mix; under the action of heat they combine to make a hideous rubber-like sludge that will quickly block up all the internal oilways in the engine. It is generally agreed that vegetable-based oil no longer has any advantage over today's high performance mineral oils and that in consequence, there is no point in using it. It is almost twice as expensive and almost impossible to obtain at normal filling stations, creating additional problems if the machine runs low in oil during a long journey. Worse still, it proves almost impossible to remove when oil leaks occur and it becomes baked on to the engine castings. But vegetable based oil still has its devotees, especially those who own ohc models where it does seem to provide particularly good lubrication. If a change has to be made from one type of oil to another (mineral to vegetable or vice-versa), the engine must be stripped and all the old oil cleaned out before the change over can be made. Note that vegetable based oil is particularly unsuitable for two-strokes that rely on a petroil mixture as it will mix with petrol in only small amounts and with great difficulty. If the petroil mix ratio is unknown, start with 16:1, then reduce to at least 20:1 if the exhaust smokes badly. These were the two ratios most commonly used in a petrol/oil system.

When on the road at last, do not forget that the machine has to be run-in very carefully, even if the cylinder has not been rebored. All the parts have to bed down again and establish a correct working relationship with each other. If the lubrication system is adjustable, set it a little on the generous side for the initial 500 miles or so. Be sure to change the engine oil (dry sump lubrication system) after the first 500 miles of running, so that any particles of swarf are drained off at the same time. After the first short run, re-check all the various running adjustments after the engine has cooled down, and re-set where necessary. Check also the many nuts, bolts and screws, since some of these too will require a little extra tightening down as the result of settlement.

Above all else, enjoy that first ride to the utmost, because it is a moment to be savoured. There is nothing to surpass the joys of taking an aged or unusually interesting machine on to the road for the very first time and giving it a new lease of life. It will more than make up for all the hard work that has gone before, making it seem worth the effort after all. But only if you have got this far without giving up!

Chapter Seventeen

Concours presentation

A visit to any of the many historic motorcycle meetings held throughout the country most weekends can prove to be a very exhilarating experience - especially for anyone having an interest in the preservation and restoration of old machines. The more so if the gathering includes a concours d'elegance contest, with awards in each separate class for the machines judged to be the best. On occasions such as this, every sympathy must be with the concours judges, who often have the greatest difficulty in making their final selection from a number of gleaming machines, each restored to a very high standard. But they are experts at their job and will be looking for the minutest imperfection that the casual onlooker (and perhaps even the average enthusiast), would fail to notice. It is often these minor points that will swing the decision in any tight-judged competition, and it is important that they are recognised by the restorer who sets his sights very high.

A fact not often appreciated is that a machine can be over-prepared almost as much as under-prepared and there is quite definitely a possibility of gilding the lily in a fit of over-enthusiasm. Examples can be seen at almost every gathering of old machines and the chances are that even the rider concerned will have no idea that he has overstepped the mark. The most frequent 'fault' is the use of chromium in place of nickel plate - justifiable perhaps, if the machine is stored in a damp garage which causes nickel plate to deteriorate very rapidly. But chromium plating did not come into widespread use until 1929 or there-abouts, which places it right out of court in the case of a veteran model. Polished brass is something else that should be eschewed, too. It was rarely seen on motorcycles in the old days because it would tarnish so readily and require frequent attention. Almost invariably, unpainted brass and copper components or accessories had a plated surface of nickel. On the other side of the fence, it is often lack of attention to detail that forms the small 'let down' which may eliminate the machine from a concours final. Phil Smith, a renowned Vintage MCC concours judge, listed several of these in an interesting series of articles in the *Official Journal of the Vintage Motor Cycle Club*, and I can do no better than to use them as examples. They include the use of plastic covered control cable outers in place of the older cotton braided type, a mixture of nickel and chromium plating, black painted spokes in one wheel and plated spokes in the other, shaky painted lines on petrol tanks, and severe wear in the ends of a rear stand such that the metal had worn right through on each foot. Each of these faults was sufficient to cause marks to be debited and a machine that was otherwise perfect stood little chance of coming out on top.

It is interesting to note that Phil is critical of even his own machine and was ashamed to find on one particularly hot day that grease from the hub of a wheel had run down one of the spokes to collect on the wheel rim - in the middle of a judging session. Moral: make sure you use high melting point grease! Another small let down is the use of a plastic covered high tension lead for the spark plug; anything that is plastic covered really stands out, even if the colour is black. Phil advocates using a rubber-covered lead like the original and going to the length of removing the spark plug and inserting an older type of the appropriate design and colour whilst the judging is in progress.

It is, perhaps, the paintwork and colour matching that causes the greatest controversy, a point already discussed in an earlier chapter. The vintage Triumph petrol tank is one of the best examples because the characteristic grey/green finish is exceptionally difficult to match with any authenticity. A look around any collection of old machines will show the variations that exist amongst the renovated models, each restorer being quite sure in his own mind that his tank exactly matches the original colour! To a lesser extent this applies to a black finish - the old John Marston Sunbeam black is an intense black that is very hard to reproduce. Refrain from adding any additional lines to the petrol tank or mudguards, even if you have acquired the technique of hand lining quite successfully, and **never** use aluminium paint in lieu of plating.

It would seem that much will depend on how the machine is transported to a meeting because if it can be cleaned and polished very thoroughly just prior to the meeting and then brought in a covered truck or van, it will have the edge over a similar machine that is ridden to the same meeting and has to be cleaned on site. However, this does not always apply. Realising that some competitors transported machines to various events in this manner and

Although of modern origin, this metal braided petrol pipe is far more acceptable than transparent plastic and is more in keeping with the period

What could have been a very nice original Gold Star BSA has been spoilt by the non-standard petrol tank and the dualseat in particular — perhaps because the owner could not trace the originals

Definitely not ready for concours presentation although its not as far away as first meets the eye. This swinging arm B31 350 BSA of Rod Grainger is running and practically original; with careful painting, rechroming and general tidying it could soon become a worthwhile entry

Shaky hand lining of this petrol tank has spoiled what would otherwise be a quite presentable effort. It is attention to small detail such as this that makes all the difference in the final count

rarely, if ever, rode them, some organisers stipulate that the machine must have travelled to the event under its own power and often, should have competed in a prior road event before it can become eligible for the concours contest. It does mean that if the weather is bad, as it often is, everyone gets an equal chance. More important, it does mean that a machine is used in the manner intended and is more than a cocooned museum piece. It is a hard fact that once the machine is used, it will start to deteriorate, no matter how well it is looked after. Those who compete regularly in concours events have to strip and restore their machines at surprisingly frequent intervals, if they are to retain their chance to win the occasional award in these events.

For reasons that should be quite obvious, keep well away from the judges whilst they are going about their task and keep your friends away from them, too. Sadly, there are one or two who take part in concours events who are very bad sports and if their beloved machine happens to be marked down, they will not be averse to using every possible excuse to explain why someone else took the main prize. It is unfortunate that it should be necessary to mention this aspect at all. However, embarrassing incidents do occur from time to time and it is as well to be aware of them.

At some time or other the question of whether to appear in period dress will arise. Broadly speaking, there is no objection at all, provided it is the correct dress and the wearer is not too flamboyant. Sometimes, this type of attire is encouraged, for carnival processions and the like, but in the main, it is more customary to wear ordinary riding gear, which is better suited to the climate. The regulations for some events specifically ban the use of certain types of clothing, especially if it is used for advertising purposes, so it is as well to make sure you understand the regulations that govern the event first of all. The use of trade plates will almost certainly be barred; this is another point worth remembering by anyone in the motorcycle trade.

It was sometimes the practice to paint a nickname of some kind on the petrol tank or rear mudguard of a machine, a fashion that has long since died out. Whilst there is no objection to this, especially if it is a continuation from the former owner, the display of such a name is unlikely to be viewed very kindly by a concours judge. To him, it is just another non-standard modification, and he will view it as such, without any sentiment. This also applies to any mascot bolted to the machine - another craze during the so-called golden years of motorcycling.

To anyone with a restored machine who has recently joined the ranks of the historic motorcycle enthusiasts the main problem is how to enter events, a problem which, fortunately, is very easily resolved. Almost every event is organised under the regulations of the Auto-Cycle Union, the body that governs most of the competitive motorcycle activities staged throughout the UK. To become eligible to take part in any of these events, the rider must be a fully paid-up member of a motorcycle club that is affiliated to the A-CU, and there is a very wide range of clubs to choose from. A club that meets locally may seem the most obvious answer, but the convenience may be outweighed by other disadvantages. For example, most local clubs have as their main interest, events of a more sporting nature, such as trials and scrambles, with the result that the owner of an old machine may be more or less neglected as far as his own interest is concerned. Furthermore, a local club will be affiliated to a certain area of the A-CU so that if the rider wishes to enter for an event outside the area, he will have to secure membership of a club in the other area unless a special invitation to his own club is included. The alternative is to join what is known as a non-territorial club such as the Vintage Motor Cycle Club or a one-make club, which covers the whole of the UK with its activities. Because clubs such as these have a large membership spread all over the country, local sections are formed wherever there are a sufficient number of enthusiasts to make regular meetings possible. This arrangement provides the advantages of a local club whilst preserving the all important interest in old machines. The Vintage Motor Cycle Club is likely to have the most advantages in this latter respect, since the one-make clubs have to cater for all types of machines, some that may have gone out of production comparatively recently. Furthermore, with a membership of well over 4,000, the VMCC is in a much

Only the purist will observe that this really beautiful 1938 KSS Velocette is fitted with front forks from a much earlier model. Circumstances dictated their fitting at the time; the owner now has the correct pattern, which are being renovated prior to fitting

stronger position to organise its own events, often on a national basis. However, the choice is yours - and there is a choice. So long as you are a member of an A-CU affiliated club, you are automatically eligible to ride in events run under their rules. The club concerned usually has advance notification of events and will frequently have copies of the regulations and entry forms. Failing this, both of the newspaper motorcycling weeklies publish lists of forthcoming events and the names and addresses of the appropriate persons to contact.

Some final advice. If you enter for an event, read the regulations carefully and make sure you understand them. This may sound elementary, but it is surprising how often an entry is submitted without an awareness of what is involved. A knowledge of what formalities have to be observed, especially if there is a competitive aspect to the event, can save a great deal of disappointment that may otherwise result from a genuine misunderstanding.

Not so many years ago, riders used to lay up their machines during the winter and were advised to coat all the plated parts with grease — a messy and somewhat tedious task, especially as all the grease had to be removed at a later date. Mention was made in an earlier Chapter of paper impregnated with a rust inhibitor, which, if hung close to the machine, will prevent rusting from occurring. This approach is much to be preferred, even if it is necessary for several enthusiasts to band together and purchase a supply of the paper, which is normally available to a minimum quantity order. If any touching-in of the paintwork is required, now is the time for this, too. Throw a dust sheet over the machine when the paintwork has had a chance to dry, not one that envelopes it completely so that the air cannot circulate. Ventilation will prove necessary on a particularly damp day, to help offset condensation. For this reason alone, do not resort to plastic sheeting, so that the machine is completely enclosed within a cocoon.

If the garage or storage place is likely to get very damp, the question of how to protect the machine's plating and paintwork needs to be answered. There are a number of lacquers on the market which, if painted over the plating, will produce a protective,

The attention to detail on this 1930 BSA Sloper is little short of incredible. It is machines such as this that have helped give the Vintage MCC a much better image, whilst actively encouraging others to restore their machines to a similarly high standard

This Morgan three-wheeler could be made very presentable with just a little extra effort. In regular, daily use, it is not so easy to keep a machine in pristine condition and one must have a little sympathy for this category of owner, who is just as keen in his own way

A nicely preserved and original ES2 Norton. There should be a transfer on the oil tank and a rubber on the kickstart pedal, otherwise it is difficult to fault the machine in any way

moisture-proof film. Unfortunately, the film will have to be removed when the machine is used once more, but this is not too difficult if the appropriate solvent is applied and the layer wiped off with a clean rag. The manufacturer who markets the lacquer will also have the remover solvent available.

Other small points to remember include the need to oil all exposed chains and to close all controls, so that there is no strain on the cables or the return springs. If a sidecar is fitted, this too should have its wheel raised clear of the ground, and should be cleaned and polished before it is covered over like the machine to which it is attached. And do not forget to lock the machine in some way so that it is difficult to remove, if it is left unattended in some remote place. Immobilising it will not be sufficient, if it can still be wheeled away without much effort.

Finally, if the garage or store room has a window, obscure it in some way, so that the machine within cannot be seen from the outside. Also have the premises checked for security quite regularly. Apart from the more obvious reasons for observing these precautions, there is much less chance of the finish fading if the machine is stored in semi-darkness. Remember above all that an elderly, well-restored machine represents an appreciable capital sum, which is steadily appreciating in value. Like any sound investment, it makes sense to take good care of it.

Chapter Eighteen

Preserving and storing an old motorcycle

Quite a number of machines, and especially those restored to a very high standard, will be used on the road fairly infrequently, so that the time spent in the garage is much greater than the time they are actually in use. The older the machine, the greater this is likely to become, and there is a danger that if the machine is left unattended for too long, some form of deterioration will occur. A few quite simple and elementary precautions, if observed, will ensure this is unlikely to happen and may even help defer the length of time between successive rebuilds, if the machine is to be kept up to a high concours standard.

The basic requirement is to store the machine in a warm, dry garage — admittedly not always feasible but very desirable, none the less. Before putting the machine away, clean and polish it thoroughly, just as though it were being prepared for a meeting the following day. Then either place it on its stands or block it up in some way so that both wheels are clear of the ground. Check that the tyres are correctly inflated at the same time. It is imperative that the machine stands securely, on level ground. The dangers of it toppling over need not be overstressed.

If the machine is likely to be left standing for some while, drain off the petrol and the oil, if it happens to be of the vegetable base (R) type. In this latter case, assuming the machine is a four-stroke, it is advisable to remove the crankcase drain plug and drain this too, before the plug is replaced. Petrol will deteriorate if left standing for too long and apart from causing difficulty in starting, will produce a characteristic smell that is quite vile and difficult to disperse. Even though modern vegetable base oils have a different composition from those generally available a decade or two ago, they will still pick up water from the atmosphere, to form an emulsion that will initiate corrosion. For similar reasons, mineral oils should be drained off too, if the machine is likely to be left for a quite lengthy period.

If the machine has electric lighting, remove the battery and make arrangements for it to be given a 'refresher' charge from a battery charger every six weeks or so. This is preferable to having it fully charged, then draining off all the acid and refilling it with distilled water. In all probability, it is best to dispose of the battery and replace it with another when the machine is used again, if the storage period is likely to be more than a year. This applies, of course, only if the battery is of the modern, plastics case type. If you are fortunate enough to have a serviceable battery of the old, hard rubber case type, there is little hope of finding a matching replacement at a later date.

If the engine is of a single cylinder, turn it over so that both valves are closed — assuming it is a four-stroke. This will not be possible on most multi-cylinder four-strokes, since one valve is bound to be off its seat, no matter what the engine position may happen to be in. Push some clean rag into the carburettor intake and into the end of the silencer — and do not forget to remove them before attempting to start the engine on the next occasion! If the machine is likely to remain unused for some while, it is a good idea to remove each spark plug and put about a teaspoonful of thin oil or upper cylinder lubricant into each bore. Rotate the engine very slowly a few times, then replace the plug. This should prevent the piston rings from rusting to the cylinder bore as the result of residual dampness in the engine, or through condensation. Should the cylinder block be of the water-cooled type, add the appropriate amount of anti-freeze to the water in the radiator, or drain off the entire water content. The former is preferred, provided the system is leaktight. Modern anti-freeze contains inhibitors, which will prevent the water channels from rusting or scaling. Furthermore, it is not always possible to ensure that every drop of water has drained from the cooling system. Some that still lurks in the odd corners may cause trouble if it happens to freeze during the winter. If anti-freeze is added, it must be thoroughly dispersed, preferably by running the engine.

A photographic gallery

This very presentable 1911 Premier is used regularly in veteran and vintage events and is close to the original manufacturer's specification. Oil leaks are more or less inevitable on elderly machines such as this, where oil seals were virtually unknown. The Premier is owned by Frank Ridealgh, of Weymouth

Although probably more suitable for sidecar work, this long wheelbase 986cc vee-twin BSA is ridden solo by Mike Hunt, of Sherborne. It is a nicely restored example of the 1926 model and is equipped with electric lighting. The forward mounted magdyno needs all the shielding it can get from the heavily valanced front mudguard

N.A. Cross, of Weymouth, is responsible for the restoration of this very nice model P Triumph of 1926 vintage. The model P was, at one time, the cheapest of the larger capacity machines on the UK market, and countless numbers were sold. Note the unusual, twin barrel carburettor of Triumph manufacture, and the double spring front forks. Engine capacity is 496cc

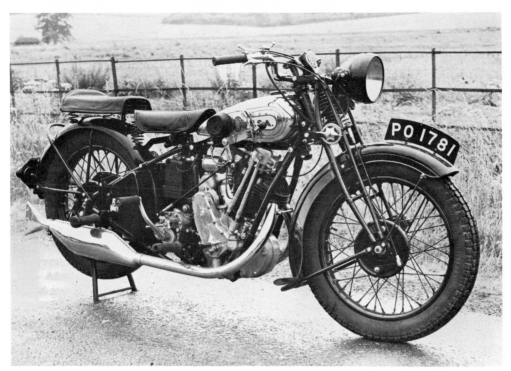

It is almost impossible to fault this 1930 493cc Sloper BSA, restored by Wally Thorn, of Yeovil. This model proved a great favourite amongst sidecar owners of the late twenties and early thirties, and is one of the best known of all BSAs

A good example of the somewhat rare 1931 490cc model 18 Norton, which has been restored by Ray Garrett, of Sturminster Newton. Outstandingly reliable, the long-stroke engine is alleged to fire every other lamp post. Few machines had a single exhaust pipe carried on the left-hand side of the machine, which necessitated a peculiar 'kink' in the pipe to clear the front down tube. The Brooklands cam silencer is, unfortunately, not of the correct period

Gerald Beddis, of Bournemouth, restored this 1935 249cc BSA, which is typical of the small capacity machines sold for a relatively low price during the early and mid-thirties. The only major departure from standard is the fitting of a Lucas Magdyno in place of the original Maglita, a modification which those in the know will consider virtually essential if the machine is used regularly

Another mount usually seen hitched to a sidecar. Keith Hunt, of Sherborne, is responsible for the restoration of this 1939 1140cc Royal Enfield which, ridden solo, is no sluggard. Note the massive crankcase, which has a special compartment for the engine oil, as evidenced by the forward mounted filler cap

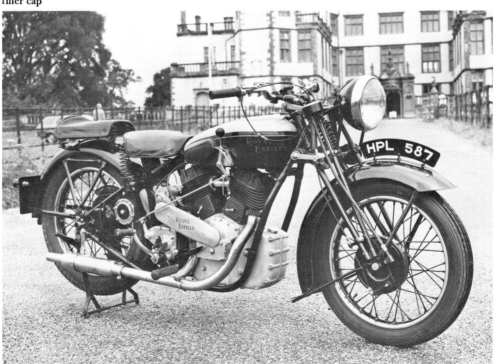

There were many admirers of this superb example of an ES2 Norton, of the type that was popular in the early fifties. Always a big bike in both size and weight, it can be argued with some truth that the ES2 was one of the last machines to have vintage characteristics. The 490cc engine has bore and stroke measurements of 79 x 100mm, retaining the longstroke characteristics always associated with the early single-cylinder Norton engines

This remarkably original 1932 150 cc New Imperial Model 23 needed only superficial tidying-up when purchased by the Author during 1979 for £160. It was a non-runner, but only because the valve timing had been incorrectly set, an easily remedied fault. This proves that 'bargains' can still be found — a line advertisement in Motor Cycle Weekly brought this machine to light

The fully renovated 1952 Triumph Tiger 100, parts of which have featured in the text. Every effort was made to rebuild to as near original specification as possible, despite the growing difficulty in obtaining new parts for the early pre-unit models. The noticeable departure from standard is the later type silencers

Although not yet eligible for acceptance as a post-war model under the ruling of the Vintage MCC, few will doubt that this 1955 596cc Scott will ultimately be accepted. A machine for the real enthusiast, the Scott has innumerable distinctive features and requires regular attention if it is to run in a satisfactory manner. The machine shown is owned by Norman Brister, of Sherborne

Bibliography

Discovering Old Motorcycles
T. E. Crowley
Shire Publications Ltd, 1974

Veteran and Vintage Motorcycles
James Sheldon
B. T. Batsford Ltd, 1961

Motorcycles: A Technical History
C. F. Caunter
Science Museum (HMSO), 1955

Motorcycles in Colour
E. E. Thompson
Blandford Press, 1974

Motorcycles and How to Manage Them
Staff of *Motor Cycle*
Iliffe and Son Ltd - various editions

Classic Motorcycles
Vic Willoughby
Hamlyn, 1975

The Restoration of Vintage and Thoroughbred Cars
R. C. Wheatley and B. Morgan
B. T. Batsford Ltd, 1971

British Racing Motorcycles
Jeff Clew
G. T. Foulis, 1976

The Motorcycle World
Phil Schilling
Hamlyn (in UK), 1974

One-Make Histories

AJS - The History of a Great Motorcycle
Gregor Grant
Patrick Stephens Ltd, 1969

Bibliography

Brough Superior - The Rolls Royce of Motor Cycles
Ronald H. Clark
Goose and Son, 1964

The Douglas Motorcycle: The Best Twin
J. R. Clew
Haynes Publishing Group, 1981

The Norton Story
Bob Holliday
Patrick Stephens Ltd, 1972

Norton
Dennis Howard
Ballantyne Books Inc., 1972

Harley-Davidson
Maurice D. Hendry,
Ballantyne Books Inc., 1972

The Scott Motorcycle - The Yowling Two-Stroke
Jeff Clew
G. T. Foulis, 1975

The Story of Triumph Motor Cycles
Harry Louis and Bob Currie
Patrick Stephens Ltd, 1975

Always in the Picture - a History of the Velocette Motorcycle
R. W. Burgess and J. R. Clew
Haynes Publishing Group, 1980

The Vincent HRD Gallery
Roy Harper
Vincent Publishing Company, 1975

The Vincent HRD Story
Roy Harper and P. C. Vincent
Vincent Publishing Company, 1975

Marque specialists and specialist repairers

Vintage MCC Members Handbook
Published annually - available free to members only

Vintage MCC Register
(Lists engine, frame and gearbox numbers of members machines - dating guide)
£2.00 to members only

Renovators and repairers

This list of names and addresses was correct at the time of going to press, but it is advisable to check the details before contacting any of the firms or individuals listed as addresses are subject to change without prior warning.

The names and addresses listed are known personally by the author and can therefore be recommended with some confidence. However, this does not imply that any liability can be attached in respect of the information given. Here again, circumstances can change and it must remain the onus of the enquirer to decide whether the standard of work will match up to expectations.

Crank, connecting rod and big-end repairs
Alpha Bearings Limited, Kingsley Street, Netherton, Dudley, Worcs
R. B. D. 9, York Place, Ilford, Essex

Exhaust pipes, including bending to pattern
 Technical Tubes Limited, Ringwood Road, Longham, Wimborne, Dorset
*Bruce's Motor Cycles, 103, Stratford Road, Birmingham 11
*Unity Special Equipe, 916, Marchester Road, Castleton, Rochdale, Lancs

Frame and forks repairs
A. L. Oliver, rear of 45, Alfreton Road, Nottingham

Magneto and dynamo repairs
Jack Cooper, 5 South Street, London S E 10

Nickel plating - DIY kits, materials and service
S. Greenway, 25, Pine Court, Cubbington Road, Leamington Spa, Warks

Plating - chrome and nickel
Barrel and Clerkenwell Plating Limited, Rosebery Avenue, London E C 1
Somerset Metal Craft, Station Road, Taunton, Somerset

*Ready-made pattern exhaust pipes and silencers only

Renovators and repairers

Saddle and seat covering
R. B. D. 9, York Place, Ilford, Essex

Speedometer and rev counter repairs, also gauges and instruments
Auto Tempo Meter Co., Ltd, 140, Kings Cross Road, London W C 1

Sprockets - new or re-toothed
Roger Maughfling Engineering, Knucklas, Knighton, Radnor

Stove enamelling
A. E. Smith, The Farringdon Enamelling and Plating Works, 17 Clerkenwell Garden, London, E.C.1

Tank painting and reconditioning
George Grou, 341, Goswell Road, London, E C 1

Wheel building and wheel repairs
J. E. Nunn, 117, Brighton Road, Surbiton, Surrey
Gordon Gill, Hill View, Houndstone Bridge, Montacute, Yeovil, Somerset

Other names and addresses are contained in the *Vintage Motor Cycle Club Handbook,* which is available free of charge to all members.

Two other directories, compiled mainly with the car restorer in mind, may also be of help to motorcycle restorers:

Thoroughbred and Classic Cars Directory of Specialist Firms and Services
Published by IPC Transport Press Ltd, Dorset House, Stamford Street, London SE1 9LU

Veteran and Vintage Directory
Published by Pioneer Publications Ltd, John Montagu Buildings, Beaulieu, Brockenhurst, Hants

Index